OPERATIONAL RESEARCH BY EXAMPLE

Colin F. Palmer

M.Sc., C.Eng., M.B.I.M., M.I.Prod.E.

Lecturer in Quantitative Methods
University of Birmingham

and

Alexander E. Innes

B.Sc. (Econ.) (Hons), D.P.A. (Lond.), Cert. Ed. (Leeds)

Senior Lecturer in Business Statistics
Liverpool Polytechnic

M

First published 1980 by
THE MACMILLAN PRESS LTD
London and Basingstoke
Associated companies in Delhi Dublin
Hong Kong Johannesburg Lagos Melbourne
New York Singapore and Tokyo

Typeset by Preface Ltd, Salisbury, Wilts

Printed in Great Britain by
Lowe & Brydone Printers Ltd, Thetford, Norfolk

British Library Cataloguing in Publication Data

Palmer, Colin F
  Operational research by example.
  1. Operations research
  I. Title   II. Innes, Alexander Edward
  658.4'034   T57.6

  ISBN 0–333–22689–5
  ISBN 0–333–22690–9   Pbk

Contents

Preface

This book introduces the nature of *operational research* and some basic techniques to students in higher and further education and to people working in business and public administration. Explanation is mainly through carefully chosen examples and exercises, occasionally simplified, but otherwise intended to be realistic in context.

Most readers are likely to have the basic knowledge needed to follow the calculations given in the text and to attempt the exercises; those with no calculus or statistics should be able to master most of the material; and those without may find the two books by A. E. Innes mentioned on page ii helpful.

Examples and exercises have been kept fairly simple. Application of the principles they use to business and to administration requires more rigorous and formalised methods, because the problems are more complex. For a complete use of operational research in a large organisation a master model will be constructed, co-ordinating the work of separate models, in each one of the specialised techniques described in this book.

Each chapter lays a simple foundation for a wide and important topic, and each bibliography contains key titles for further study. Readers will find that deeper penetration into specialised branches often depends upon more complex mathematical methods.

The authors are glad to acknowledge the great help received in planning and writing the book. Mr Shaie Selzer, one of the publisher's editors, was concerned with the birth of the book, and its early upbringing, and his successor, Mr Nicholas Brealey, saw it into publication. Mrs Sonia Yuan, B.A., M.Sc., Senior Lecturer in Statistics at Oxford Polytechnic, discussed with the authors the general proposals and saw some of the manuscript, and her advice has proved most valuable. Our three typists served in this taxing field most competently; they were Mrs Joan Jones and Miss Anne Westover, both of the Institute of Local Government Studies, Birmingham University, and Mrs Beryl Perry.

The authors have worked closely together to make the book useful, accurate and up to date, ideals in a developing quantitative field easier to set than to achieve; for any shortcomings they take full responsibility.

C. F. PALMER
A. E. INNES

Acknowledgements

The authors and publisher wish to thank the following, who have kindly given permission for the use of copyright material:

The Bank of England for an extract from *Bank of England Statistical Abstract*, no. 1, 1970.

The Controller of Her Majesty's Stationery Office for tables from *Monthly Digest of Statistics,* no. 375 (1975); *United Kingdom Energy Statistics* (1973); *Annual Abstract of Statistics* (1975), and *Housing and Construction Statistics*, no. 3.

The London and Cambridge Economic Service, University of Cambridge, for tables from *The British Economy Key Statistics 1900–1970*.

McGraw-Hill Book Company (U.K.) Ltd for a table from *Discounted Cash Flow*, 2nd ed. by M. G. Wright, © 1973.

Every effort has been made to trace all the copyright-holders, but if any have been inadvertently overlooked the publishers will be pleased to make the necessary arrangement at the first opportunity.

1

Introducing Operational Research

Operational research, or operations research (to use the American term), describes the application of specialised quantitative techniques to solving problems met in industry, in commerce and in administration. For many years separate statistical and mathematical methods had been used to guide decision-making in these fields, but it was the impetus of the Second World War in Great Britain and America that began to bring together teams of mathematicians, statisticians, psychologists, physicists and other scientists to tackle problems demanding over-all strategies of enquiry and application. Calculations of manpower and material needed to land and maintain combatant forces on hostile territory and of civilian food requirements in a siege economy were two examples of the fields in which operational research developed. Peaceful applications have been made in most countries of the world on lines described in the remaining chapters of this book.

Operational research studies *systems*, a term readily recognised but not easy to define. A fleet of lorries regularly delivering goods from a warehouse to a firm's customers constitutes a system. The term could properly be applied to surgeons working together in a hospital, with the anaesthetists, sisters and nurses working with them, and the equipment they use. In business, study of the behaviour of a system usually involves study of related sub-systems: the production-line of a factory is an identifiable system; but a change in its working would involve changes in the supplies of raw materials, in the employment of workers and perhaps in the storage of finished products. Essentially, therefore, a system is a group of people engaged in joint, purposeful activity, together with material means used to achieving it, within the general context of industry, commerce or administration; and such a system is likely to be supported by, or associated with, other systems called sub-systems.

Groups and sub-groups thus described rarely lend themselves to direct experiment of the kind carried out in laboratories in the natural sciences. A Birmingham firm, for example, with a new product to export may need to choose between Liverpool, Bristol and London as its outlet. It cannot set up three separate dock offices and in the light of experience choose the most suitable. A government may need to decide whether £100 million is better spent on electrifying the railway between two major cities or upon improving the road system between them. Not only are the issues at stake very complicated, but for the government there is little scope for crucial experiment, as the scientist would understand it. Both kind of problem are suitable for operational research, and insight would be obtained by setting up *models*.

Iconic models, i.e. those which give a physical resemblance to the original, are often used in engineering, architecture and other branches of study. The nautical properties of a proposed oil-tanker, for example, can be studied by constructing a small-scale model and simulating stormy weather in a laboratory. Operational research uses a variety of quantitative models and formulae which are mathematical or statistical in origin. A firm deciding upon its stock-ordering policy could use the simple model derived on page 90:

$$Q = \sqrt{\left(\frac{2DP}{SC}\right)}$$

where Q is the most economical size of batch in which to order stock, D is the total annual demand, P is the cost of placing one order, S is a measure of stock-holding costs and C is the unit cost of the items. This is an *a priori* model, a general description constructed from first principles. The expression

$$P = \frac{80}{Q + 65}$$

where Q is the number of units of a commodity demanded, and P is the unit price, is a simple model showing how prices change as demand changes, and which is likely to have been obtained by observing a number of pairs of values of P and Q for this commodity and fitting a relationship which best suits them. Such a model is *empirical* or *a posteriori*, though the general shape of the model, and in particular the positions of P and Q, reflect simple economic theory. The letters in both models indicate variables. Those which are determined by factors outside the defined system are called *exogenous*; for example, in the stock model, D, total demand, and the other factors on the right-hand side are determined by the size of the firm's market, salaries of order clerks, etc. Q, in this context, is an *endogenous* variable, because it influences the system from within. The batch size, for example, will affect the firm's storage and transport policies. In the second model Q will be exogenous and P endogenous.

The reason for constructing an operational research model is *optimisation*, i.e. the calculation of the best value for a particular set of conditions. In the stock model Q gives the size of batch which will give the lowest average figure of unit cost when the combined effect of purchase, ordering and holding are taken into account. An optimum may be a maximum value: we may, for example, in planning vehicle routes between a series of towns served by a delivery system choose that plan which makes the greatest use of vehicle capacity.

The two models quoted so far are comparatively simple. They are *static* in the sense that the only interrelationship between the factors involved is that described by the model; the effect does not itself influence the values of the factors causing it. But this is not always so. Consider the second model. In the long run a change in price will induce changes in quantities being produced for sale, and a more sophisticated model would be needed to do justice to the situation. Models which make allowance for changes induced in the system by its own operation are called *dynamic*. Where a model incorporates an allowance for the time taken for one factor to affect another, the variables are said to be *lagged*.

Where operational research methods are applied to large organisations the great problem is to reconcile the policies which models describing the separate parts would suggest. In a large manufacturing firm a model may show the scale of output which will minimise average production costs: but a model of the market may suggest a different figure for maximum profits. Neither of these levels may be consistent with the level of production which best suits the firm's capital structure and financial resources. Overall models which attempt to cover all the variables are sometimes constructed. Of necessity they are computer operated, and they constitute important tools of management. Operational research is scientifically based. Facts are studied objectively, hypotheses framed, tested and re-framed if necessary. Models which are constructed have the same logical status as theories in the natural sciences. Today they are indispensable tools of management. But the successful running of large enterprises, whether for public good or private profit, depends upon informed personal judgement, so that management becomes an art and not merely a science.

Bibliography

Most of the following books deal not only with the nature of operational research but also with the main topics covered by the other chapters of this book.

R. L. Ackoff and M. W. Sasieni, *Fundamentals of Operations Research* (New York: Wiley, 1968).
W. T. Bane, *Operational Research Models*, Occasional Paper No. 8 (London: H.M.S.O., 1968).

E. S. Buffa, *Operations Management* (New York: Wiley, 1976).

D. Gale, *Theory of Linear Economic Models* (New York: McGraw-Hill, 1960).

F. S. Hillier and G. T. Lieberman, *Introduction to Operations Research*, 2nd ed. (San Francisco: Holden–Day, 1974).

M. S. Makower and E. Williamson, *Operational Research – Problems, Techniques and Exercises*, 3rd ed. (London: Hodder & Stoughton, 1975).

G. H. Mitchell, *Operational Research: Techniques and Examples* (London: English Universities Press Ltd, 1972).

P. G. Moore, *Basic Operational Research*, 2nd ed. (London: Pitman, 1976).

F. Ricaferrera, *Operations Research Models for Business and Industry* (Cincinatti: South-Western Publishing Company, 1964).

P. Rivett, *Principles of Model Building: The Construction of Models for Decision Analysis* (New York: Wiley, 1972).

J. Singh, *Operations Research* (Harmondsworth: Penguin, 1971).

2

Queueing and Waiting-time Problems

An early application of operational research methods was to the problems of queueing. The queues formed in a modern supermarket by customers waiting to pay for baskets of goods typifies quantitative problems found in other business and industrial situations. Each cash-till is approached by a single *service-channel*, each customer is a *unit*, and the service-channels and tills or *service-points*, to use a more general term, form a *system*. The fundamental problem is to strike the right balance between customers' demands for services and the organisation's supply of service somewhere between the extremes of excessive queueing and uneconomical manning of service-points. The first example shows that even when the arrival rates of customers and the service times are fixed – a simple situation rarely met in practice – the system is very sensitive to small changes in rates or times.

Example 2.1   The stores of a large organisation issues material at the constant rate of 10 orders per hour. The stores open at 9.00 a.m. and workers arrive in succession at the rate of 8 per hour, as soon as the store opens. Assuming a single service-channel:
  (i) For what proportion of the first hour will the storekeeper be issuing material?
  (ii) What change in (a) arrival rate *or* (b) service rate would result in the storekeeper being fully employed without queueing occurring?
  (iii) Investigate the queueing that would arise at the original service rate, but with workers arriving at a new rate of 12 per hour.

  (i) An issue rate of 10 per hour means that one worker can be supplied in 6 min. But if workers arrive at 8 per hour, they will arrive at 60 min./8 = $7\frac{1}{2}$ mins., and there will be a gap of $(7\frac{1}{2} - 6)$ min. = $1\frac{1}{2}$ min. after each. Queueing will not occur, and the storekeeper will be employed

$$\frac{8 \times 6 \text{ min.}}{60 \text{ min.}} \times \frac{100}{1} = 80\% \text{ of the time}$$

  (ii) Either (a) the storekeeper slows down to 8 per hour (the arrival rate), or (b) the workers increased their arrival rate to 10 per hour (the service rate).

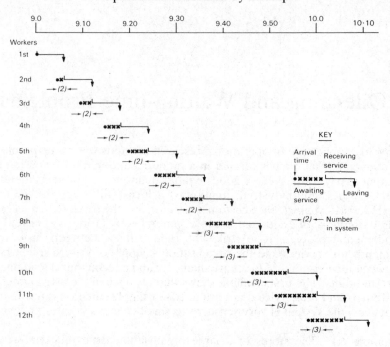

FIG. 2.1   Workers queueing at stores

(iii) Figure 2.1 shows how a queue would build up gradually. The second worker, arriving at 9.05 a.m., would queue for 1 min. before the storekeeper was free to start supplying him at 9.06 a.m. After 9.20 a.m. at least 2 people would be in the system. At 9.35 a.m. 3 would be in the system for a short time, and after 9.45 a.m. there would never be fewer than 3, until the arrival of workers stopped. Congestion would increase progressively and successive workers would have to wait increasingly longer. The twelfth worker, for example, would spend 16 min. in the system. With a single service point the number 'in the system' = 1 being served plus number waiting, so that from 9.45 a.m. the queue would contain 2 workers.

Under these simplified conditions whether queueing occurs depends upon the *traffic intensity*, a quantity indicated by ρ (Greek – pronounced rho), and calculated by dividing by the average number of units arriving in unit time λ (Greek lambda) divided by μ (Greek mu), the average number of services completed in unit time, i.e.

$$\rho = \frac{\lambda}{\mu}$$

In Example 2.1 the opening value of ρ equals

$$\frac{8 \text{ arrivals/hour}}{10 \text{ orders/hour}} = 0.8$$

for (ii) (a) $\frac{8}{8} = 1$ and (b) $\frac{10}{10} = 1$

and for (iii) $\frac{12}{8} = 1.5$

Where both μ and λ are unvarying the three cases just studied demonstrate that if $\rho < 1$ no queueing will occur and if $\rho = 1$ the service facility will be in continuous use, and if $\rho > 1$ queueing will start with the second arrival and will increase with subsequent arrivals.

In practice the above calculations have been oversimplified: no allowance has been made for the time that must elapse between finishing one service and starting the next. Initially this might appear trivial, but after several services a cumulative and disruptive lag would develop. An even more serious criticism can be made: neither the arrival rates nor the service times are likely to be rigid; variations in either will upset the neat calculations made so far and, where variations are combined, the disturbance to the original system will be great. In general if queueing is occurring, any increase in arrival rate or service time will make it worse, whereas a reduction in service time will only improve the situation if constantly matched with an increase in arrival rate.

If the two variables were completely random, queueing calculations would be almost impossible to make, though, given the limits of variation, methods of simulation (see Chapter 3) might be used. Fortunately, input and output in queueing situations can often be described by two statistical distributions, the first being introduced by the next example.

Example 2.2 Assume that the arrivals of workers in Example 2.1 follow the Poisson distribution, with $\lambda = 8$ per hour, and calculate the separate probabilities of 4, 5, 6, etc., up to 12 workers arriving in 1 hour.

The Poisson formula gives the probability of X events as follows:

$$P(x) = \frac{e^{-m}m^x}{X!},$$

when $X = 4$, $P(x) = \dfrac{e^{-8}8^4}{4!} = \dfrac{0.0003546 \times 4096}{4 \times 3 \times 2 \times 1} = 0.057$

and

when $X = 5$, $P(x)$ $\dfrac{e^{-8}8^5}{5!} = 0.092$

Other values, directly calculated, or more conveniently calculated by the recursion method (see *Business Statistics by Example*, by A. E. Innes (Macmillan, 1974, pp. 238–9), give

$$P(4) = 0.057$$
$$P(5) = 0.092$$
$$P(6) = 0.122$$
$$P(7) = 0.140$$
$$P(8) = 0.140$$
$$P(9) = 0.124$$
$$P(10) = 0.099$$
$$P(11) = 0.072$$
$$P(12) = 0.048$$

Probabilities decrease either side of the 4–12 range, which can be seen to account for 89.4 per cent of the probabilities. Hence, we can expect some divergency, but well over 50 per cent of the time arrivals are likely to be in the (6–10) per hour range. The use of formulae, to be stated presently, does not require Poisson calculations, but study of probabilities of the kind calculated above will show why queueing sometimes occurs well before ρ approaches unity.

The Poisson distribution calculates the frequency of events over set periods of time. Calculation of varying service times depends upon a distribution which is a kind of obverse of Poisson, because it deals with lengths of times between events. The next example introduces it.

Example 2.3 (i) Take the service times for Example 2.1 to be exponentially distributed, with expected frequency of 10 per hour. Calculate and graph the probabilities of service times of less than 6 min. and more than 6 min. (ii) Calculate by integration the proportion of service times that can be expected to be (a) between 5 min. and 7 min., and (b) between 3 min. and 9 min.

The probability density function for the exponential distribution is

$$Y = \mu e^{-\mu x}$$

where Y is the probability density, μ is the expected number of events in unit time and X the number of units of time that will elapse before the recurrence of an event, on the assumption that an event has just occurred.

Working in minutes, if 10 services occur in 1 hour, 1 occurs in 6 min., and in 1 unit of time, i.e. 1 min., 1/6 of a service will occur. Assuming no break occurs between the ending of a service and the beginning of the next, x is a service time. When $x = 0$ min.

$$Y = \frac{1}{6}e^{-1/6 \times 0} = \frac{1}{6} \times 1 = \frac{1}{6}$$

when $x = 1$ min.,

$$Y = \frac{1}{6}e^{-1/6 \times 1/1} = 0.1411$$

The following table summarises these and similarly calculated values:

Service time (min.)	Probability density
0	0.1667
1	0.1411
2	0.1194
4	0.0857
6	0.0613
8	0.0439
10	0.0315
20	0.0059
30	0.0011

(ii) (a) The required probability is given by the shaded area in Figure 2.2, and is obtained as the value of the probability density function integrated between the limits $x = 5$ and $x = 7$:

$$\int_5^7 \frac{1}{6}e^{-x/6}\,\mathrm{d}x = \frac{1}{6}\left[1 - e^{-x/6}\right]_5^7 = \frac{1}{6}$$

$$\{(1 - 0.3114) - (1 - 0.4346)\} = 0.02053$$

(b) For the wider limits

$$\frac{1}{6}\left[1 - e^{-x/6}\right]_3^9 = 0.0639$$

Hence, the wide variations in service times are illustrated, only 2.053 per cent lying within a minute either side of the average, and only 6.39 per cent within 3 min. either side.

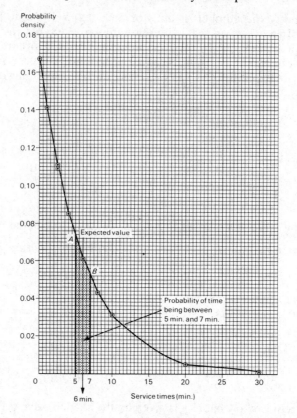

FIG. 2.2   Exponential distribution of service times

Such wide random variations in arrival and service times show why the approach of Example 2.1 needs considerable modification and why the measurements of queueing situations are usually in terms of probability. The combination of Poisson and exponential conditions has produced a series of formulae used to solve quantitative problems and the next examples introduce them.

Example 2.4   A tyre centre is open 10 hours per day for repairing punctures, the average repair time being 20 min. Customers arrive at an average rate of 20 per day. Calculate (i) the probability that a motorist has to wait upon arrival, and (ii) the number of hours during a 6-day working week when punctures are not being repaired.

(i) The probability, P, is the traffic intensity ρ already defined.

$$\lambda = 20 \text{ per 10-hour day} = 2/\text{hour}$$
$$\mu = \text{average number of services in 1 hour} = 60 \text{ min.}/20 \text{ min.} = 3$$
$$\text{Therefore } P = 2/3 \ (= 66.7 \text{ per cent})$$

(ii) The probability of a motorist being 'in the system', i.e. either having a puncture repaired or waiting for it to be repaired, is given by ρ. Punctures will not be repaired when there is no one in the system, i.e.

the probability is $1 - P = 1 - 2/3 = 1/3$

in a full week for $\dfrac{6 \times 10}{3}$ hours $= 20$ hours.

Excessive queueing can be to the disadvantage of management not only because of physical congestion, but because customers may *renage*, i.e. leave the queue before being served. The next example introduces another formula used in such situations.

Example 2.5 A cashier at a supermarket check-out points deals with customers at an average rate of 30 per hour: (i) with customers arriving at an average rate of 25 per hour, calculate the average length of queue when a queue of 1 or more forms; (ii) what improvement is needed in service time if the average queue-length is to be reduced by 1?

(i) The formula for average length of queue is

$$\frac{1}{1 - \rho}$$

$\lambda = 25/\text{hour}$, $\mu = 60 \text{ min.}/2 \text{ min.} = 30/\text{hour}$, giving

$$\rho = \frac{25}{30} = \frac{5}{6}$$

and average length is

$$\frac{1}{1 - 5/6} = 6$$

Note that the formula is based on the number of queues and does not reflect occasions when no queue occurs.

(ii) If the average is to be $(6 - 1) = 5$

$$\frac{1}{1 - \rho} = 5$$

i.e. $1 = 5 - 5\rho$, giving $\rho = 0.8$

$$\frac{25}{\mu} = 0.8,$$

i.e. $\mu = \dfrac{25}{0.8}$/hour,

giving an improved service time of

$$\frac{60}{25/0.8} \text{ min.} \simeq 1 \text{ min. } 55 \text{ sec.}$$

The next example introduces a formula which takes into account times when the queue length $= 0$ as well as occasions when it is greater than 0.

Example 2.6 (i) Use the data in Example 2.5(i) to calculate the average queue length on the basis just described. (ii) If the shop is open from 9.0 a.m. to 5.30 p.m., using the unimproved service rate, calculate the number of hours when no queue can be expected.

(i) The formula is

$$\frac{\rho^2}{1 - \rho}$$

For $\rho = 5/6$, the average is

$$\frac{(5/6)^2}{1 - 5/6} = \frac{25}{6} = 4\tfrac{1}{6}$$

(ii) By the method of Example 2.4 (ii)

$$1 - \rho = 1 - 5/6 = 1/6$$

Total hours $= 8\tfrac{1}{2}$, giving $8\tfrac{1}{2}/6$ hours $= 1\tfrac{1}{4}$ hours without a queue.

Often we shall need to know the chance that a queue will be a particular length between nil and its maximum state. The probability of n people being in the system is given by

$$P(n) = (1 - \rho)\rho^n$$

and the next example uses it.

Example 2.7 Patients arrive at a doctor's surgery at the average rate of 8 per hour and the waiting-room seats 9 patients. The average time of consultation is 6 min.

(i) For what proportion of surgery time is the waiting-room likely to be just full?
(ii) What is the probability that (a) 1 patient and (b) 2 patients are queueing outside the waiting-room?

The system is the consulting room + waiting room, so that when the waiting room is just full, $n = (1 + 9) = 10$:

$$\rho = 8/10 = 0.8$$

$$P(10) = (1{-}0.8) \times (0.8)^{10} = 0.021$$

i.e. 2.1 per cent of surgery time.

(ii) (a) The system has been extended, $n = 1 + 9 + 1$ (outside) $= 11$

$$P(11) = (1{-}0.8) \times (0.8)^{11} = 0.0172$$

(b) Multiplication by 0.8 gives the new probability as

$$0.8 \times 0.0172 = 0.0138.$$

Where employees of an organisation are forced to queue to draw stores, collect new work or deliver completed work, to give a few examples, loss of productive effort occurs, and to measure it two more formulae are useful.

$$\text{The expected number in the system} = \frac{\rho}{1 - \rho}$$

The average time spent by one unit (e.g. worker) in the system

$$= \frac{1}{\mu - \lambda}$$

The next example uses them.

Example 2.8 The work of a Senior Executive in a large organisation is to validate claims, each being brought by an Administrative Assistant, who remains with the Executive to help him until validation is completed. The average time of validation is 12 min, and Assistants arrive on the average 7 every 2 hours. The cost of the Executive's time to the undertaking is £5/hour, for that of an assistant, £2.25/hour. Calculate the hourly loss to

the undertaking: (i) through queueing and validations by Assistants; and
(ii) through the Executive waiting for claims.

(i) $\lambda = 7$ every 2 hours $= 3.5$/hour
     $\mu = 60/12 = 5$/hour.
     Therefore $\rho = 3.5/5 = 0.7$.
     The expected number of Assistants in the system equals

$$\frac{\rho}{1-\rho} = \frac{0.7}{1-0.7} = 2\tfrac{1}{3}$$

     The average time spent by each Assistant in the system is

$$\left(\frac{1}{\mu-\lambda}\right) \text{hours} = \left(\frac{1}{5-3.5}\right) \text{hours} = \tfrac{2}{3} \text{hours}$$

     Therefore the loss to the firm equals

$$(2\tfrac{1}{3} \times \tfrac{2}{3} \times \text{£2.25}) \text{ per hour} = \text{£3.50/hour}$$

(ii) The Executive will be waiting for claims when no one is in the system.
     Following the method of Example 2.4 (ii) the probability is
     $1 - \rho = 1 - 0.7 = 0.3$. Therefore the loss/hour $= 0.3 \times £5 = £1.5$.

If the organisation takes the different view that an Assistant's time is only
lost when he is queueing, and is not lost when with the Executive, then the
figure calculated in (i) will overstate the loss.
     The average number of Assistants queueing is

$$\frac{\rho^2}{1-\rho} = \frac{(0.7)^2}{0.3} = 1.63$$

The average queueing time will be

$$\frac{\rho}{\mu(1-\rho)} = \frac{0.7}{5 \times (1-0.7)} = 0.47 \text{ hours}$$

giving the lower figure of loss

$$(1.63 \times 0.47 \times \text{£2.25})/\text{hour} = \text{£1.72}$$

All examples used so far have described *single-channel* situations. The
organisation in the last examples, faced with such losses, would begin to
consider appointing an extra Senior Executive to share the work of validation. Assuming his functions to be identical with those of the first, the new
system would be *multi-channel* with greatly complicated equations to
describe it. The effect of providing two service-points is not simply to halve

a queue length or double the number of customers served in unit time. This would be so if two entirely independent service routes developed.

The next example shows the complications and benefits produced by extending service capacity.

Example 2.9 Vehicles approach a road tunnel by a single carriageway at an average rate of 3 per minute, toll being taken at a single booth at the average rate of 15 sec./vehicle. Discuss the effect of installing extra booths upon (i) the probability that no vehicle is in the system, (ii) the average number of vehicles in the system, and (iii) the average delay per vehicle.

(i) For a single-channel system

$$\lambda = 3/\text{min.}, \ \mu = (60/15)/\text{min.} = 4/\text{min.}$$

so that $\rho = 3/4 = 0.75$, giving $P = 0.25$. For a multi-channel system, ρ becomes

$$\frac{\lambda}{C\mu}$$

where $C =$ the number of channels. If 1 more booth is installed $C = 1 + 1 = 2$, making

$$\rho = \frac{0.75}{2} = 0.375$$

But the new probability is obtained by putting this value in the formula

$$\frac{C!(1-\rho)}{(\rho C)^c + C!(1-\rho)\{\sum_{r=0}^{C-1} \frac{1}{r!}(\rho C)^r\}}$$

r in the denominator indicates the term being summated. For our immediate problem we let $r = 0$, note the { } value and add to it the { } value for $r = 2 - 1 = 1$. If we had been calculating the probability for 8 booths, r would have taken the successive values of 0, 1, 2, . . ., 7.

For $r = 0$

$$\{\text{expression}\} = \frac{1}{0!}(0.375 \times 2)^0 = 1$$

For $|r = 1$

$$\{\text{expression}\} = \frac{1}{1!}(0.375 \times 2)^1 = 0.75$$

Therefore complete summation $= 1 + 0.75 = 1.75$, giving the probability as

$$\frac{2 \times 1(1 - 0.375)}{(0.375 \times 2)^2 + (2 \times 1)(1 - 0.375)(1.75)} = 0.45$$

For 3 booths

$$\rho = \frac{0.75}{3} = 0.25$$

In the denominator, for $r = 0$ $\{\ \} = 1$

For $r = 1$ $\dfrac{1}{1!}(0.25 \times 3)^1 = 0.75$

„ $r = 2$ $\dfrac{1}{2!}(0.25 \times 3)^2 = \dfrac{0.28}{2.03}$

so that the new probability is

$$\frac{3!(1 - 0.25)}{(3 \times 0.25)^3 + (3!) \times (0.75)\{2.08\}} = \frac{4.5}{9.78} = 0.46$$

(ii) For the single booth, the average is

$$\frac{1}{1 - 0.75} = 4$$

For the multi-channel system, we use P_0, the probability calculated in (i). This, as we have seen, will depend upon the number of channels. The value is then used in the formula

$$\frac{\rho(\rho C)^C}{C!(1 - \rho)^2} P_0 + \rho^0 C$$

to give the required average. For 2 channels $P_0 = 0.45$, giving

$$\frac{0.375(2 \times 0.375)^2}{2!(1 - 0.375)^2} \times \frac{0.45}{1} + (2 \times 0.375) = 0.82 \text{ vehicles}$$

For 3 channels $P_0 = 0.46$, giving

$$\frac{0.25(3 \times 0.25)^3}{3!(1 - 0.25)^2} \times \frac{0.46}{1} + (3 \times 0.25) = 0.76 \text{ vehicles}$$

(iii) Ignoring the delay caused by vehicles decelerating to enter the system and in accelerating upon leaving it, the delay will be the average time in the system. For the single channel the delay will be

$$\frac{1}{4-3} \text{min./vehicle} = 1 \text{ min./vehicle}.$$

For the multi-channel system the average time formula, as before, includes P_0, and is

$$\frac{\mu(\rho C)^C}{C!(1-\rho)^2 C\mu} P_0 + \frac{1}{\mu}$$

giving for 2 booths

$$\left\{ \frac{(2 \times 0.375)^2}{2!(1-0.375)^2 \times 0.375 \times 4} \times \frac{0.45}{1} \right\} + \frac{1}{4} = 0.39 \text{ min.}$$

and for 3 booths

$$\left\{ \frac{(2 \times 0.25)^3}{3!(1-0.25)^2 \times 0.25 \times 4} \times \frac{0.46}{1} \right\} + \frac{1}{4} = 0.27 \text{ min.}$$

The formula for calculating the average time in the queue in such a situation is

$$\frac{(\rho C)^c}{C!(1-\rho)^2 C\mu} P_0$$

The methods given so far are valid, however many people have required a service, and although in practice the number will be limited, for theoretical purposes the queues are regarded as *infinite*. The next example introduces a different situation where the queue is of inanimate items awaiting the service of one or more operations.

Example 2.10   A baker looks after 3 similar ovens, each producing equal size batches of the same product. Each oven takes 5 min. to load and 10 min. to unload, and the baking process takes 15 min. If he starts work at 8.0 a.m., analyse the use of his time in the first hour.

Figure 2.3 shows one possibility. He loads the three ovens consecutively, finishing the last, no. 3 at 8.15 a.m., with a break until 8.20 a.m., the earliest time when he can start unloading no. 1. Having completed this at

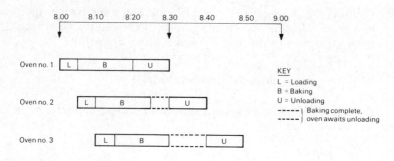

FIG. 2.3   The 'three ovens' problem

8.30 a.m., he starts to unload no. 2, which was ready at 8.25 a.m. At 8.40 a.m. the baker is free for any one of the following operations.

   (i) reload 1
  (ii) reload 2
 (iii) unload 3

If he follows (iii) he will be free at 8.50 a.m. for (i) or (ii).
   Baker's and oven times are summarised below:

| | *Baker* | | | *Oven* | |
	Working	*Waiting*		*In use*	*Waiting*
	55 min.	5 min.	1	(30 min. + 5 min.)	25 min.
			2	(30 min. + 5 min.)	25 min.
			3	(30 min.)	30 min.
	Total 55 min.	5 min.		100 min.	80 min.

Hence 8.3 per cent of the baker's time and 44.4 per cent of the oven time is spent in waiting. If the baker's duties are only loading and unloading the ovens, then there is a slight loss of his time. Oven capacity is greatly underused, but whether employment of another baker is justified depends upon other factors not stated.

   As it is the problem has been oversimplified. In practice variations in the complete cycle time of $\frac{1}{2}$ hour and in times of the separate operations are likely to occur: allowance should be made for the baker changing from one operation to another; and most important of all, the baker is likely to be overseeing the performance of the ovens when all three are baking at the same time. To allow for random variations in the routine operations and for the baker to attend to a non-routine incident, e.g. the over-heating of an oven, we need formulae based on probabilities. The application of queueing theory to situations where one or more operative looks after more than one machine is called *machine interference* because we need to estimate how often and for how long an operative must interrupt his general care of one machine to attend to another.

The next example shows how the general demand for an operative's services may be calculated.

Example 2.11 A fitter looks after a bank of 5 similar machines and the probability of a machine requiring attention is 1/8. Use the biomial distribution to show how, in theory, his services will be needed. (Readers needing revision of the distribution are referred to the authors' two books mentioned on page ii.)

If $p = {}^1/_8$ is the probability that a machine will require attention, then $q = 1 - {}^1/_8 = {}^7/_8$ is the probability that it will not: and the 6 possible situations have probabilities given by the successive terms of the expansion $(p + q)^5$, i.e.

$$({}^1/_8 + {}^7/_8)^5$$

$$= ({}^1/_8)^5 + 5({}^1/_8)^4({}^7/_8)^1 + 10({}^1/_8)^3({}^7/_8)^2 + 10({}^1/_8)^2({}^7/_8)^3 + 5({}^1/_8)({}^7/_8)^4 + ({}^7/_8)^5$$

Calculating the values of the separate terms, summarising and calculating as percentages we obtain the information contained below:

No. of machines		*Relative	Percentage of
Needing attention	Not needing attention	frequency	Total time
5	0	1	0.003
4	1	35	0.107
3	2	490	1.495
2	3	3430	10.468
1	4	12005	36.636
0	5	16807	51.291
		32768	100.000

*Calculated for convenience by multiplying each probability by 8^5. Hence for slightly over half his time the fitter can expect all machines to be running satisfactorily, for just over 36 per cent can he expect to have one machine to deal with and for less than 2 per cent of the time will 3 or more machines need attention.

But such calculations only show very generally the probable demand for the service. For a practical judgement of the situation we need to consider the average service time and the distribution of variations about it. Furthermore, as we are considering a time schedule composed of successive pairs

of events, each being (occurrence of break-down + retification of it), we
need to use, not a fixed value of $p = \frac{1}{8}$, which is in nature an 'arrival rate',
but, rather, random variations about it. The picture given by Example 2.11
is incomplete, and likely to be optimistic.

In such problems we can often assume that breakdowns occur with Poisson frequency and that service times are distributed exponentially. We need
to calculate a quantity, λ, a servicing factor, which is comparable with ρ in
earlier problems, from the relationship:

$$\lambda = \mu\alpha$$

where μ = mean number of stops per hour and α = mean service time
per stop.

Machine interference arises from two different causes: (i) routine attention at set intervals, with little variation about an average time, e.g. to
restock a bin with raw material which the machine uses; and (ii) break-
downs, adjustments and similar causes occurring at widely varying intervals, and requiring widely varying amounts of an operative's time to rectify.
The servicing factor for a particular machine is likely to be the sum of two
different products, and for a bank of machines the problems may well
differ for machines of the same type, e.g. an older machine may break
down more often than a newer one and take more time to put right. The
next example illustrates the problem.

Example 2.12   A machine making electrical components must be stopped
every 5 min. to replace a spool of wire, an operation which takes on the
average 20 sec. Furthermore, each time a control needs readjusting, the
operative stops the machine, an event occurring on average every 12 min,
with an average time of 45 sec. Calculate the service factor for replacing
the spools.

λ = (mean stops/hour) × (mean service time), which equals

$$\frac{60}{5} \times \frac{20}{60 \times 60} = \frac{1}{15}$$

and for control readjustment

$$\frac{60}{12} \times \frac{45}{60 \times 60} = \frac{1}{16}$$

giving a total service factor of $1/15 + 1/16 = 31/240$. Hence, in every hour
the machine will be down, i.e. not running for a total of

$$\frac{60 \times 31}{240} \text{ min.} = 7\frac{3}{4} \text{ min.}$$

If we have n machines, and a single value of λ, then P_0, the probability that all machines are running, is given by

$$P_0 = \frac{1}{1 + n\lambda + n(n-1)\lambda^2 + \ldots n!\lambda^n}$$

and the next example uses it.

Example 2.13 A machine, on the average, needs an operative's service once every 10 minutes for $1^1/_8$ minutes. If he had 4 such machines to look after, how long during an hour would he be likely to be free?

$\lambda = $ (no. of stops) $\times$ (mean service time), which equals

$$\frac{60}{10} \times \frac{1^1/_8}{60} = \frac{9}{80}$$

The operative would be likely to be free when all machines were running. For $n = 4$

$$P_0 = \frac{1}{1 + (4 \times 9/80) + \{4 \times 3(9/80)^2\} + \{4 \times 3 \times 2(9/80)^3\} + \{4 \times 3 \times 2 \times (9/80)^4\}}$$

$$= 0.61$$

Therefore, he would be likely to be free for 36 min. 36 sec. each hour.

Note that on this limited data we are not to judge whether an economical balance between use of manpower and employment of machines has been reached. On the face of things service capacity is greatly underused: yet during the theoretical 23 min. 24 sec. when one or more machines is down, the loss of output may reach an undesirable level. The next example introduces a formula which allows us to analyse such a situation more closely.

Example 2.14 A firm owns 5 delivery vehicles and, excluding major services, each requires minor maintenance or repair twice every 100 running hours for 20 min. on each occasion. Calculate the proportion of time that 0, 1, 2 and 3 vehicles are out of commission.

As before $\lambda = \dfrac{2}{100} \times \dfrac{1}{3} = \dfrac{1}{150}$ (hours)

$$P_0 = \frac{1}{1 + (5 \times 1/150) + (5 \times 4)(1/150)^2 + (5 \times 4 \times 3)(1/150)^3 + (5 \times 4 \times 3 \times 2)(1/150)^4 + (5 \times 4 \times 3 \times 2 \times 1)(1/150)^5}$$

$$= 0.9668$$

The probability that r machines (in this case vehicles) are stopped is calculated as:

$$P_r = \frac{n!}{(n-r)!} \times \lambda^n P_0$$

When $r = 1$

$$P_1 = \frac{5 \times 4 \times 3 \times 2 \times 1}{4 \times 3 \times 2 \times 1} \times \left(\frac{1}{150}\right)^1 \times 0.9668 = 0.0322$$

$$P_2 = \frac{5 \times 4 \times 3 \times 2 \times 1}{3 \times 2 \times 1} \times \left(\frac{1}{150}\right)^2 \times 0.9668 = 0.000859$$

$$P_3 = \frac{5 \times 4 \times 3 \times 2 \times 1}{2 \times 1} \times \left(\frac{1}{150}\right)^3 \times 0.9668 = 0.0000172$$

Hence, for 96.68 per cent of the time all vehicles are running, for 3 per cent $(5 - 1) = 4$ are running, and the times when 3 and 2 only are running are so small as to be of little practical importance. Even in the P_0 calculation the last term in the denominator was so small that it could be ignored.

Although some of the calculations shown in this chapter appear formidable, exact mathematical descriptions of the situations would need to take other factors into account. For example, we have assumed a very simple *queue discipline*, the term used to describe the order in which waiting items pass through the system. In our calculations items have passed through the system in their order of entry, F.I.F.O., 'first in, first out'. But alternative arrangements often produce more complicated calculations. Certain items may have priority, either going to the head of the queue upon arrival, or in an extreme system going before the item being serviced. Where at one point the services being offered are of two or more kinds, some advantage may be gained when installing an extra service-point if each point specialises in a particular kind of service. A large bank, for example, will reduce the extent of queueing by reserving one till for personal cheque payments only. Furthermore, equations used so far do not always describe the behaviour of service channels when first opened: for example, when a supermarket first opens in the morning ρ is likely to be small, but it will fluctuate during the day. Fortunately, we can often solve quantitative problems of this kind without involving even more sophisticated formulae. The techniques of *simulation*, to be explained in the next chapter, are being increasingly used to this end.

Exercises 2

2.1 In a large organisation workers are paid by two clerks, each taking $\frac{1}{2}$ min. to pay a worker. Workers arrive at a steady rate of 3 per min. If both clerks are free, or the two queues are equal, a worker will go to either; otherwise, a worker will choose the clerk with the smaller queue. Use the graphical method of Example 2.1 to investigate for the first 10 minutes (i) the extent of queueing under present arrangements, and (ii) the effect on queueing of (a) a clerk taking a 5 min. break after a service for 2 min., (b) a 1 min. break in the arrival of workers after 4 min., and (c) both (a) and (b) occurring.

2.2 Customers arrive at a launderette at the average rate of 8 per 10 hours and, on the average take 35 min. each to use its services. Calculate (i) the average time each customer has to wait before using the services, and (ii) the percentage of opening time when the launderette is not being used.

2.3 (i) Explain the importance of *traffic intensity*.
(ii) A garage specialises in fitting new exhaust systems to cars, taking on the average $\frac{3}{4}$ hour over one car. Customers arrive at the average rate of 3 every 4 hours. What is the average number of motorists in the system?
(iii) Calculate what changes in (a) arrival rate, and (b) service rate would reduce the traffic intensity in (ii) by 10 per cent.

2.4 A road organisation has requests from motorists members who have broken down on the average 4 times every 24 hours. On the average it can cope with 11 demands in 2 days. Use the appropriate Poisson distribution to estimate the number of days in 1977 (i) when it could not cope with all the demands, and (ii) when no demands were made.

2.5 The times which Electricity Board collectors take to empty domestic meters are distributed exponentially, the average being 5 per hour. By calculating a few typical probabilities show that variations in service times are likely to be wide. How, in general, would variability be affected by an increase in rate of emptying?

2.6 A self-service petrol station has one 4-star pump. The average customer takes $1\frac{1}{2}$ min. to draw petrol from the pump and to leave the pump ready for use by the next motorist. At peak time motorists arrive at the average rate of 30 per hour. Using various methods shown in the chapter calculate values of interest to the garage-owner and to the motorists. Your account should explain and illustrate the difference between *the system* and *the queue*. When would such a difference matter very little?

2.7 Claimants arrive at a government office on the average at 15 min. intervals, and are paid by a clerical officer at the average rate of 10 min. each claimant. An extra clerk, with the same average rate as the first, is appointed.

(i) Calculate as percentages the changes brought by the new arrangements:
   (a) in the average queue length;
   (b) in the average time each claimant takes to pass through the office;
   (c) in the average time a clerk is not dealing with a claimant.
(ii) Discuss briefly in general terms whether queueing can be completely abolished by the appointment of more clerks.

2.8 Explain with simple examples why the characteristics of each of the following statistical distributions are important in queueing calculations:
   (i) exponential
   (ii) Poisson
   (iii) binomial

2.9 (i) Explain the terms *machine interference* and *service factor*.
   (ii) State important points to be taken into account in deciding how many service machines can be looked after by one operative.
   (iii) Repeat Example 2.12, using the following new figures:

   service – once every 12 min.
   each service takes $1\frac{1}{4}$ min.
   let the operative have 5 machines to look after.

   Compare in a few sentences the new situation with the old.

2.10 A workman looks after 4 machines. On the average a machine must be stopped for service every 20 min., and it takes 8 min. before the machine is running again. In an 8-hour day (i) estimate the time when the workman will not be attending a machine, and (ii) estimate the time when no machine will be running.

Content

Bibliography

D. R. Cox and W. L. Smith, *Queues* (London: Chapman & Hall, 1971).

D. R. Cox and W. L. Smith, *Queues* (London: Chapman & Hall, 1971).
D. Gross and C. M. Harris, *Fundamentals of Queueing Theory* (New York: Wiley, 1974).
A. M. Lee, *Applied Queueing Theory* (London: Macmillan, 1966).
P. M. Morse, *Queues, Inventories and Maintenance* (New York: Wiley, 1958).
E. Page, *Queueing Theory in Operational Research* (London: Butterworth, 1972).
N. Y. Prabhu, *Queues and Inventories* (New York: Wiley, 1965).
J. Riordan, *Stochastic Service Systems* (New York: Wiley, 1962).
F. L. Saaty, *Elements of Queueing Theory* (New York: McGraw-Hill, 1961).
L. Takacs, *Introduction to the Theory of Queues* (New York: Oxford University Press, 1962).

3

Simulation

Operational research techniques, as we have already seen, use quantitative models for the study of business and other systems. Such representation is one kind of *simulation*, other kinds being the construction of physical models, e.g. of the hull of a new boat to test navigational characteristics or of working drawings used to estimate the cost of a new reservoir. Rarely in the field of operational research can a system be described by a simple equation or set of equations which give a unique and absolutely correct value for one set of variables: each variable is likely to assume a value within a stated or estimated range, and the way in which particular values of different variables combine is unlikely to follow a set pattern. To estimate final values under such conditions simulation methods are often used in preference to mathematical methods, where the uncertainties of the data would produce calculations of great and sometimes impossible complexity. Systems which have to be described in terms of such uncertainties are studied by *Monte Carlo* methods. The first example shows how two simple devices may be used to solve a business problem by representing its uncertainties.

Example 3.1 A firm uses whichever of its 4 vehicles is available to convey stock to its branches. The vehicles have average petrol consumption as follows:

Vehicle	Consumption
A	15 m.p.g.
B	18 m.p.g.
C	24 m.p.g.
D	20 m.p.g.

Lengths of return journeys to its branches are as follows:

Branch	Miles
I	60
II	80
III	105
IV	120
V	164
VI	188

Assume choices of destinations and vehicles occur at random, simulate 10 trips and hence estimate average petrol consumption per trip.

The use of each vehicle is equally probable. To simulate the choice of vehicle, the author tossed two coins, of equal value, but distinguishable by date, and chose according to the following scheme:

1954 coin	1963 coin	Vehicle
Head	Head	A
Head	Tail	B
Tail	Head	C
Tail	Tail	D

To choose a branch the author noted the position of the second hand on his watch, and used the following table:

Time (sec.)	Branch
0 –	I
10 –	II
20 –	III
30 –	IV
40 –	V
50 – (60)	VI

The first throw produced Tail – Tail and vehicle D was chosen. The time was 34 sec., which gave Branch IV. The second throw gave Tail (1954) – Head (1963) and the time was 26 sec., giving vehicle C travelling to Branch III. The remaining 8 pairs of values, similarly obtained, are recorded in cols (4) and (5) below. Care was taken to avoid a regular pattern of throw–time observations, in case the times and hence choice of branches began to assume a non-random pattern.

(1) Trip no.	(2) Vehicle	(3) Branch	(4) m.p.g.	(5) Miles	(6) Gallons
1	D	IV	20	120	6.00
2	C	IV	24	105	4.38
3	C	V	24	164	6.83
4	B	III	18	105	5.83
5	A	I	15	60	4.00
6	D	VI	20	188	9.40
7	C	IV	24	120	5.00
8	B	II	18	80	4.44
9	C	IV	24	120	5.00
10	D	III	20	105	5.25
					56.13

Consumption for each trip, stated in col. (6), is calculated by dividing the col. (5) value by the col. (4) value.

The average consumption/trip = 56.13/10 gallons = 5.613 gallons.

The author repeated the calculation by a technique to be shown in the next example and obtained a value of 5.93 gallons. In practice a much greater number of trips would be used for the estimate.

Example 3.2 Sales of joints of meat by a large butcher's shop over a period of time were summarised as follows:

Daily sales (no. of joints)	%age days	Weight (kilos)	%age joints	Price (pence/kilos)	%age joints
40	18	1	16	120	14
50	10	1.25	23	122	17
60	29	1.50	35	124	38
70	22	1.75	10	126	9
80	16	2.00	9	128	22
90	5	2.25	7		100
	100		100		

Estimate by using random numbers average price/joint on the basis of (i) 5 days' sales, (ii) 10 days' sales.

1 day's sales will be calculated as

> (a number of joints between 40 and 90) × (a weight between 1 kilo and 2.25 kilo) × (a price between 120p and 128p)

with a minimum value of (40 × 1 × 120) pence = £48 and a maximum of (90 × 2.25 × 128) = £259.20

Although in the calculation for 1 day either of these estimates is feasible, as is any other combination of (number × weight × price), our overall estimate must acknowledge the probabilities with which different values occur. The first table, for example, shows that the chance of selling 60 joints in a day is 5.8 times the chance of selling 90 (29/5 = 5.8) and the second that we ought to allow for one-tenth of the joints sold having a weight of 1.75 kilos. To select the required values we use Tables (p. 210). Consider the ten digits, 0, 1, 2, . . . , 9, and imagine an enormous collection of these, thoroughly mixed, but with equal numbers of each digit. We pick one blind-folded, as it were. It is '2', and we enter it on the first row of the page. We pick a second '8' and put it next to it. Our third choice is '8', the fourth a '9', and so on. The first row completed we continue on the second, to complete a page of 50 rows of 50 columns, i.e. 2500 separate figures. The arrangement in pairs and blocks has no special significance and is only for the convenience of the user. For this example we take pairs of digits. Note that if we picked out all pairs from 00, 01, 02, . . . , 98, 99 we should have one hundred different numbers, which could represent 1 per cent, 2 per cent, . . . , 100 per cent. To use this relationship we cumulate the percentages in each of the three data tables and allocate 2-digit random numbers to match, as follows:

Sales (no.)	%	Cum.%	Random numbers	Weight (kilos)	%	Cum.%	Random numbers
40	18	18	00–17	1	16	16	00–15
50	10	28	18–27	1.25	23	39	16–38
60	29	57	28–56	1.50	35	74	39–73
70	22	79	57–78	1.75	10	84	74–83
80	16	95	79–94	2.00	9	93	84–93
90	5	100	95–99	2.25	7	100	94–99
	100				100		

Price (pence)	%	Cum.%	Random numbers
120	14	14	00–13
122	17	31	14–30
124	38	69	31–68
126	9	78	69–77
128	22	100	78–99
	100		

(i) To estimate 5 days' sales we need five 2-digit random numbers between 00 and 99 (incl.) and we select Block A–I and the first row, to give

    28
    30
    95
    01
    10

28 is in the 28–56 range, so it indicates sales of 60; 30 also indicates 60; 95 indicates 90; 01, 40; and 10, 40.

When a random number table is used extensively on one exercise, the starting-point and method of selection should be changed as often as possible so that the risk of bias, e.g. including a series of digits more than once, is at a minimum. Various alternatives will be shown in this chapter.

To choose five random weights take the last pair of digits in Block J–V and every other pair in the column, moving upwards. Random numbers and associated weights are as follows:

Random number	Weight (kilos)
29	1.25
66	1.50
38	1.25
03	1
97	2.25

For price, start at 16, the first pair in F–II and move diagonally south-west:

Random number	Price (pence)
16	122
84	128
98	128
39	124
52	124

Multiplication and averaging give the required estimate:

Day	No.	Weight (kilos)	Price (pence)	Total (pence)
1	60	1.25	122	9150
2	60	1.50	128	11520
3	90	1.25	128	14400
4	40	1	124	4960
5	40	2.25	124	11160
	290			51190

Therefore, average price per joint $= \dfrac{£511.90}{290} = £1.765$

(ii) If data for days 6–10 (incl.) is added to the above, a 10 days' average can be obtained.

Three other methods of obtaining the random numbers are now shown.

Number

C–II. Take the last digit on the first row and pair it with the first digit in C–III. Read the next four pairs downwards to give:

> 75
> 79
> 24
> 81
> 93

Weight

Read the second row in H–III backwards:

> 57
> 27
> 45
> 58
> 50

Price

Start at the top of the last column in J–IV, read in pairs turning up the first column in J–V to complete the series and give:

    86
    17
    61
    65
    89

The corresponding values are entered and processed below:

Day	No.	Weight (kilos)	Price (pence)	Total (pence)
6	70	1.50	128	13440
7	80	1.25	122	12200
8	50	1.50	124	9300
9	80	1.50	124	14880
10	80	1.50	128	15360
	360			65180

For 10 days the average price per joint equals

$$\frac{(51190 + 65180)\text{p}}{290 + 360} = £1.79$$

Note that a random choice is not inconsistent with the concept of a stated distribution. The allocation of random numbers in accordance with the cumulative percentages reconciles the two principles. Consider the price distribution in the last example. The last column classifies 100 random numbers. If the printed table distribution and method of selection are perfectly random, the probability of picking a number from 31 to 68 (incl.) = 38 per cent and this will ensure that a price of 124p is selected in 38 per cent of the choices; this is what the original distribution would require.

The next example shows simulation used to solve a problem even less accessible to formal methods than the last.

Example 3.3 Output and deliveries of a firm's product over 50 typical days were as follows:

Units produced	Number of days	Vehicles available	Number of days
400	2	3	6
450	8	4	17
500	12	5	9
550	19	6	8
600	6	7	6
650	3	8	4
	50		50

Each vehicle makes 1 trip a day and can deliver 102 units when fully laden. As many vehicles as possible are loaded full each day. Units in excess of total vehicle capacity are stored overnight and added to the next day's output for delivery. Simulate 10 days' operations by the firm and derive averages and other values of use to management.

Doubling the frequencies produces percentages for simulation and representation by random numbers as follows:

Units produced				Vehicles available			
Units	%	Cum.%	Random numbers	Number	%	Cum.%	Random numbers
400	4	4	00–03	3	12	12	00–11
450	16	20	04–19	4	34	46	12–45
500	24	44	20–43	5	18	64	46–63
550	38	82	44–81	6	16	80	64–79
600	12	94	82–93	7	12	92	80–91
650	6	100	94–99	8	8	100	92–99
	100				100		

Random numbers were selected by methods already shown as follows:

Day	Output	Vehicles
1	56	38
2	24	69
3	36	97
4	18	95
5	90	59
6	75	36
7	28	44
8	13	11
9	04	08
10	42	06

Hence on the first day, because 56 is in the 44–81 output random number class, the output would be 550 units. 38 is in the 12–45 vehicle random number class, so that 4 vehicles are available. 4×102 units = 408 units, so that 550 units − 408 units = 142 units are stored overnight and added to Day 2 output. These and other values simulated for the 10 days are given in Table 3.1, giving averages and other useful summaries obtained from them:

TABLE 3.1

(1) Day	(2) Simulated output (units)	(3) Undelivered from day before (units)	(4) Total for delivery (units)	(5) Simulated number of vehicles available	(6) No. of full vehicles used	(7) Capacity of (6) (units)	(8) Load of partly filled vehicle (units)	(9) No. of unused vehicles	(10) Stored overnight units
1	550	—	550	4	4	408	—	—	142
2	550	142	692	6	6	612	—	—	80
3	500	30	580	8	5	510	70	2	—
4	450	—	450	8	4	408	42	3	—
5	600	—	600	5	5	510	—	—	90
6	550	90	640	4	4	408	—	—	232
7	500	232	732	4	4	408	—	—	324
8	450	324	774	3	3	306	—	—	468
9	450	468	918	3	3	306	—	—	612
10	500	612	1112	3	3	306	—	—	806
	5100			48	41				2754

Total col. (2) = 5100 units, so therefore average daily output = 5100/10 units = 510 units.

Total col. (5) = 48 vehicles, so therefore average number of vehicles available = 48/10 = 4.8.

Total number of vehicles fully used (col. (6) = 41; of the remainder, 5 were unused and 2 underused – see data for Days 3 and 4 – i.e. by a total amount of $(2 \times 102) - (70 + 42)$ units = 92 units. Total of col. (10) = total units stored overnight = 2754, i.e. an average of 275.4 units/day or 2754/8 = 344.25 units, if based on the 8 days when the store was used.

In general, on the simulated figures, because 5100/48 units = 106.25 units, we would expect the cumulative build up of undelivered units experienced over the second half of the simulated period. The original figures show that in the long run increasing the capacity of each vehicle to 105 would be likely to avoid a prolonged build up. However, for a better understanding of the problem the simulation should be extended.

In the last example simulation has estimated undelivered output and underused vehicle capacity. The next example simulates time delays through a disparity between input and output in a single-channel situation. Instead of applying queueing formulae of the kind given in the last chapter observed frequencies are used. We are not therefore assuming theoretical distributions; furthermore, in more involved queueing problems simulation reduces the complexity of calculation.

Example 3.4 In a factory items arrived for processing by machine A in accordance with the following schedule:

Frequency of arrival	%age of items
every 8 min.	16
„ 9 min.	19
„ 10 min.	23
„ 11 min.	28
„ 12 min.	14
	100

The processing time for items is described by the following distribution:

Time (min.)	% of items
7	7
8	9
9	15
10	45
11	16
12	8
	100

By simulating the processing of 10 items, investigate possible queueing and underuse of the machine.

As before, percentages are cumulated, and random numbers allocated, to give:

Frequency of arrival	%age	Cum.%	Random numbers
8 min.	16	16	00–15
9 min.	19	35	16–34
10 min.	23	58	35–57
11 min.	28	86	58–85
12 min.	14	100	86–99

Processing time (min.)	%age	Cum.%	Random numbers
7	7	7	00–06
8	9	16	07–15
9	15	31	16–30
10	45	76	31–75
11	16	92	76–91
12	8	100	92–99

Random numbers for use are:

Item	Arrival	Processing
1		08
2	16	75
3	48	56
4	08	36
5	07	55
6	88	89
7	98	18
8	71	79
9	88	51
10	11	04

Let the first item arrive at 0 min. time. Its processing random number is 08, so that it takes 8 min. to process. But item no. 2 arrives at (0 + 9) min., so that the machine is unused for 9 min. − 8 min. = 1 min. Thereafter, it is used continuously with items queueing if their arrival time is before the time when the last item leaves the machine. These and other details are set out below:

Item	Arrives	Queues	Enters	In process	Leaves	Unused
No. 1	0 min.	0 min.	0 min.	8 min.	8 min.	–
No. 2	9 min.	—	9 min.	10 min.	19 min.	1 min.
No. 3	19 min.	—	19 min.	10 min.	29 min.	—
No. 4	27 min.	2 min.	29 min.	10 min.	39 min.	—
No. 5	35 min.	4 min.	39 min.	10 min.	49 min.	—
No. 6	47 min.	2 min.	49 min.	10 min.	59 min.	—
No. 7	59 min.	1 min.	60 min.	9 min.	69 min.	—
No. 8	70 min.	—	70 min.	11 min.	81 min.	1 min.
No. 9	82 min.	—	82 min.	10 min.	92 min.	1 min.
No. 10	90 min.	2 min.	92 min.	7 min.	99 min.	—
		11 min.				

Hence 5 items queue for a total of 11 min. an average time of 11/5 min. = 2.2 min. each. The average, based on all 10 items, will be 11/10 min. = 1.1 min. The machine was unused on 3 separate occasions of 1 min. each, i.e. a total of 3 min. As a percentage of the running time this is

$$\frac{3}{99} \times \frac{100}{1} = 3.03 \text{ per cent}$$

No allowance is made for movement to or from the machine, so that in practice the queueing could well be worse and the percentage of unused machine time smaller.

The next example uses simulation to describe a multi-channel queueing situation where *a priori* methods would lead to very complicated calculations.

Example 3.5 Members of the public arrive at a government office with a frequency described by the following distribution:

Interval after last arrival (min.)	%
4	7
5	10
6	52
7	20
8	11
	100

A porter directs each person to one of rooms A, B, or C, where the same business is done, but at service times which are distributed as follows:

A		B		C	
Time (min.)	%	Time (min.)	%	Time (min.)	%
8	18	10	18	12	15
9	22	11	19	13	22
10	33	12	35	14	36
11	27	13	28	15	27
	100		100		100

Where more than one room is vacant alphabetical order determines the porter's choice. Distributed at random amongst the arrivals are 'special cases', which in the long run account for 10 per cent of all cases. Each takes 4 min. longer to service. Simulate 10 arrivals and show waiting times and use of the different rooms.

Percentages are cumulated, and random numbers allocated, as follows:

Arrivals (min.)	Cum.%	Random numbers	A min.	Cum.%	Random numbers
4	7	00–06	8	18	00–17
5	17	07–16	9	40	18–39
6	69	17–68	10	73	40–72
7	89	69–88	11	100	73–99
8	100	89–99			

B min.	Cum.%	Random numbers	C min.	Cum.%	Random numbers
10	18	00–17	12	15	00–14
11	37	18–36	13	37	15–36
12	72	37–71	14	73	37–72
13	100	72–99	15	100	73–99

The arrival time of each citizen will be given by a 2-digit random number. If randomisation is perfect, each of the digits 0, 1, 2, . . ., 9 will occur in the second place with equal frequency. To choose one digit at random the author noted that in Table 5 (p. 210) the first pair of digits was '28'. He therefore chose the eighth digit in the second row, i.e. '5'. Any citizen with an arrival random number ending in 5 was to be treated as a special case.

Random numbers were selected as follows:

Citizen	Arrival	Service
1	(14)	00
2	46	99
3	11	20
4	66	19
5	60	32
6	90	40
7	33	20
8	65	01
9	72	68
10	92	87

The first citizen's arrival was at 0 min., so that an arrival random number was not needed for this purpose; but one was included to indicate whether or not it was a 'special case', hence maintaining the 10 per cent assumption required by the problem.

Citizen 1 would go, by the priority rule, to room A. Random number '00' gives a service time of 8 min.

Citizen 2 arrives after a time to correspond with random number '46', i.e. 6 min. Room A is still occupied. He goes to B, where a random number of '99' indicates a service time of 13 min.

The table below describes the outcome of all 10 arrivals. Note that Citizen 8 (arrival random number '65') is a 'special case'.

Time-table showing use of Offices A, B *and* C

Citizen no.	Enters at	Room	Waiting	Service time	A Enters	Leaves
1	10.00 a.m.	A	—	8 min.	10.00 a.m.	10.08 a.m.
2	10.06 a.m.	B	—	13 min.		
3	10.11 a.m.	C	—	13 min.		
4	10.17 a.m.	A	—	9 min.	10.17 a.m.	10.26 a.m.
5	10.23 a.m.	B	—	11 min.		
6	10.31 a.m.	A	—	10 min.	10.31 a.m.	10.41 a.m.
7	10.37 a.m.	B	—	10 min.		
8	10.43 a.m.	A	—	12 min.*	10.43 a.m.	10.55 min.
9	10.50 a.m.	B	—	12 min.		
10	10.58 a.m.	A	—	11 min.	10.58 a.m.	11.09 a.m.

*Special case 8 min. + 4 min. = 12 min.
Total time taken for all ten citizens = 69 min.

Analysis of this table

(i) 10 citizens received service in a total time of 69 min. Overall average service time = 69/10 min. = 6.9 min.
(ii) No queueing occurred, i.e. upon the arrival of a citizen one office was always free.
(iii) The performance of the different offices is analysed below:

	A	B	C
No. services	5	4	1
Total service time	50 min.	46 min.	13 min.
Average service time	10 min.	11.5 min	13 min.
Total time office unused	14 min.	23 min.	56 min.
% unused time	20.3%	33.3%	81.2%

Note that performance of B is at a slight disadvantage because of No. 8, the 'special' case. In the long run these would be likely to be equally distributed between A, B and C. The model just used could yield other information, e.g. continuity of service, average intervals between services, etc.

Where the solution of a problem depends upon the values of items which are normally distributed, Table 6 (p. 212) may be used. The next example illustrates their use.

B		C	
Enters	Leaves	Enters	Leaves
10.06 a.m.	10.19 a.m.		
		10.11 a.m.	10.24 a.m.
10.23 a.m.	10.34 a.m.		
10.37 a.m.	10.47 a.m.		
10.50 a.m.	11.02 a.m.		

Example 3.6 The average annual mileage of a firm's fleet of cars is normally distributed with an arithmetic mean of 12500 miles and a standard deviation of 320 miles. The cost per mile of running each vehicle varies with the annual mileage in accordance with the following distribution:

Annual mileage	Cost/mile (pence)
Less than 10000	5
10000–	4.75
10500–	4.5
11000–	4.2
11500–	4.0
12000–	3.8
12500–	3.9
13000–	4.0
13500–	4.1
14000–	4.4
14500 and more	4.8

The firm runs 145 cars. Estimate the annual cost of running them from a random sample of 10 cars.

To use the tables we need 10 random numbers, each of 3 digits. Take the first such number in Block H–II in Table 5 (p. 210), and use the 9 others immediately above. This gives:

(1)	(2) Random sample no.	(3) Table no.	(4) Normal deviate	(5) Milage	(6) Cost/mile	(7) Total cost
Car						
1	931	431	−0.782	12250	3.8	£465.5
2	482	482	+0.012	12504	3.9	£487.7
3	654	154	+0.334	12607	3.9	£491.7
4	842	342	−0.533	12329	3.8	£468.5
5	594	094	+1.322	12923	3.9	£504.0
6	889	389	+1.787	13072	4.0	£522.9
7	699	199	+0.033	12511	3.9	£487.9
8	081	081	−0.522	12332	3.8	£468.7
9	519	019	−0.722	12269	3.8	£466.2
10	898	398	+0.415	12633	3.9	£492.7
						£4855.8

In col. (3) we note the remainder after each random sample number is divided by 500. The first 2 digits of the table, col. (3) p. 212 above show the row to be selected, and the last digit the column in the normal deviates table (Table 6, p. 210). Hence 431 gives −0.782. Call this value X.

Then the required mileage is

Arithmetic Mean $+(X \times$ standard deviation)

giving for Car 1 12500 miles $+\{(-0.782 \times 320$ miles)$\} = 12250$ miles (entered in col. (5)).

The distribution of costs shows that the rate is 3.8p per mile, entered in col. (6). The total cost to be entered in col. (7) = £465.5.

For Car 2 482 gives a value of $+0.012$ for col. (4). Therefore, mileage equals

$$[12500 + (0.012 \times 320)] \text{ miles} = 12504.$$

The rate is 3.9p and total cost = $(12504 \times 3.9\text{p}) = £487.7$.

Other table values are similarly calculated. The total of col. (7) is £4855.8, so that the estimated cost for all 145 cars is

$$\frac{4855.8 \times 145}{10} = £70409$$

The next example shows simulation used to calculate an area bounded by a curved line.

Example 3.7   Plot the following curve on a graph:

x	y
0	0
0.10	0.46
0.20	0.58
0.30	0.67
0.40	0.74
0.50	0.79
0.60	0.84
0.70	0.89
0.80	0.93
0.90	0.97
1.00	1.00

By simulation calculate the area lying between the curve and the x-axis over the range $x = 0, x = 1$.

An x value is simulated by taking a 2-digit random number from Table 5 (p. 210) and dividing by 100. Dividing another 2-digit random by 100 gives a y value. The point represented by $x = 0.88$, $Y = 0.48$ is plotted on

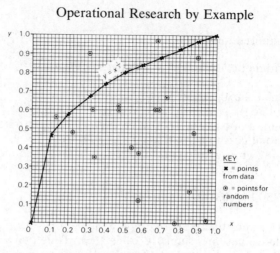

FIG. 3.1   Area under a curve – simulation

Figure 3.1. The following table was used to plot a total of 20 points.

No. of point	x	y
1	0.88	0.48
2	0.67	0.61
3	0.95	0.12
4	0.90	0.88
5	0.22	0.48
6	0.47	0.62
7	0.73	0.67
8	0.69	0.60
9	0.33	0.60
10	0.58	0.12
11	0.78	0.00
12	0.58	0.37
13	0.34	0.35
14	0.47	0.60
15	0.33	0.90
16	0.97	0.39
17	0.86	0.17
18	0.54	0.40
19	0.68	0.97
20	0.13	0.56

Figure 3.2 shows the curve and the points plotted. Every point defined by a pair of values of x and y chosen at random will fall into a rectangle with opposite corners at the origin and at the point of maximum values of x and

y. As all the points fall at random, the proportion falling in a particular
sector will represent the sub-area in question. Counting these points and
comparing their total with the overall total gives an estimate of the area of
the sector: but we could only guarantee absolute accuracy if an infinite
number of points were plotted.

An estimate of the area between the curve and *x*-axis is obtained from
the ratio:

$$\frac{\text{Number of points under curve}}{\text{,,}\quad\text{,,}\quad\text{,,}\quad\text{in complete square}}$$

which equals $17/20 = 0.85$. This is only a rough estimate. The curve is
described by the equation

$$Y = x^{1/3}$$

The area, from the integral $\int_0^1 X^{1/3}\,dx$, is

$$[\tfrac{3}{4} X^{4/3}]_0^1 = 0.75$$

The more points used for the estimate, the nearer should we get to the true
value. This follows from the statistical *law of large numbers*. This is true of
the earlier examples: the more times we repeat a particular calculation, the
more confident can we be of the estimate. The separate calculations used
so far have been comparatively simple. They have been repeated by hand,
but for good estimates the arithmetic would soon become very laborious.
Hence large simulation operations are usually performed on an electrical
digital computer, because of the ease and speed with which calculations can
be repeated. Random numbers must be available. Table 5 contains
$50 \times 50 = 2500$ digits and in theory these and the contents of other pages
could be stored in a computer to be drawn upon when required. For
full-scale business operations, however, the claim on storage space would
be exorbitant. A financial simulation, for example, might involve the
accounts of 10000 customers, with the possibility of having to use random
numbers from 00000 to 99999 and using 50000 digits. In practice computers are programmed to generate *pseudo-random numbers*. By feeding original digits into the system, a series of numbers of the required digits, e.g.
2-digit, 3-digit, etc., having some of the qualities of random numbers will
be produced. The method is deterministic, so that when the original combination of digits occurs again the whole series will be repeated. If the cycle
is long, however, little disadvantage arises. A compensating advantage of a
deterministic series is that a complex set of calculations can be repeated
with the same random numbers and hence the effect of varying causal
factors can be measured. The next example shows two methods of generat-
ing pseudo-random numbers.

Example 3.8 Generate (i) ten 4-digit random numbers by the additive
congruential method using the values 4236 and 9318 to start with; (ii) ten
2-digit random numbers by the mean square method, using (a) 1496 to
start with, (b) 3500 to start with, and comment.

(i) To generate 4-digit random numbers we need a 5-digit number as a
   divisor; and we choose, for simplicity, 10001. First, add the given
   4-digit numbers

$$4236 + 9318 = 13554$$

Then divide by 10001 to give 1.355264474. Thus 3552 is the first
random number. The second is formed by adding it to 3854 – the
figures of corresponding order from the first total. To continue the
series add the last 4 digits thus obtained to the 4 digits before. Full
calculations are:

3854		
+ 3552	1st random number	
7406	2nd	,,
(1)0958	3rd	,,
8364	4th	,,
9322	5th	,,
(1)7986	6th	,,
(1)7008	7th	,,
(1)4994	8th	,,
5694	9th	,,
(1)0688	10th	,,

Note that the 1s to the left are discarded.

(ii) (a) First, square the starting number:

$$1496^2 = 2238016$$

Place '0' to the left, as the number of digits must be even:

02238016

Select the two central digits, i.e. '38', as the first random number.
Square these, and take the central two digits of the product as the
second random number:

$$38 \times 38 = (1)44(4)$$
$$44 = \text{second random number}$$

Continue to square, using central pairs of digits, discarding outer digits and adding '0' where the product has 3 digits only:

$$44 \times 44 = (1)93(6) \qquad \text{3rd random number} = 93$$
$$93 \times 93 = (8)64(9) \qquad \text{4th random number} = 64$$
$$64 \times 64 = (4)09(6) \qquad \text{5th random number} = 09$$
$$09 \times 09 = 81 \qquad \text{6th random number} = 81$$
$$81 \times 81 = (6)56(1) \qquad \text{7th random number} = 56$$
$$56 \times 56 = (3)13(6) \qquad \text{8th random number} = 13$$
$$13 \times 13 = (0)16(9) \qquad \text{9th random number} = 16$$
$$16 \times 16 = (0)25(6) \qquad \text{10th random number} = 25$$

(b)
$$3500^2 = (122)50(000) \qquad \text{1st random number} = 50$$
$$50 \times 50 = (2)50(0) \qquad \text{2nd random number} = 50$$
$$50 \times 50 = (2)50(0) \qquad \text{3rd random number} = 50$$

and the method would produce only a series of 50s. Therefore, steps are needed to avoid this and certain other combinations of digits.

Various tests are available to discover whether series of digits are random. The first is the frequency test. If a set of digits is taken, then 0's, 1s, 2s, etc. should occur with equal frequency. Two blocks of Table 5 were taken at random and are summarised below in the first two columns:

Digit	Total number (0)	E	$(0 - E)^2/E$
0	12	10	0.40
1	9	10	0.10
2	9	10	0.10
3	11	10	0.10
4	10	10	0.00
5	10	10	0.00
6	12	10	0.40
7	9	10	0.10
8	12	10	0.40
9	6	10	1.60
	100		$3.20 = \chi^2$

$$\nu = 10 - 1 = 9$$

The table value of χ^2 for $\nu = 9$ is 14.684 at the 10 per cent level. If the distribution of frequencies were perfectly random, we would expect each digit to occur $100/10 = 10$ times. The observed values, i.e. those that have been counted, show slight differences from 10, but the test can be interpreted as showing that the departures from the expected values are most likely to have arisen by chance, and are not so large that we ought to look for bias in the frequencies of the digits.

The following arrangement of digits would satisfy a frequency test:

$$01 \quad 23 \quad 45 \quad 67 \quad 89$$
$$98 \quad 76 \quad 54 \quad 32 \quad 10$$

for 0's, 1s, etc. occur with equal frequency. But the values would be dangerous to use for simulations because the digits could not be regarded as independent of one another. The ordering of the first row shows perfect serial correlation, and the same is true of the second row; taken in vertical pairs, the digits show perfect inverse correlation. Such an arrangement would fail one of the other tests used, for example the *poker test*, which is based on the frequencies with which digits are arranged in particular groups of 5, e.g. 5 all different, 5 containing 2 pairs, etc. A large number of theoretical tests can be devised to test the effectiveness of randomisation of numbers printed in tables or generated by computers; and it has been impossible so far to devise sets of numbers which satisfy all tests. Small areas of tables of random numbers can sometimes be found below the required standard of heterogeneity. Safety in simulation usually lies in numbers, i.e. in repeating the calculations a number of times so that final estimates rest on a fair representation of varying situations met in practice.

Exercises 3

Note: Each quantitative exercise below can produce more than one correct answer because random numbers will be used. The answers (pp. 178 and 179) will, in the main, be outlines of methods rather than giving numerical values.

3.1   A wholesale greengrocer's cabbage business over 50 days was as follows:

Purchases		Demand	
Number of cabbages	*Number of days*	*Number of cabbages*	*Number of days*
800	8	700	3
850	11	750	5
900	14	800	6
950	10	850	7
1000	7	900	18
	50	950	5
		1000	4
		1050	2
			50

(i) Simulate 6 days' transactions, stating for each the number of cabbages unsold or the excess of demand over purchases.

(ii) Discuss briefly the importance of the order in which random numbers are used by repeating the calculation, but reversing the order, i.e. using the 6th day's demand numbers for the first day, the 5th for the second day, and so on.

(iii) Show that, on the whole, the greengrocer's purchasing policy is sound.

3.2 A store noted that customers at a busy time reached the cash-tills to pay for their goods at the following rates:

Interval (min.)	Percentage of customers
$\frac{1}{4}$	21
$\frac{1}{2}$	43
$\frac{3}{4}$	18
1	10
$1\frac{1}{4}$	5
$1\frac{1}{2}$	3

They paid at either of two check-out points, which had the following service times:

Time (minutes)	Percentage of customers	Time (min.)	Percentage of customers
$\frac{1}{2}$	5	$\frac{1}{2}$	3
$\frac{3}{4}$	30	$\frac{3}{4}$	28
1	33	1	30
$1\frac{1}{4}$	26	$1\frac{1}{4}$	24
$1\frac{1}{2}$	3	$1\frac{1}{2}$	6
$1\frac{3}{4}$	2	$1\frac{3}{4}$	5
2	1	2	4
	$\overline{100}$		$\overline{100}$

Investigate the extent of queueing by simulating the arrival of 10 customers.

3.3 The average daily output of standard metal fittings made by a factory is 200, with a standard deviation of 12. Each fitting has an average weight of 15 kilos. with a standard deviation of 0.8 kilos. Assuming that numbers and weights are normally distributed, estimate by 5 simulations the average daily weight of output and the range of variation.

3.4   Each of four similar machines requires a fitter's attention with frequencies as follows:

Attention needed after	Percentage of times
5 min.	10
6 ,,	34
7 ,,	27
8 ,,	16
9 ,,	8
10 ,,	5
	100

Two fitters of similar ability are available. The service each gives varies in accordance with the following distribution:

Service time	Percentage of services
$\frac{1}{2}$ min.	15
$\frac{3}{4}$,,	29
1 ,,	24
$1\frac{1}{4}$,,	11
$1\frac{1}{2}$,,	9
$1\frac{3}{4}$,,	7
2 ,,	5
	100

Assume that a machine stops automatically when needing a service and does not restart until the completion of the service. Where more than one machine has stopped, the first to stop will be the first to be served. Simulate enough services to show how effectively machines and fitters are being used.

3.5   A tunnel spans a horizontal width from K to L of 20 metres, and has a curved roof, d is the horizontal distance from K of a point along KL, and h is the vertical height above that point. Plot a vertical section of the tunnel on graph paper from the following data:

d (metres)	h (metres)
0	0
4	25.6
8	38.4
10	40.0
12	38.4
16	25.6
20	0

By simulation estimate the cross-sectional area of the tunnel.

Bibliography

J. W. Forrester, *Industrial Dynamics* (Cambridge, Mass.: M.I.T. Press, 1961).

J. M. Hammersley and D. C. Handscomb, *Monte Carlo Methods* (London: Methuen, 1964).

G. W. King, 'The Monte Carlo Method as a Natural Mode of Expression in Operations Research', *Journal of Operations Research in America*, vol. 1, no. 2.

H. A. Meyer (ed.), *Symposium on Monte Carlo Methods* (New York: Wiley, 1956).

R. P. Rich, 'Simulation as an Aid to Model Building', *Journal of Operations Research in America*, vol. 3, no. 1.

P. Rivett, 'Trends in Operational Research', *Product Engineer*, vol. 44, no. 109.

K. D. Tocher, *The Art of Simulation* (London: English Universities Press, 1963).

4

Forecasting

Success in business and administration depends greatly on the ability to estimate future values of such variables as sales, output of commodities and demand for social services. The construction and use of models has made forecasting a branch of operational research. *Forecasting* describes methods of analysing existing data and carrying forward suggested patterns into the future, i.e. *extrapolation*, to use the technical term. *Prediction* (literally 'saying beforehand') describes methods based on individual or collective judgement by methods mentioned later in the chapter. Important decisions are usually reached by an amalgam of both techniques.

The first example shows a typical *time series*, as observations made at regular intervals of time such as weeks, months or years are called. Published data is widely used in illustration because of its availability, but readers with access to a firm's private records will find the methods suitable for this data.

Example 4.1 Graph each of the following time series and estimate the required value by continuing the curve in the pattern suggested by the values plotted.

(i) *Vehicle licences current (private cars) U.K.*

Year	Number (000s)
1945	1521
1946	1807
1947	1983
1948	2003
1949	2179
1950	2308
1951	2433
1952	2565
1953	2825
1954	3177
1955	3610
1956	3981
1957	4283
1958	4651

Year	Number (000s)
1959	5081
1960	5657
1961	6114
1962	6706
1963	7547
1964	8436
1965	9131

Source: *The British Economy: Key Statistics 1900–1970*, published for the London and Cambridge Economic Service by Times Newspapers Ltd (n.d.).

Derive an estimate for 1969.

(ii) *Manufacturers' sales of slippers, etc.*

Year	Quarter	Sales (million pairs)
1973	1st	6.3
	2nd	9.3
	3rd	11.9
	4th	13.5
1974	1st	3.5
	2nd	8.8
	3rd	12.6
	4th	14.8
1975	1st	7.2
	2nd	8.0
	3rd	11.6
	4th	11.9

Source: C.S.O., *Monthly Digest of Statistics,* London, H.M.S.O., no. 375, March 1977, table 10.6.

Derive an estimate for the third quarter of 1976.

(iii) *Industrial Production, U.S.A. (index numbers, average 1963 = 100)*

Year	Index number
1920	21
1921	17
1922	20
1923	24
1924	23
1925	25
1926	27
1927	27
1928	29

Year	Index number
1929	31
1930	26
1931	21
1932	17
1933	20
1934	21
1935	25
1936	29
1937	32
1938	25
1939	31
1940	35
1941	45
1942	56
1943	66
1944	65
1945	56

Source: *The British Economy: Key Statistics 1900–1970*, published for the London and Cambridge Economic Service by Times Newspapers Ltd (n.d.).

Derive an estimate for 1952.

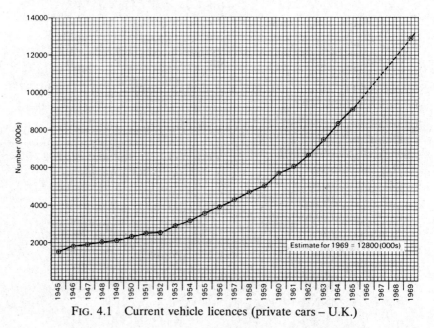

FIG. 4.1   Current vehicle licences (private cars – U.K.)

(i) Figure 4.1 shows the figures plotted and an estimate of 12800 (000s) obtained by extrapolation. The estimate is unlikely to be very accurate as the curve changes shape several times and we cannot be very certain about its course beyond 1965. We experiment by calculating and plotting $\log_{10}$ number (000s) against year, attempting only 2-place accuracy. Values are:

Year	Log_{10} number (000s)
1945	3.18
1946	3.26
1947	3.30
1948	3.30
1949	3.34
1950	3.36
1951	3.39
1952	3.41
1953	3.45
1954	3.50
1955	3.56
1956	3.60
1957	3.63
1958	3.67
1959	3.71
1960	3.75
1961	3.79
1962	3.83
1963	3.88
1964	3.93
1965	3.96

Figure 4.2 shows the semi-logarithmic graph. Extrapolating the straight line which appears to fit the curve gives a 1969 estimate of antilog 4.11 (000s), i.e. 12882 (000s). A straight line is more readily extended than a curve. The true figure for 1969 was 11504 (000s).

(ii) Figure 4.3 shows a strongly marked seasonal pattern, sales being their lowest for the first quarter of each year and rising to their highest in the fourth. 3 years' figures are hardly enough to show the trend with confidence but give the impression of a line with a slight upward bow with an ultimate decline. Extrapolation of the line sketched through the 3 third quarters' figures estimates the required sales as 9.9 (million pairs).

(iii) Figure 4.4 shows an overall rise in the index, but subject to cyclical movements – which economic theory would lead us to expect. These movements are less regular than seasonal patterns, and variations of

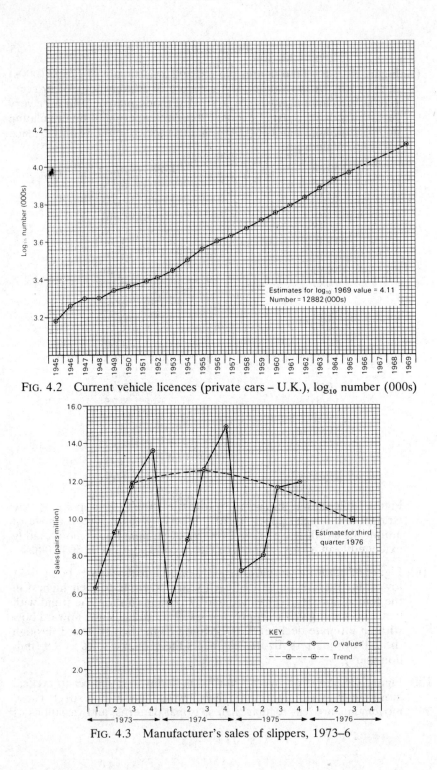

FIG. 4.2 Current vehicle licences (private cars – U.K.), $\log_{10}$ number (000s)

Estimates for $\log_{10}$ 1969 value = 4.11
Number = 12882 (000s)

Estimate for third
quarter 1976

KEY
⊙———⊙ O values
⊡----⊡ Trend

1973   1974   1975   1976

FIG. 4.3 Manufacturer's sales of slippers, 1973–6

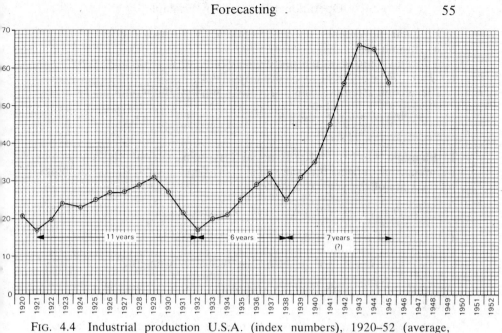

FIG. 4.4 Industrial production U.S.A. (index numbers), 1920–52 (average, 1963 = 100)

the order shown, i.e. 11 years (or 3 years and 8 years perhaps), 6 years and 7 years, are found in other economies. The 1946 figure was in fact, below that for 1945, but an upswing started in 1947 so that 7 years (?) was, in fact, 8 years. In 1945 estimation of the 1952 index would have been statistically hazardous.

The trend took a sharp upwards turn from 1932, and on this basis an estimate of about 100 is suggested for 1952, but if the cyclical pattern of the 7 years before is repeated a fall of 10 points would be expected, and an estimate of $100 - 10 = 90$ is suggested. This value is over-optimistic, the recorded value being 68.

A graph of past figures will usually suggest the general pattern to be followed in making a forecast. But graphical extrapolation is likely to be highly subjective and not always convenient and the first step towards reliable forecasting is to construct a model.

In Example 4.1 (i) our first attempt to forecast implied the model

$$O = T + R$$

where O = original or observed values, i.e. number of licences (000s), T = trend, the relatively long-term movement, and R = random, residual or irregular movements – variations taking the strongly marked trend out of its smooth path.

A formal forecast would therefore require us to find suitable numbers for T and R, a problem to be discussed later.

The second attempt, using logarithms, implied the model

$$\log O = \log T + \log R$$
$$= \log TR$$

In Example 4.1 (ii), if S = seasonal variations, i.e. the element in our estimates that reflects that sales of slippers depend, amongst other things, on the time of the year, the model is

$$O = T + S + R$$

In Example 4.1 (iii), the descriptive model would be

$$O = T + C + R, C \text{ being the cyclical movement.}$$

Forecasts of O are obtained by combining separate forecasts of T, C, S and R.

Graphs drawn so far have shown the predominant element to be the *trend*, and measuring it is usually the next step in analysing the data from which the forecast will spring. Again, a model is used, as the next example illustrates.

Example 4.2   (i) Plot the following data on a natural-scale graph:

Year	No. of electricity consumers — shops (000s)
1965	691
1966	690
1967	692
1968	696
1969	680
1970	666
1971	667
1972	669

Source: Department of Trade and Industry, *United Kingdom Energy Statistics 1973*, London: H.M.S.O., 1973, table 85.

 (ii) Calculate and insert on the graph the linear regression trend.
(iii) Check the equation in (ii) by the averages method.
(iv) Calculate and examine R values.

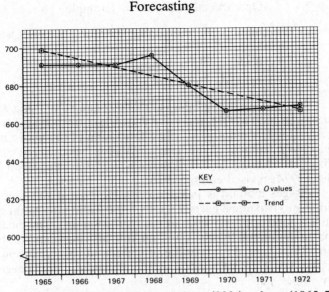

FIG. 4.5   Number of electricity consumers (000s) – shops (1965–72)

(i) Figure 4.5 shows the original values with the linear regression line inserted.

(ii) If y = number of shops, and x = number of the year, taking 1965 as 0, 1966 as 1, and so on, then we can set up the general linear regression model for the trend as $y = a + bx$, the parameter a being the y-axis intercept and b the slope of the line. Values of a and b are obtained by solving simultaneously the standard equations.

$$\Sigma y = Na + b\Sigma x$$
$$\Sigma xy = a\Sigma x + b\Sigma x^2$$

N being the numbers of pairs of values in the data, here 8, and the Σ quantitities being obtained by tabulating the data in the columns

$x_2 \quad x \quad xy \quad y$

and taking the totals indicated. This gives the following equation:

$$y = 696.50 - 4.32x$$

To plot the trend on the graph, plot two points:

For 1965, $x = 0$; therefore $y = 696.50$

For 1972, $x \times 7$, giving $y = 696.50 - (7 \times 4.32) = 666.26$

An alternative method for calculating the trend equation is from

$$Y - \bar{y} = \left\{ \frac{\Sigma(x - \bar{x})(y - \bar{y})}{\Sigma(x - \bar{x})^2} \right\}(X - \bar{x})$$

where X and Y are the variables in the final equation, x and y are data values as defined earlier, and $\bar{x}$ and $\bar{y}$ are the corresponding arithmetic means. (Readers requiring further illustration of the above methods, and a convenient way of reducing calculations should read chapter 10 in *Business Statistics by Example* by A. E. Innes, published by Macmillan, 1974; revised edition 1979.)

(iii) The averages method is based on the fact that if the time span is divided into two equal parts, a straight line joining the mean centre of each is a good approximation of the regression line. The mean centre is the point defined by $(\bar{x}, \bar{y})$. For the first half the years will be 1965, 1966, 1967 and 1968, giving x values of 0, 1, 2 and 3 and $\bar{x} = (0 + 1 + 2 + 3)/4 = 1.5$. $\bar{y}$ will be the average of the corresponding y values, i.e.

$$(691 + 690 + 692 + 696)/4 = 692.25$$

Hence, one point satisfied by the equation is $(x_1 y_1)$, i.e. (1.5, 692.25). Similarly, calculated values for the second half of the data give $(x_2 y_2)$ as (5.5, 670.5). Insertion of these values in the general equation $y = a + bx$ gives two simultaneous equations:

$$692.25 = a + 1.5b$$
$$670.5 \ = a + 5.5b$$

to give $b = -5.44$ and $a = 700.41$, i.e. a rough estimate of the trend equation is $y = 700.41 - 5.44x$.

(iv) Tabulate original values, the two *trend* values already calculated and 6 other similarly calculated values. The model is now $O = T + R$, i.e. $R = O - T$, – subtraction gives R values calculated in the last column:

Year	O	T	R
1965	691	696.50	−5.50
1966	690	692.18	−2.18
1967	692	687.86	+4.14
1968	696	683.54	+12.46
1969	680	679.22	+0.78
1970	666	674.90	−8.90
1971	667	670.58	−3.58
1972	669	666.26	+2.74
			−0.04 = ΣR

Note that 4 O values lie above the trend and 4 below. The R values are comparatively small and summate to $\simeq 0$. We have good grounds for supposing that the variations about the straight-line trend are random, and that therefore the trend fits the O values well.

Although the techniques of Example 4.2 could be used to construct a straight-line trend for the next example, a curve would represent the growth of sales better, and a more elaborate technique is introduced.

Example 4.3 (i) Plot the following values on a graph. (ii) Plot the trend as $y = 11.69x^2 + 92.18x + 897.67$, where y = sales (£000s) and x = year, measured from 1969.

Manufacturers' sales of ballpoint refills

Year	Sales (£000s)
1964	700
1965	730
1966	741
1967	810
1968	772
1969	921
1970	970
1971	1147
1972	1195
1973	1544
1974	1630

Source: C.S.O., *Annual Abstract of Statistics,* London, H.M.S.O., no. 112, 1975, table 20.

(i) Figure 4.6 shows the *original* values, with the *trend*, calculated in (ii), inserted.

(ii) To calculate the 1964 *trend* value, take x as $(1964 - 1969) = -5$, and insert it in the model

$$y = 11.69x^2 + 92.18x + 897.67$$

to give

$$292.25 - 460.9 + 897.67 = 729.02$$

Now, for 1964:

$$R = O - T = 700 - 729.02 = -29.02$$

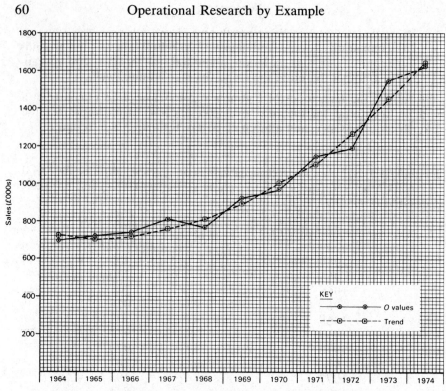

FIG. 4.6 Manufacturer's sales of ballpoint refills (quadratic trend)

This and similarly calculated T and R values are given below:

Year	T	R
1964	729.02	−29.02
1965	716.02	+13.98
1966	726.34	+14.66
1967	760.07	+49.93
1968	817.18	−45.18
1969	897.67	+23.33
1970	1001.54	−31.54
1971	1131.79	+15.21
1972	1279.42	−84.42
1973	1453.46	+90.54
1974	1650.82	−20.82
		−3.33 = ΣR

The low value of ΣR confirms the impression given by the graph that the *quadratic* or *second-order* trend is a good fit. For a rigorous test of the suitability of the curve, as we shall see, ΣR^2 should be considered. The equation used was obtained from the model:

$$y = ax^2 + bx + c$$

Values of the parameters a, b and c are obtained by solving simultaneously the standard equations:

$$\Sigma y = Na + b\Sigma x + c\Sigma x^2$$
$$\Sigma xy = a\Sigma x + b\Sigma x^2 + c\Sigma^3$$
$$\Sigma xy = a\Sigma x^2 + b\Sigma x^3 + c\Sigma x^4$$

the summated values being obtained by an extension of the tabulation described in the answer to Example 4.2 (ii). The method is quite general and can be extended to fit cubic curves, i.e. of the family $y = a + bx + cx^2 + dx^3$, which would involve $(3 + 1) = 4$ simultaneous equations, and curves of higher order. Where x^n is the highest power $n + 1$ equations will be used. Calculation and use of such equations becomes cumbersome, even when an electronic computer is used.

Where the seasonal pattern is strongly marked, as in Example 4.1 (ii), the trend can be calculated by the *moving-average* method, and the next example illustrates the methods used.

Example 4.4 Graph each of the following series, calculate an unweighted moving-average trend for each and plot it on the graph. A centred trend is needed for (ii).

(i) *Total daily traffic, Road A (00s) vehicles)*

Day	Week 1	Week 2	Week 3
Monday	8	10	12
Tuesday	9	11	12
Wednesday	12	15	17
Thursday	7	9	11
Friday	6	8	10
Saturday	10	13	16
Sunday	3	5	7

(ii) *Production of compound feeding stuffs (calf food)*

Year	Quarter	tons (000s)
1973	1	44.2
	2	35.0
	3	27.4
	4	40.8

Year	Quarter	tons (000s)
1974	1	39.3
	2	28.2
	3	24.2
	4	34.6
1975	1	34.7
	2	26.1
	3	21.9
	4	35.5
1976	1	38.7
	2	28.4
	3	26.0
	4	41.2

Source: C.S.O., *Monthly Digest of Statistics*, no. 375, London, H.M.S.O., March 1975, table 5.6.

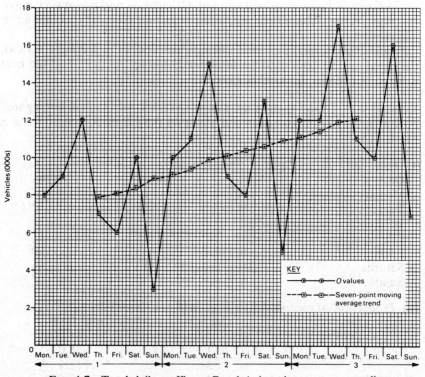

FIG. 4.7   Total daily traffic on Road A (moving-average trend)

(i) Figure 4.7 shows a marked 'seasonal' pattern 7 days long; for example, Wednesday is always the busiest day, and Sunday the least busy. To facilitate explanation plot each O value at the mid-point of each day. Total the traffic for the first 7 consecutive days, to show 55 in col. (4) below. The total is placed at the mid-point of 7 days, which coincides with the mid-point of Thursday, i.e. opposite the O value, 7 (00's vehicles), and $55/7 \simeq 7.9$, giving the first moving average value in col. (5). The next moving total is given by omitting Monday's O value in week 1, i.e. 8, and including Monday's O value in week 2, 10, and $(9 + 12 + 7 + 6 + 10 + 3 + 10) = 57$, and the derived moving average 8.1 is placed opposite to Friday week 1. Calculations continue until the last group of 7 consecutive O values are taken, ending the moving-average trend with 12.1, placed opposite to Thursday in week 3. The complete values are as follows:

Week (1)	Day (2)	O (3)	7-point moving total (4)	Moving-average trend (5)
1	Monday	8		
	Tuesday	9		
	Wednesday	12		
	Thursday	7	55	7.9
	Friday	6	57	8.1
	Saturday	10	59	8.4
	Sunday	3	62	8.9
2	Monday	10	64	9.1
	Tuesday	11	66	9.4
	Wednesday	15	69	9.9
	Thursday	9	71	10.1
	Friday	8	73	10.4
	Saturday	13	74	10.6
	Sunday	5	76	10.9
3	Monday	12	78	11.1
	Tuesday	12	80	11.4
	Wednesday	17	83	11.9
	Thursday	11	85	12.1
	Friday	10		
	Saturday	16		
	Sunday	7		

Figure 4.7 shows *original values* and the *trend*.

(ii) Plotting the original values suggests a strong seasonal pattern of 4 quarters' duration. A 4-point *moving total* is therefore plotted in col. (4) below, but the first value, 147.4, must be plotted at mid-1973, i.e. cutting the line separating the second and third quarters. This brings it between two O values, and not opposite one, so that further analysis on the lines of $O - T$ and illustrated in Example 4.2 (iv) and following Example 4.3 would be impossible, for O and T refer to different times. Instead of dividing the 4-point total by 4, we therefore add consecutive pairs of such totals putting the new 8-point total $(2 \times 4 = 8)$ in the next column. But the new total must come mid-way

Centred moving-average calculations for calf food data (000s tons)

(1) Year	(2) Quarter	(3) O	(4) 4-point moving total	(5) 8-point centred moving total	(6) Moving-average trend
1973	1	44.2			
	2	35.0			
			147.4		
	3	27.4		289.9	36.2
			142.5		
	4	40.8		278.2	34.8
			135.7		
1974	1	39.3		268.2	33.5
			132.5		
	2	28.2		258.8	32.4
			126.3		
	3	24.2		248.0	31.0
			121.7		
	4	34.6		241.3	30.2
			119.6		
1975	1	34.7		236.9	29.6
			117.3		
	2	26.1		235.5	29.4
			118.2		
	3	21.9		240.4	30.1
			122.2		
	4	35.5		246.7	30.8
			124.5		
1976	1	38.7		253.1	31.6
			128.6		
	2	28.4		262.9	32.9
			134.3		
	3	26.0			
	4	41.2			

between the points in time set for the old totals, which brings it opposite to an original value, e.g. 147.4 (2/3 quarter line for 1973) and
142.5 (3/4 quarter line for 1973) to give 289.9, opposite to third
quarter, 1973. Division by 8 of these centred totals yields 36.2, the
first value in a *centred* moving-average trend shown in the last column.
The complete tabulation is on page 64.

Figure 4.8 shows O values and the centred moving-average trend.

Both series analysed above are represented by the model

$$O = T + S + R$$

To use the models in forecasting, we first need to forecast the *trend*.
Unfortunately, the method does not give a trend equation and extrapolation on the graph would be required. To measure seasonal effects we
note from the model that

$$S = O - T - R$$

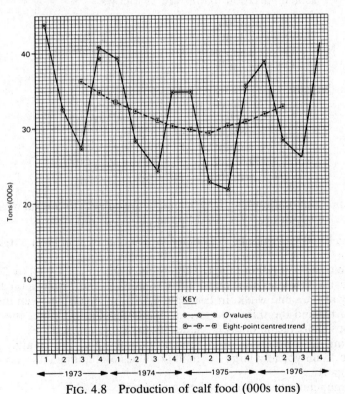

FIG. 4.8 Production of calf food (000s tons)

i.e. we subtract the trend figures from the O values, recognising that the seasonal differences are still unrefined measures subject to R influences. To obtain seasonal variation figures all the seasonal difference figures are averaged for their respective classes, e.g. for Mondays, for Tuesdays, etc., in (i) above, and for the 1st quarter, the 2nd quarter, etc. for (ii). Any such set should balance to O, so that in applying them separately to a trend, no bias is introduced. The individual adjustment that may be needed is explained in A. E. Innes, *Business Statistics by Example*, chap. 10. The next example shows how seasonal variation figures are used in forecasting.

Example 4.5 Trend values for a firm's sales were forecast as follows:

$$
\begin{array}{lll}
1979 & Q1 & £85000 \\
& Q2 & £83200 \\
& Q3 & £80000 \\
& Q4 & £79700
\end{array}
$$

Quarterly seasonal variation figures are as follows:

$$
\begin{array}{ll}
Q1 & -£8300 \\
Q2 & +£2100 \\
Q3 & +£13500 \\
Q4 & -£7300
\end{array}
$$

Forecast the values for 1979.

	T		S		Forecast
Q1 =	£85000	+	(−£8300)	=	£76700
Q2 =	£83200	+	(£2100)	=	£85300
Q3 =	£80000	+	(£13500)	=	£93500
Q4 =	£79700	+	(−£7300)	=	£72400

Forecasts based on simple moving averages are subject to certain weaknesses, some of which are illustrated by the above examples:

(i) The trend can only be conveniently forecast by graphical extrapolation.

(ii) The trend lags behind the O values, e.g. in Example 4.4 (i) by 3 days, because O values start on Monday in week 1, and T values on Thursday of the same week. In Example 4.4 (ii) the lag is between the first quarter and the third quarter, i.e. 6 months. Furthermore, the trend stops short of the latest O values by the same amount.

(iii) Using the unweighted arithmetic mean makes the trend unduly sensitive to untypically large or small O values and impairs its smoothing property.

(iv) Large amounts of data need to be stored.

(v) In calculating a single trend value all N items, earlier, current and later, count equally, yet for the next calculation one is lost and a new one is suddenly considered.

One method of meeting (v) is to apply *triangular weights* in constructing a moving average. The next example illustrates the method.

Example 4.6 A firm records its output every four months. Estimate the trend for 1980 by using a moving average with triangular weights for the following data:

	Period beginning	Output (000s units)
1974	Jan	20
	May	28
	Sep	21
1975	Jan	23
	May	32
	Sep	25
1976	Jan	27
	May	35
	Sep	29

Figure 4.9 shows the short series to have a strong 3-point seasonal pattern. Weights already used for moving averages have been *rectangular*. If applied to the above data, the pattern would be

$$\left. \begin{array}{l} 20 \times 1 \\ 28 \times 1 \\ 21 \times 1 \end{array} \right\} \rightarrow 69 \div 3 = 23$$

and the same answer would be obtained by

$$\left. \begin{array}{l} 20 \times 1/3 \\ 28 \times 1/3 \\ 21 \times 1/3 \end{array} \right\} \rightarrow 23$$

In triangular weighting we arrange for the oldest O value to carry the least weight – call it 1. The second value carries a weight of 2, and the most recent a weight of 3.

To employ the technique just demonstrated, we express weights as fractions, as follows:

			Weight
Oldest	1		$1/6$
Next	2	2/6 =	$1/3$
Most recent	3	3/6 =	$1/2$
	$\overline{6}$		$\overline{1}$

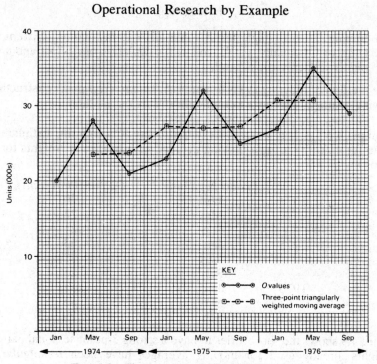

FIG. 4.9   Firm's output, 1974–6 (000s units)

Two values are worked out below:

$$
\begin{array}{llll}
1974 & \text{Jan} & 20 \times {}^1/_6 = & 3^2/_3 \\
 & \text{May} & 28 \times {}^1/_3 = & 9^1/_3 \\
 & \text{Sep} & 21 \times {}^1/_2 = & 10^1/_2 \\
\hline
 & & & 23^1/_2
\end{array}
\Big\} \rightarrow 23.5
$$

$$
\begin{array}{llll}
1974 & \text{May} & 28 \times {}^1/_6 = & 4^2/_3 \\
 & \text{Sep} & 21 \times {}^1/_3 = & 7 \\
1975 & \text{Jan} & 23 \times {}^1/_2 = & 11^1/_2 \\
\hline
 & & & 23^1/_6
\end{array}
\Big\} \rightarrow 23.7
$$

Decimals are used only in the final stages of calculation to minimise errors due to rounding.

These, and other similarly calculated values, are tabulated below:

Year	Period beginning	O	Triangularly weighted moving average
			(000s units)
1974	Jan	20	
	May	28	23.5
	Sep	21	23.7
1975	Jan	23	27.2
	May	32	27.0
	Sep	25	27.2
1976	Jan	27	30.7
	May	35	30.7
	Sep	29	

Instead of using weights which decreased with the age of the O values, we could let them decrease symmetrically either side of the centre of the set of O values being weighted using binomial coefficients (see *Business Statistics by Example*, pp. 147–54, and *Business Mathematics by Example*, pp. 30–1).

For example to find 5 binomially related weights we note that the coefficients of $(x + a)^4$ are

$$1 \quad 4 \quad 6 \quad 4 \quad 1$$

These could be applied directly, with weighted totals being divided by 16, or, better, weights of

$$1/16 \quad 4/16(=^1/_4) \quad 6/16(=^3/_8) \quad 4/16(=^1/_4) \quad 1/16$$

could be applied to give a total needing no division.

The next example introduces a method of weighting which offers marked advantages over earlier methods and becoming increasingly prominent in modern forecasting.

Example 4.7 Estimate for each month, starting with February 1965, the percentage yield on short-dated British Government stock, each estimate to be calculated as

$$(0.2 \times \text{actual value}) + (0.8 \times \text{last estimate})$$

Take as the estimate for January 1965 the average for the last 12 months (=5.54 per cent). Also, calculate the error in the estimated values.

British Government stocks, short-dated redemption yields (%)

1965			1966		
	Jan	6.45		Jan	6.22
	Feb	6.41		Feb	6.45
	Mar	6.57		Mar	6.71
	Apr	6.63		Apr	6.57
	May	6.72		May	6.62
	June	6.70		June	6.80
	July	6.77		July	7.11
	Aug	6.73		Aug	7.25
	Sep	6.59		Sep	6.96
	Oct	6.39		Oct	6.91
	Nov	6.38		Nov	6.88
	Dec	6.53		Dec	6.72

Source: *Bank of England Statistical Abstract*, no. 1, 1970, table 30.

Jan 1965 – Actual value = 6.45%
$$\begin{array}{r} \times\ 0.2 \\ \hline 1.29\% \end{array}$$

Forecast (see data)   = 5.54%
$$\begin{array}{r} \times\ 0.8 \\ \hline 4.432\% \end{array}$$

Therefore, the forecast for February = 1.29% + 4.432% = 5.722%. This is used in forecasting the March value:

Actual for Feb = 6.41%
$$\begin{array}{r} \times\ 0.2 \\ \hline 1.282\% \end{array}$$

Last forecast = 5.722%
$$\begin{array}{r} \times\ 0.8 \\ \hline 4.578\% \end{array}$$

March forecast = 1.282% + 4.578% = 5.86%

These and similarly calculated values are tabulated below: (see also Figure 4.10):

		Actual %	Forecast %	Error %
1965	Jan	6.45	5.54	−0.91
	Feb	6.41	5.722	−0.688

		Actual %	Forecast %	Error %
	Mar	6.57	5.860	−0.710
	Apr	6.63	6.002	−0.628
	May	6.72	6.128	−0.592
	June	6.70	6.246	−0.454
	July	6.77	6.337	−0.433
	Aug	6.73	6.424	−0.306
	Sep	6.59	6.485	−0.105
	Oct	6.39	6.506	+0.116
	Nov	6.38	6.483	+0.103
	Dec	6.53	6.462	−0.068
1966	Jan	6.22	6.476	+0.256
	Feb	6.45	6.425	−0.025
	Mar	6.71	6.43	−0.28
	Apr	6.57	6.486	−0.084
	May	6.62	6.503	−0.117
	June	6.80	6.527	−0.273
	July	7.11	6.582	−0.528
	Aug	7.25	6.688	−0.562
	Sep	6.96	6.800	−0.16
	Oct	6.91	6.832	−0.078
	Nov	6.88	6.848	−0.032
	Dec	6.72	6.854	+0.134

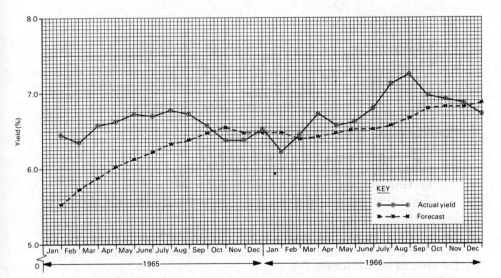

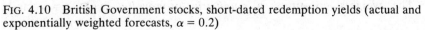

FIG. 4.10   British Government stocks, short-dated redemption yields (actual and
exponentially weighted forecasts, $\alpha = 0.2$)

The method used is *exponential smoothing*, and the value of 0.2 was the *smoothing constant* conventionally represented by α and $0.8 = 1 - \alpha$. Substituting in the instruction given in the example and using the word 'forecast' instead of 'estimate':

$$\text{New forecast} = (\alpha \times \text{actual value}) + \{(1 - \alpha) \times \text{old forecast}\}$$

Multiplying out and simplifying the right-hand side terms gives

$$\text{New forecast} = \text{old forecast} + \alpha\,(\text{actual value} - \text{old forecast})$$

so that the method has the important advantage that the new forecast makes some allowance for any recent change in direction of the series revealed by the difference between the last forecast and the true value. The next example reveals an important property of the weights used in exponential smoothing.

Example 4.8 Trace the weights used in forecasting May sales for the following values if the constant α is used, and hence calculate the sum of the weights in an infinite series:

	Sales (£00s)	
	Actual	Forecast
Jan	6	(4)
Feb	5	
Mar	8	
Apr	9	

February forecast = $(\alpha \times 6) + (1 - \alpha)4$
March forecast = $(\alpha \times 5) + (1 - \alpha)\{(\alpha \times 6) + (1 - \alpha)4\}$
April forecast   = $(\alpha \times 8) + (1 - \alpha)[(\alpha \times 5) + (1 - \alpha)\{(\alpha \times 6)$
                 $+ (1 - \alpha)4\}]$
May forecast   = $(\alpha \times 9) + (1 - \alpha)(\text{April forecast})$

Consider 6, the actual value for January:

In February forecast it is multiplied by α
In March forecast it is multiplied by $\alpha(1 - \alpha)$
In April forecast, it is multiplied by $\alpha(1 - \alpha)^2$
And expansion would show the corresponding value for May to be $\alpha(1 - \alpha)^3$

These values are weights, and as α and $(1 - \alpha)$ are both positive and less than 1, the January actual value enters proportionately less into a forecast the later in time it occurs.

The weights constitute a *geometric progression* with $a = \alpha$ and

$r = (1 - \alpha)$, so

$$\underset{\infty}{S} = \frac{a}{1 - r} = \frac{\alpha}{1 - (1 - \alpha)} = 1$$

Hence, in an infinite period of time the system would not produce bias.

Any value of α may be chosen between 0 and 1. In practical business situations, where values followed no neat pattern, experiment would show which value tended to produce the best forecasts. If the original data shows periodicity where we would use a simple moving average based on N units, then the same degree of smoothing will be given by making

$$\alpha = \frac{2}{n + 1}$$

Earlier years' data used in Example 4.7 showed no simple pattern. The higher the value of α, the more responsive is the forecast to recent values. Exercise 4.5 will show that a higher value of α will reduce the error in the forecast. On the whole the errors produced for $\alpha = 0.2$ showed that too often the yield was being underestimated.

Although the exponential smoothing method is best used in short-term forecasting, measuring the trend is comparatively simple, and applying it may improve the quality of the forecasts obtained. Trend values are simply obtained as the difference between one forecast and the forecast for the period immediately before. We illustrate with a few calculations based on the data of Example 4.7:

		Forecast %		*Trend* %
1965	Jan	5.54		
	Feb	5.722	$(5.722 - 5.54) =$	+0.182
	Mar	5.860	and so on	+0.138
	Apr	6.002	,,	+0.142
	May	6.128	,,	+0.126
	June	6.246	,,	+0.118

Where the later forecast is smaller, the trend will be downwards, e.g. the trend for December 1965 is $(6.462 - 6.483)\% = -0.021$ per cent.

A great virtue of the exponential method is economy in data storage. The whole mathematical history of a series is contained in the last forecast figure, and to continue only the value of α and the actual figure are needed. Not only can trend values be calculated and allowed for, but in computing systems the performance can be constantly checked and α itself adjusted to meet new secular conditions.

Earlier models have been additive, i.e. the forecast is based upon adding or subtracting constituent elements. The exponential model is multiplicative because in making each forecast part of the last forecast is multiplied by $1 - \alpha$. Replacing $+$ signs by $\times$ signs in the simple model used in Example 4.4 gives

$$O = T \times S \times R$$

or if cyclical changes occur

$$O = T \times C \times S \times R$$

with O and T being measured in original units and C, S and R as numbers greater or less than 1 according to whether the trend is to be increased or decreased. If R values are purely random and the model fits well, individually they would differ little from 1 and their extended product, i.e. $R_1 \times R_2 \times \ldots \times R_N$ would tend to 1. The first model is encountered commonly, as the next example illustrates.

Example 4.9 Plot the following values on a graph, and explain why the multiplicative model is more suitable than the additive one:

Firm's sales (£000s)

Year	Quarter	Sales
1970	1	466
	2	568
	3	650
	4	331
1971	1	317
	2	378
	3	412
	4	191
1972	1	170
	2	175
	3	151
	4	53

Given that the *quarterly index numbers* are

$$Q1 = 84$$
$$Q2 = 110$$
$$Q3 = 139$$
$$Q4 = 78$$

and that the *trend* equation is

$$y = 600 - 44x$$

where y = sales (£000s) and x takes consecutive values of $1, 2, \ldots, n$ (where n is the consecutive number of the quarter, Q1 (1970) being 1), forecast the sales for the first quarter of 1973, and examine the nature of R for 1971.

In the additive model every first quarter would be the same distance from the trend, the value being called the *seasonal variation*. All the second quarters would be equal distances from the trend, and so on, so that we would expect the graph to show waves of equal amplitude about the trend, whereas the data and Figure 4.11 show clearly that this is not so. As the trend falls, the waves close in on it.

The trend value for the first quarter 1973 is

$$£\{600 - (44 \times 13)\}(000s) = £28000.$$

An index is a percentage figure, so that Q1 = 84 means that each first quarter value is trend × 84/100, and hence

$$£28000 \times 0.84 = £23520$$

The trend value for the first quarter 1973 is

$$600 - (44 \times 5) = 380$$

From $O = T \times S \times R$

$$R = \frac{O}{T \times S}$$

But S is given as 84/100.

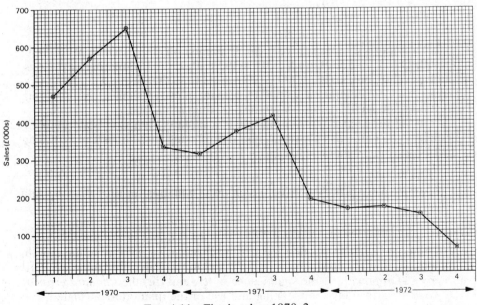

FIG. 4.11   Firm's sales, 1970–2

Therefore

$$R = \frac{317}{380 \times 0.84} = 0.993$$

Trend for the second quarter $1971 = 380 - 44 = 336$, and

$$R = \frac{378}{336 \times 1.10} = 1.023$$

and by similar calculations for the third and fourth quarters respectively

$$R = 1.015 \text{ and } 0.987$$

The individual values are reasonably close to 1, and their product is 1.018. If we take more than one group of 4, we shall find that the product is even closer to 1. Hence the model would appear to be a reasonable fit.

In Example 4.2 (iv) inspection showed that R values were individually small in relationship to O, and collectively $\Sigma R \simeq 0$. We assumed correctly that the trend line was a good fit. But the test was not rigorous, and in series like the following $\Sigma R = 0$ would prove an unsatisfactory criterion of the trend fit:

Year	Sales(£000s)
1970	10
1971	20
1972	80
1973	90

Earlier methods would give a linear regression trend of $y = 50$ (£000s) with $O - T$ values of $-40, -30, +30, +40$, $\Sigma R = 0$. Squaring deviations gives values of $+1600, +900, +900, +1600$, so that $\Sigma R^2 = £^2 5000$ (000s): there are no minus($-$) values to balance plus($+$) values, and squaring penalises large deviations more heavily than small ones.

In the next example the principle is used in conjunction with sampling theory to enable us to measure the risk of using fitted lines and of basing estimates upon them.

Example 4.10 The linear regression trend equation for the following data is

$$y = 6.23 + 0.81x$$

where y = number of sales and x is the consecutive number of the month, January counting as 0, February as 1, and so on. Calculate (i) the *standard error of estimate*, (ii) the significance of '*b*', and (iii) the *standard error of forecast*, explaining the meaning and use of the quantities calculated.

Month	Sales (units)
Jan	6
Feb	7
Mar	9
Apr	8
May	9
June	10
July	12
Aug	13
Sep	11
Oct	14

(i) S_{yx}, the standard error of estimate, equals

$$\sqrt{\left\{\frac{\Sigma(Y - y_c)^2}{n - k}\right\}}$$

where y = observed values of Y, y_c = the calculated values, n = number of values and k = number of parameters, i.e. constants in the equation used in calculation. For January $y_c = 6.23 + \{(0.81) \times (0)\} = 6.23$, and for February $y_c = 6.23 + 0.81 = 7.04$. These and similarly calculated values are summarised below, enabling us to calculate $\Sigma(Y - y_c)^2$:

	Y	y_c	$(Y - y_c)^2$
Jan	6	6.23	0.0529
Feb	7	7.04	0.0016
Mar	9	7.85	1.3225
Apr	8	8.66	0.4356
May	9	9.47	0.2209
June	10	10.28	0.0784
July	12	11.09	0.8281
Aug	13	11.90	1.21
Sep	11	12.71	2.9241
Oct	14	13.52	0.2304
			7.3045

$n = 10$, $k = 2$ because the equation contained 2 parameters, $a + b$. Therefore

$$S_{yx} = \sqrt{\left\{\frac{7.3045}{10 - 2}\right\}} = 0.956$$

An alternative method of calculation is

$$S_{yx} = \sqrt{\left\{\frac{\Sigma y^2 - b\Sigma xy}{n - 2}\right\}}$$

where $y = Y - \bar{Y}$ and $x = X - \bar{X}$. S_{yx} measures how close the estimate obtained by using the equation is to the original data. The numerator under the square-root sign measures the closeness, but in theory we are supposing that we have taken at random a 10-month run out of an infinite number of such runs. They constitute a sampling distribution, and S_{yx} is its standard deviation. It is used to calculate (ii) and (iii) below.

(ii) b measures the average change in y associated with a given change in x. If $b = 0$, one would assume that the two changes are dissociated from one another. Although here $b = 0.81$, we rely on a sample for our value, and it is possible that sampling error may have accounted for this value. The standard error of b is

$$\frac{S_{yx}}{\sqrt{\Sigma x^2}}$$

with $x = X - \bar{X}$, as above. X takes values 0, 1, ..., 9:

$$\bar{X} = \frac{\overset{9}{\underset{n=0}{\Sigma}} x}{10} = 4.5$$

Therefore, $\Sigma x^2 = (-4.5)^2 + (-3.5)^2 \ldots + (3.5)^2 + (4.5)^2 = 82.5$, and the standard error of b equals

$$\frac{0.956}{9.083} = 0.105$$

To test whether the calculated value of b is significant, we use Student's t test. Difference $= 0.81 - 0.0 = 0.81$ (between observed b and 0, the value of b if x and y are uncorrelated).

$$t = \frac{\text{Difference}}{\text{Standard error}} = \frac{0.81}{0.105} = 7.714, \nu = 10 - 2 = 8$$

Therefore b is significant at the 0.05 per cent level, i.e. we have very strong grounds for supposing that the relationship between y and x has not arisen by chance.

(iii) Suppose we use the equation to estimate sales for next January; then

$X = 12$ and $y = 6.23 + (0.81 \times 12) = 15.95$. We may need to know what degree of certainty we can put on our estimate. Using the theory of confidence intervals, we can be 95 per cent certain that the value will fall within

$15.95 \pm (1.96 \times$ standard errors)

But here we need the standard error of individual forecast (S_f), which takes into account S_{yx}, already calculated, and n and x, and which equals

$$ S_{yx} \sqrt{\left\{ 1 + \frac{1}{n} + \frac{x^2}{\Sigma x^2} \right\}} $$

$$ = 0.956 \sqrt{\left\{ 1 + \frac{1}{10} + \frac{(12 - 45)^2}{82.5} \right\}} = 1.276 $$

To apply it we could be 95 per cent confident that our estimate would lie within

$15.95 \pm (1.96 \times S_f) = 15.95 \pm (1.96 \times 1.276)$

i.e. between 13.449 and 18.451.

So far, forecasts have been made by applying quantitative methods to past figures, with the only subjective element being the choice of one model rather than another, e.g. of a linear pattern rather than a quadratic curve; and if a criterion were required, significance tests already shown could settle between alternatives. On this basis forecasting could be automatic. But the reliability of the method rests upon the certainty with which the pattern of past figures continues into the future. Hence, an alternative method of forecasting uses the collective judgement of teams of individuals to estimate future figures. A *synthetic forecast*, for example, might be made by a paint manufacturer on the basis of the separate judgements of sales managers in different parts of the country. Often, the final forecast will represent a projection of past figures, described earlier in the chapter, tempered by the subjective but informed assessment of groups of executives.

The distinction is usually made between short-term and long-term forecasts, but no final rule can be given. In general a forecast is long term when it contemplates fundamental changes in the conditions determining the variable being measured; for example, a long-term forecast in the price of milk would be based on changes in dairy-herd size brought about by the prospect of higher or lower prices. A short-term forecast assumes that the underlying conditions will remain unchanged, but that random variations will affect constituent factors. The simplest methods of exponential smoothing are short-term techniques.

Long-term forecasts rely on complicated models and electronic computers to use them. Simulation, as discussed in the last chapter, is increasingly used in forecasting.

Exercises 4

4.1 Plot the following data on a time-series graph:

Year	Telephone calls, trunk – U.K. (millions)
1964	624
1965	736
1966	842
1967	932
1968	1069
1969	1207
1970	1352
1971	1517
1972	1699
1973	1944
1974	2138

Source: C.S.O., *Annual Abstract of Statistics 1975*, London, H.M.S.O., 1975, table 293.

(i) Estimate the 1977 figure:
    (a) by extrapolating a free-hand curve;
    (b) by the method of Example 4.2 (iii);
    (c) by using the equation $y = 382.2 + 149.3x$ taking x as the consecutive number of the year, 1964 = 0, 1965 = 1, etc.
(ii) Calculate for the 1964–74 values $\Sigma(Y - y_c)$ for (i)(b) and for (i)(c). What do you conclude?

4.2 (i) From the following data, plot log y against x on a semi-logarithmic graph.
    (ii) Calculate the average annual rate of growth of electricity generation.
    (iii) Estimate from (ii) the 1970 figure, compare it with the actual figure of 228.3 (000s in kWh) and comment.

Year	Electricity generated (000s kWh)
1955	81.2
1956	88.3
1957	92.2
1958	99.8
1959	106.6
1960	120.5
1961	129.4
1962	143.6
1963	156.0
1964	164.6

Source: *The British Economy: Key Statistics 1900–1970*, Times Newspapers Ltd, n.d., table c.

4.3 (i) Plot the following data on a graph and calculate and insert on the graph a 4-point centred moving-average trend.

(ii) Discuss the problems of forecasting deliveries for the four quarters of 1970 on the basis of your graph and calculations.

Year	Quarter	Index (1963 = 100)
1965	1	120.3
	2	100.8
	3	96.8
	4	90.9
1966	1	90.3
	2	94.4
	3	97.7
	4	86.3
1967	1	101.8
	2	107.6
	3	104.9
	4	107.9

Brick deliveries, Great Britain

Source: Department of the Environment, *Housing and Construction Statistics*, no. 3, third quarter 1972, London H.M.S.O., 1972, table 1.

4.4 Repeat Example 4.3, but use the following data, taken from the same source:

Manufacturer's sales of ballpoint pens

Year	Sales (£000s)
1964	3838
1965	4254
1966	4605
1967	4872
1968	5428
1969	5570
1970	6106
1971	5583
1972	6843
1973	7849
1974	10286

The trend, with y and x defined as before, is

$$y = 5338 + 504x + 59x^2$$

Discuss whether knowing both sets of sales facilitates your forecasts of the separate products. Directly paired, the sales of the two products show a product-moment coefficient of correlation of $+0.937$.

4.5 Repeat Example 4.7, using the following data, which are from the same source, but taking $\alpha = 0.4$:

Industrial ordinary shares – earnings yield %

1965			1966	
Jan	8.92		Jan	7.49
Feb	9.27		Feb	7.51
Mar	9.57		Mar	7.55
Apr	9.83		Apr	7.34
May	10.07		May	6.95
June	10.75		June	6.85
July	10.98		July	7.85
Aug	8.48		Aug	8.32
Sep	7.99		Sep	8.15
Oct	7.58		Oct	8.41
Nov	7.73		Nov	8.21
Dec	7.77		Dec	7.93

Discuss, in the light of both examples, the problem of selecting a suitable value for α.

4.6 The total sales of a product for separate 4-month periods are shown below:

Year	4-month period	Sales (000s)
1970	1	200
	2	35.5
	3	48
1971	1	137.5
	2	25
	3	36
1972	1	100
	2	17.5
	3	24

The firm has noted that over a long period the sales/trend ratio is as follows:

4-month period	Ratio (%)
1	250
2	50
3	80

  (i) Show that the ratios are consistent with a constant seasonal pattern.

 (ii) Calculate the trend for the 3 years quoted.

(iii) Estimate sales for each 4-month period of 1973.

4.7 State the statistical factors likely to affect the accuracy of forecasts, and explain how the degree of accuracy may be measured.

Bibliography

A. Battersby, *Sales Forecasting* (London: Cassell, 1968).

G. Box and G. Jenkins, *Time Series Analysis, Forecasting and Control* (San Francisco: Holden-Day, 1970).

R. Brown, *Statistical Forecasting for Inventory Control* (New York: McGraw-Hill, 1959).

R. Brown, *Smoothing, Forecasting and Prediction of Discrete Time Series* (Englewood Cliffs, N.J.: Prentice-Hall, 1963).

G. A. Coutie *et al.*, *Short-Term Forecasting* (Edinburgh: Oliver & Boyd, 1966).

M. Ezekiel and K. A. Fox, *Methods of Correlation and Regression Analysis* (New York: Wiley, 1959).

W. Gilchrist, *Statistical Forecasting* (London: Wiley, 1976).

J. V. Gregg, C. H. Hassell and J. T. Richardson, *Mathematical Trend Curves: An Aid to Forecasting* (Edinburgh: Oliver & Boyd, 1964).

A. E. Innes, *Business Statistics by Example* (London: Macmillan, 1974).

A. E. Innes, *Business Mathematics by Example* (London: Macmillan, 1977).

M. Kendall, *Time Series* (London: Griffin, 1973).

W. A. Spurr and C. P. Bonini, *Statistical Analysis for Business Decisions* (Homewood, Ill.: Irwin, 1967).

5
Stock and Inventory Control

The successful working of most firms and large organisations depends upon keeping stocks: of goods for sale, as with a multiple-shop system; material for internal use, as with stationery for a government office; or raw materials, components and semi-finished goods, as with a production factory. The term *inventory* describes stock held to meet some future need, and unless rule-of-thumb methods are followed quantitative methods will be used to guide management in two types of decision, the level of stock to be aimed at and the re-ordering policy which will best achieve it. For solving such problems operational research brings in techniques of model-making and optimisation.

The first example shows the calculation of *average stock*, a quantity needed in most calculations.

Example 5.1   At the beginning of each 28-day month a firm's stock is at a level of 500 units, and at the end of the month it is nil.

(i) Calculate the average stock level (a) assuming that stock is used at an even rate, (b) assuming that the stock level (y, in units) is given by

$$y = 500 + 2x - \left(\frac{139}{196}\right) x^2$$

x being the number of days ($x > 2$).

(ii) When during the month will the level be 100 units under assumptions (a) and (b) above?

(i) (a) In Figure 5.1 AB shows the regular fall of stock level through the month, and intuitively we could estimate the average stock correctly as $\frac{1}{2}$ (opening stock + closing stock) = $\frac{1}{2}$ (500 + 0) units = 250 units. More formally, the through-put of stock = time × stock = area of $\triangle AOB = \frac{1}{2}$ (28 × 500) units = 7000 units. If y_0 = average stock level, then through-put at this level must make the area of rectangle the same, i.e. area of rectangle $OCDB$ = 7000 units, i.e. 28 y_0 = 7000 units, giving y_2 = 250 units, as above.

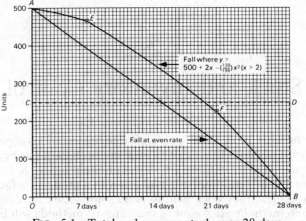

FIG. 5.1   Total and average stock over 28 days

(b) Values of $x = 0$ and $x = 28$ show that the model gives values coinciding with A and B. But when $x = 7$, $y = 500 + (2 \times 7) - (139/196) \times 7^2 = 479.25$ units, and for $x = 21$, $y = 500 + (2 \times 21) - (139/196) \times 21^2 = 229.3$ units, and assuming the distribution is continuous we can draw a curve $AEFB$. Let $\bar{y}$ be the average stock (units), then

$$28\,\bar{y} = \text{area } AEFBO$$

$$= \int_{0}^{28} \left\{ 500 + 2x - \left(\frac{139}{196}\right) x^2 \right\} dx$$

$$= \left[500x + \left(\frac{2}{2}\right) x^2 - \frac{1}{3} \times \left(\frac{139}{196}\right) x^3 \right]_{0}^{28}$$

$$= 9594.67 \text{ units}$$

Dividing by 28 gives $\bar{y} = 342.7$ units.

(ii) (a) Let x_3 days give a stock level of 100 units. Then, by similar triangles,

$$\frac{28 - x_3}{28} = \frac{100}{500}$$

giving $x_3 = 22.4$ days.

(b) $y = 500 + 2x - \left(\frac{139}{196}\right) x^2$

We need the value of x which makes $y = 100$ units:

$$100 = 500 + 2x - \left(\frac{139}{196}\right) x^2$$

Solving this quadratic equation gives $x = 25.20$, the negative solution being rejected. As expected, the stated level is reached later than with (a), i.e. at 25.2 days, the stock being used at a slower rate. If the firm sets too low a stock level, it takes the risk of *stocks-out*, i.e. of running out and being unable to meet the whole or part of an order, and prejudicing future business. It may also reduce the size of order it can place, reducing the benefit brought by trade (i.e. quantity) discounts. A high level, however, can be costly in storage space, in the provision of special facilities such as refrigeration or air-conditioning, and in security and insurance costs. Stock stored ties up capital which may more profitably be used in the business or invested elsewhere. If the current rate of interest is 9 per cent, an average stock of £20000 over 6 months (26 weeks) represents a weekly expenditure of

$$\frac{9}{100} \times \frac{1}{2} \times \frac{1}{26} \times \frac{£20000}{1} = £34.62$$

Stock stored too long may deteriorate or become obsolete. If prices are falling, profits are reduced or changed to losses when stock is sold, but rising prices will favour a policy of retaining stock.

The next example introduces a rule which is useful when trade discount is the only factor to consider.

Example 5.2 A dealer buys 100 articles each month at £30 each. His office and related costs are £8 for each order placed. Stock-holding costs are 18 percent on average stock per annum. His supplier introduces a discount scheme as follows:

Size of order	Discount allowed
100	Nil
120	5%
150	7%

Assuming that whatever the size of order stock sells at a steady rate and reaches zero just before the next order is taken, advise the dealer on the size of order to place.

Total cost without discount = $12 \times 100 \times £30 = £36000$. Average stock will be $(100 + 0)/2 = 50$, giving stock-holding costs for the year as 18 per cent of $50 \times £30 = £270$. He will order 12 times a year, incurring ordering costs of $12 \times £8 = £96$. Total annual costs will be (£36000 + £270 + £96)

= £36366. To claim 5 per cent discount, he will have to order

$$\frac{12 \times 100}{120} \text{ times}$$

i.e. 10 times a year, with order costs $10 \times £8 = £80$. Average stock will be higher, at 60 units, and holding costs will be £324. New costs are lower, i.e. $0.95 \times £36000 = £34200$, making the new total costs £34604.

For the 7 per cent discount, corresponding calculations give a cost of £33480, to which are added £405 holding costs and £64 ordering costs. The new total is £33949, so that the trader should accept 7 per cent discount.

To meet a given total demand for goods over a period of time, a firm may choose between ordering in small quantities fairly frequently and ordering in larger quantities less frequently. The next example illustrates how *batch size*, i.e. size of one order, affects unit cost.

Example 5.3 From the following data, assuming that discount is not a critical factor, which policy is the more economical for a firm ordering and holding stock? (The symbols are used in the next example.)

	Policy A	Policy B	Symbol
Total annual demand	500 units	500 units	D
Unit cost	£4	£4	C
Cost of placing 1 order	£8	£8	P
Stock-holding cost per annum (%age of total + ordering cost for average stock)	18%	18%	S
Size of order	50 units	125 units	Q

Policy A
Total purchase cost = $500 \times £4 = £2000$.
No. of orders placed = 500 units/50 units = 10.
Total order cost for 1 year = $10 \times £8 = £80$.
Therefore, average cost per unit (purchase + ordering)

$$= (£2000 + £80)/500 = £4.16$$

Cost of holding 1 unit or stock = 18 per cent of £4.16 = £0.7488.
As the stock is renewed regularly 10 times a year, the average time each unit is in stock is

$$\frac{50}{2 \times 500} \text{ (year)} = \frac{1}{20} \text{ (year)}$$

Therefore, the average annual cost of holding 1 unit of stock is

$$\frac{1}{20} \times \frac{£0.7488}{1} = £0.03744$$

Therefore, required unit cost = £4.16 + £0.03744 = £4.19744.

Policy B
Stock will be ordered 500/125 = 4 times per year, at a cost of 4 × £8 = £32 and a (purchase + ordering) average of

$$(£2000 + £32)/500 = £4.064$$

The average time each unit is in stock higher

$$\frac{125}{2 \times 500} \text{ (year)} \quad \frac{1}{8} \text{ (year)}$$

giving the stock-holding element in unit cost as

$$\frac{1}{8} \times \frac{18}{100} \times \frac{£4.064}{1} = £0.09144$$

Therefore, new average = £4.064 + £0.09144 = £4.15544.

Therefore, Policy B is the more economical.

For purposes of exposition the averages have been calculated to a degree of accuracy which may not be justified by the data.

   As the batch size increases, one element in the final average will increase but another will decrease. The next example shows how to calculate the *optimum batch size*, i.e. that size of order which minimises unit cost.

Example 5.4   (i) Using the symbols in Example 5.3 produce a formula for final unit cost, and hence for the optimum batch size. (ii) Calculate it for the data in Example 5.3.

   (i) Frequency of ordering $= P/Q$. Therefore, cost of ordering and purchasing 1 unit $= (C + P/Q)$. Average time a unit is in stock is $Q/2D$. Final unit cost

$$= \left(C + \frac{P}{Q}\right) + \left\{\frac{S}{1} \times \frac{Q}{2D}\left(C + \frac{P}{Q}\right)\right\} = Y \text{ (say)}$$

We are assuming that D, C, P and S are given, and wish to find the value of Q which makes Y a minimum. Maximum and minimum values of Y are given by $dy/dQ = 0$. Multiplying out and differentiating gives

$$0 - \frac{P}{Q^2} + \frac{SC}{2D} = 0$$

i.e. $-\dfrac{P}{Q^2} = -\dfrac{SC}{2D}$

$$Q = \sqrt{\left(\frac{2DP}{SC}\right)}$$

Consideration of d^2Y/dQ^2 shows that its value will always be positive, so that the formula gives a minimum value for Q.

(ii) Substituting

$$Q = \sqrt{\left(\frac{2 \times 500 \times £8}{0.18 \times £4}\right)} = 105.4$$

Hence, the firm would aim to order 105 units each batch.

Another balance to be struck in deciding stock policy is between the cost of holding stock and the cost of running out. The next example illustrates a simple situation.

Example 5.5 A firm stocks items which cost £150 each. It receives 80 items at the beginning of each month and sells them all by the end. Stock-holding costs are £2.4 per item per year. Experience has shown that when the level falls below 10 items it is likely to run out, thus incurring a shortage cost of £25/item/annum. (i) Calculate the combined stock-holding and shortage average charge per item for year. (ii) Recalculate the value assuming that the total ordered is unchanged, but it orders 120 a batch instead of 80, the stock-out point being unchanged.

(i) Figure 5.2 shows the stock level for January and February. For January BC represents the time when stock-holding costs are incurred, and it will clearly be

$$\frac{AB}{AO} \text{ of 1 month} = \frac{80 - 10}{80} \text{ (month)} = \frac{7}{8} \text{ (month)}$$

The average stock will be $\frac{1}{2}(80 + 10)$ items at a cost of

$$\frac{7}{8} \times \frac{45}{1} \times \frac{£2.4}{12}$$

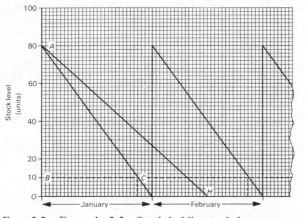

FIG. 5.2 – Example 5.5   Stock-holding and shortage costs

remembering that the rate quoted was annual, i.e. £7.875. Shortage charge will occur for $\frac{1}{8}$ (month) for an average stock of

$$\frac{1}{2}(0 + 10) = 5 \text{ units}, \quad \frac{1 \times 5 \times £25}{8 \times 12} = £1.302$$

giving a combined annual average of 12 (£7.875 + £1.302) = £110.124.

(ii) Total stocks received at 80/month = 12 × 80 = 960. Hence, under the new scheme stock will be renewed every

$$\frac{120}{960} \times 12 \text{ (months)}$$

i.e every 1.5 months.

Triangle AOH represents one stock cycle, and stock is held for

$$\frac{120 - 10}{120} \text{ of 1.5 months} = \frac{11}{12} \times \frac{3}{2} = 1\frac{3}{8} \text{ months}$$

The average stock is (120 + 10)/2 = 65 items, giving a monthly stock-holding cost of

$$\frac{11}{8} \times \frac{65}{1} \times \frac{£2.4}{12} = £17.875$$

Shortage cost will be for $(1\frac{1}{2} - 1\frac{3}{8})$ months, i.e. $\frac{1}{8}$ month. It will affect an average stock of 5 items, as before, with a charge of

$$\frac{1}{8} \times \frac{5}{1} \times \frac{£25}{12} = £1.3021$$

The new cycle will occur 8 times a year, giving a total charge of

$$8 \times (£17.875 + £1.3021) = £153.4168$$

which is considerably more than the 12-month basis figure.

In the next example we show how to optimise Q to give the minimum holding cost.

Example 5.6 (i) Use the following symbols

D = Total annual demand (units)
L = Stock level below which stock-out occurs (units)
C_s = Cost of holding 1 unit of stock for 1 year (£s)
E = Shortage cost for 1 unit of stock for 1 year
Q = Order quantity

to construct a model which gives average (stock-holding + shortage) cost for 1 unit for 1 year.

(ii) Calculate an expression for the optimum value of Q, and apply it where $L = 10$ units, the cost of holding one unit of stock for 1 year is £2.4, and the annual cost of running out of 1 unit of stock for 1 year is £25.

(i) Figure 5.3 shows 1 stock cycle, the unshaded right-angled triangle FKJ showing stock being held, and the right-angled triangle JHG representing the stock-out situation, OG, the length of the cycle = Q/D years, and

$$\frac{KJ}{OG} = \frac{FK}{FO} = \frac{Q-L}{Q}$$

making $KJ = \dfrac{Q-L}{D}$ and

$$JH = \frac{Q}{D} - \left(\frac{Q-L}{D}\right) = \frac{L}{D}$$

Cost of holding or shortage = average stock × time × unit cost. For stock-holding FKJ), average stock

$$= \tfrac{1}{2}\{(Q-L) + C\} = \frac{Q-L}{2}$$

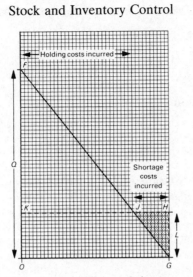

FIG. 5.3   Stock-holding and shortage costs

Therefore, cost

$$= \left(\frac{Q-L}{2}\right)\left(\frac{Q-L}{D}\right)\frac{C_s}{1}$$

and for shortage (JHG), average stock

$$= \tfrac{1}{2}(O + L) = \tfrac{1}{2}$$

and cost

$$= \left(\frac{L}{2}\right)\left(\frac{L}{D}\right)\frac{E}{1}$$

No. of cycles in 1 year $= D/Q$. Therefore, the model is

$$Y = \frac{D}{Q}\left\{\frac{(Q-1)^2}{2D} \, C_s + \frac{L^2 E}{2D}\right\}$$

$$= \frac{C_s}{2}\frac{(Q-L)^2}{Q} + \frac{L^2 E}{2Q}$$

Y being the average cost per unit per year, taking both stock-holding and shortage into account.

(ii) Q is a maximum or minimum when $dY/dQ = 0$. Differentiating the model w.r.t. Q gives the condition:

$$Q = \sqrt{\left(\frac{C_s L^2 + L^2 E}{C_s}\right)} = \sqrt{\left\{\frac{(£2.4 \times 100) + (100 \times £25)}{£2.4}\right\}}$$

$$= 33.79 \text{ units}$$

so that in theory the firm would order in batches of 34. But 960/34 gives an inconvenient frequency, so that probably 960/32 times/year, i.e. 30 times/year, would be more suitable.

Systems of stock replenishment illustrated so far are simple examples of the *cyclical review policy*, or (t, S) to use the conventional symbols: t stands for the fixed time interval between replenishment and S is the ceiling to which the replenishment takes the stock. Because we have assumed demand operating at a constant rate the replenishment amounts have been identical: but the policy also describes systems where demand and hence replenishment rates vary. A system which replenishes stock to level S when it falls to a lower predetermined level is called the re-order level policy, designated (s, S). A simple example is the *two-bin system*, using two equal-sized bins, say A and B. Both are full to start and stock is withdrawn from A. When empty A is returned for replenishment and stock is drawn from B. When A comes back full B is topped up from it, to act once more as a reserve until A is emptied and the cycle repeated. The system is useful for small components which can be conveniently handled and counted.

A more sophisticated replenishment policy embodies characteristics of (t, S) and (s, S). Stock is reviewed at regular intervals and is made up if the observed level is below a predetermined amount. Where an organisation carries a range of items of stock, the general policy is likely to be a compromise between the different requirements for different items. A wholesale grocer, for example, who uses his own transport to collect supplies may order an item earlier than strict theory would require for the sake of using a vehicle which is picking up other items.

Variations in *lead-time*, i.e. the lapse of time between placing and delivering an order, and in demand rate, either separately or together, require modifications to the *deterministic* models used so far. The final example shows the kind of *probabilistic* approach required.

Example 5.7 A timber yard has a capacity of 1000 standards of timber:
   (i) Assuming that it takes 6 days to replace used stock and stock is sold at a steady rate of 40 standards per day, calculate the minimum level of stock that should be maintained.
   (ii) Calculate at the 95 per cent confidence level revised minimum stock levels on the following assumptions:
        (a) lead time varies about an average of 6 days with a standard

deviation of 1.4 days, with demand still steady at 40 standards per day;

(b) lead time is steady at 6 days, but demand varies with an average of 40 standards per day and standard deviation of 3.7 standards;

(c) both lead time and demand vary as in (a) and (b).

(i) We need at least 6 days reserve, i.e. 6×40 standards $= 240$ standards, so this is the minimum stock level.

(ii) (a) We assume that each of the variables is normally distributed. From normal curve of distribution tables, 5 per cent = area of 0.05. This corresponds with a cut-off point of 1.645 standard deviations above the mean:

6 days + (1.645 × 1.4 days) = 8.303 days

giving a revised reserve of

8.303 × 40 standards = 332.12 standards

(b) Similarly, the level needed will be

$6 \times \{40 + (1.645 \times 3.71)\}$ standards $= 276.618$ standards

(c) We are not compelled to provide for the worst case (maximum lead time × maximum demand) as that would occur in less than 5 per cent of the cases. We use an expression which depends upon the additive property of the variance (variance = standard deviation)^2, so that the combined standard deviation is

$\sqrt{\{(6 \times 1.4^2) + (40 \times 3.7^2)\}}$ (standards) $= 23.651$ standards

so that the new safety level would be

$\{(6 \times 40) + (1.645 \times 23.651)\}$ standards $= 278.91$ standards

Where stock problems introduce variable factors, as above, simulation techniques become suitable. Example 3.3 (p. 31) illustrate their use.

Exercises 5

5.1 (i) In the first quarter of 1975 a firm used 5000 gallons of heating oil costing 40p per gallon at a steady rate. Estimate the average value of oil in stock for (a) January, (b) February, and (c) March.

(ii) Assume that the level of oil at any time is given by

$(5000 - e^{0.094635x})$ gallons

where $x = 1, 2, \ldots, 90$, representing the end of the 1st, 2nd, etc. day of the quarter. Estimate the average value of oil being held (a) for the quarter, (b) for February.

Explain briefly why answer (i) (c) differs from (ii) (b).

5.2 A dealer buys 400 articles each month at £70 each. An order costs £9 to set up and his annual stock-holding costs are 20 per cent per annum. Can he take advantage of the following discount scheme by ordering the same number of articles each year, but with a different frequency? Assume for the purpose of calculation any new frequency to be regular.

Size of order	Discount allowed
600	5%
800	$7\frac{1}{2}$%

5.3 What would be the most economical stock-ordering policy for a firm to pursue with a total annual demand of 1200 units at £8 each, where each order costs £10 to place, stock-holding costs are 15 per cent per annum of the cost of the stock, and discount was not a factor? How, in general, would policy be affected by a change in the cost of placing an order?

5.4 (i) The total demand for a firm's product is 2000 units per year. On the average each unit costs £1.25 to hold in stock for a year. If the level falls below 40 units, a shortage cost of £6.0 per year per unit occurs. Advise the firm on its stock policy. (ii) What are the main elements likely to enter into shortage costs?

5.5 (i) An engineering stores can accommodate 400 of item x. Replacement is subject to a lead time of 4 days, with a standard deviation of 1.2 days. Demand averages 50 items daily, with a standard deviation of 4.6 items. Estimate the 95 per cent confidence level at which stock level should be maintained. (ii) If the firm worked to this level, could it be certain of (a) not being overstocked, (b) running out of stock?

Bibliography

A. Battersby, *A Guide to Stock Control*, 2nd ed. (London: Pitman, 1971).
R. G. Brown, *Decision Rules for Inventory Management* (New York: Holt, Rinehart & Winston, 1967).
H. G. Hadley and T. M. Witin, *Analysis of Inventory Systems* (Englewood Cliffs, N.J.: Prentice-Hall, 1964).
F. Hanssmann, *Operations Research in Production and Inventory Control* (New York: Wiley, 1968).

C. D. Lewis, *Scientific Inventory Control* (London: Butterworths, 1971).

J. F. Magee and D. M. Boodman, *Production Planning and Inventory Control,* 2nd ed. (New York: McGraw-Hill, 1967).

A. Morrison, *Storage and Control of Stock* (London: Pitman, 1970).

S. Vajda, *Problems in Linear Programming* (New York: Griffin, 1973).

H. Wagner, *Statistical Management of Inventory Systems* (New York: Wiley, n.d.).

6

Linear Programming

Programming problems are concerned with the efficient use or allocation of limited resources to meet desired objectives. These problems are characterised by the large number of solutions that satisfy the basic conditions of each problem. A solution that satisfies some desired objective, subject to certain restraints, is termed 'an optimum solution'. The *objective* might be to increase profits, reduce costs, or manufacture certain quantities of a product. *Restraints* are restrictions within which the problem must be resolved. They may arise from a variety of reasons, e.g. limitations on financing, facilities, quality, sales restrictions and so forth.

Linear programming is concerned with the minimising or maximising of an objective function in those situations where this function and the associated restrictions can be stated mathematically in terms of linear expressions.

Linear programming problems will be divided into three main groups, each of which have slightly different methods of calculation. In this chapter two methods will be considered: (1) the *graphical method*; (2) the *simplex method*. A third method, the *transportation method*, is considered in the next chapter. As in most methods of solutions each has its advantages and some limitations.

Graphical method

Example 6.1 A company manufactures two products A and B. The products must pass through two processes I and II. It takes 7 hours on process I and 4 hours on process II to manufacture 100 units of product A. It requires 6 hours on process I and 2 hours on process II to manufacture 100 units of product B.

It is possible for process I to take 42 hours and process II 16 hours of this work. The profit that can be realised per 100 units of product A is £5.50p and £2 per 100 units of product B.

To obtain maximum profit, how many of product A and B should be produced? (The sales department have declared that there is no problem in selling all products made.)

It is necessary to develop a mathematical model of the problem and it can be expressed by linear equations.

Let the number (00's) of product A to be produced $= x$
Let the number (00's) of product B to be produced $= y$

Our objective is to maximise profit (P); thus our *objective function* is to maximise $P = £5\frac{1}{2}x + £2y$, which is subject to certain restrictions forced upon us. For process I 42 hours are available and for process II 16 hours. Note that in the objective function $5\frac{1}{2}x$ represents the profit from selling a number of 100s of product A and $2y$ from product B.

In linear programming we are often more concerned with inequalities rather than equations and symbols can assist us to shorten the statement of the problem, such as:

$\leq$ means less than or equal to
$\geq$ means greater than or equal to
$<$ means less than
$>$ means greater than
$\simeq$ approximately equal to

The restriction on process I is $7x + 6y \leq 42$ and restriction on process II is $4x + 2y \leq 16$.

As it is not possible to produce negative quantities of x or y, therefore x and y are to be ≥ 0.

Therefore, our mathematical 'model' is now:

Restriction process   I $7x + 6y \leq 42$
Restriction process II $4x + 2y \leq 16$
Restriction product x $x \quad\ \ \geq\ 0$
Restriction product y $\quad\ y \geq\ 0$
Objective function $5\frac{1}{2}x + 2y = $ *Maximum Profit*

If the two relationships for the restrictions on Processes I and II are considered as equations

$7x + 6y = 42$
$4x + 2y = 16$

they can be plotted as shown in Figure 6.1.
Line AC can be defined as the locus of points satisfying the equation

$4x + 2y = 16$

With x and y requiring values ≥ 0, these values for x and y in $4x + 2y$ can

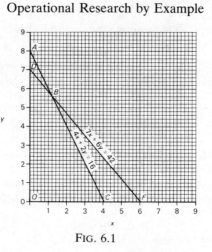

FIG. 6.1

be any amount, providing the total sum is ≤ 16, i.e. $4x + 2y \leq 16$. Thus a series of parallel lines to the left-hand side of ABC could be formed, and therefore because values for x and y which would satisfy $4x + 2y \leq 16$ can only be found in the area AOC, it is called a 'feasible region'. The area to the right-hand side of line AC is called a 'non-feasible region' (see Figure 6.2).

Similarly, line DF can be defined as the locus of points satisfying the equation $7x + 6y = 42$. The same reasoning applies to this line and the area to the left-hand side of DF is the 'feasible region' and to the right-hand side the 'non-feasible region' (see Figure 6.3).

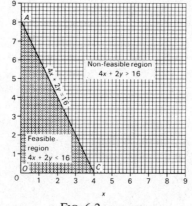

FIG. 6.2

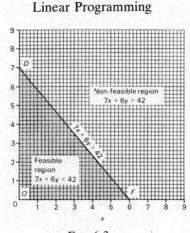

FIG. 6.3

The area that is common to both inequalities is $DOCB$, which represents the locus of points satisfying the system

$$7x + 6y = 42$$
$$4x + 2y = 16$$

and therefore this area contains the solution to the problem.

To obtain the pair of values x and y that optimises the solution, we must consider the objective function $5\frac{1}{2}x + 2y$. To revise our algebra one of the general forms of a two-variable linear equation is

$$y = ax + c$$

where x and y = the variables, a = the slope, c = the y intercept (value of y when $x = 0$).

To return to our objective function $5\frac{1}{2}x + 2y = maximum\ profit$, the slope can therefore be obtained thus:

$$y = -\frac{5\frac{1}{2}}{2}x + \frac{\text{maximum}}{2}$$

$$\therefore \quad a = -\frac{5\frac{1}{2}}{2}$$

The profit function can be represented by a number of parallel lines with $a - 5\frac{1}{2}/2$ slope. The negative sign describes a straight line which slopes down to the right and up to the left. The $5\frac{1}{2}/2$ signifies that, for every $5\frac{1}{2}$ divisions vertically, the line is offset 2 divisions horizontally.

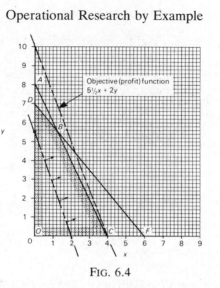

Fig. 6.4

If the profit function line with the $-5\frac{1}{2}/2$ slope was placed on the graph shown in Figure 6.4, then this line could be seen as a locus of points which give the same profit. To obtain the maximum value of the function, which is the maximum profit, the line must be as far away as possible from the origin, or zero, but still satisfy the equations $7x + 6y \leq 42$ and $4x + 2y \leq 16$. The farthest point the profit function touches from the origin, and still contains a point in area $DOCB$, is at point C. This is where $x = 4$ and $y = 0$.

The optimum solution for this problem, which is the maximum profit, is

$$5\frac{1}{2}(4) + 2(0) = £22$$

i.e. 400 of product A and zero of product B.

A problem concerned with obtaining a minimum cost will now be considered, with an additional constraint to be included in our 'model'.

Example 6.2 A company produces two ingredients A and B; these cost respectively, £11 and £8 per 100 lb. Each of the ingredients contains three nutrients but these are in different amounts and are shown below:

Amount of each nutrient in 100 lb of

	Ingredient A	*Ingredient B*
Nutrient 1	10 lb	2 lb
Nutrient 2	3 lb	3 lb
Nutrient 3	4 lb	9 lb

It is necessary to obtain the following amounts of each nutrient:

at least 20 lb of nutrient 1
at least 18 lb of nutrient 2
at least 36 lb of nutrient 3

What is the minimum cost that will meet these requirements?

Developing a mathematical 'model':

Let the number of 100 lb of ingredient $A = x$
Let the number of 100 lb of ingredient $B = y$

Our objective function can be expressed in this example as

minimum cost $= C = £11x + £8y$
or   minimum cost $= 11x + 8y$

From the table the restrictions can be obtained to form the linear inequalities:

Nutrient 1 $10x + 2y \geq 20$
Nutrient 2 $3x + 3y \geq 18$
Nutrient 3 $4x + 9y \geq 36$

In the problem x and y can be greater than or equal to zero and therefore the complete model can be stipulated:

Objective function   min $C = 11x + 8y$

subject to $10x + 2y \geq 20$
$3x + 3y \geq 18$
$4x + 9y \geq 36$
$x \geq 0$
$y \geq 0$

The first restriction $10x + 2y \geq 20$ is plotted in Figure 6.5. All values not inside the triangle AOB will satisfy the equation $10x + 2y \geq 20$. The remaining restrictions are shown on Figure 6.6.

To satisfy our restrictions points lying on the perimeter $ACDE$ or to the right of it would be acceptable and give us a feasible solution. To obtain the optimum solution we need to consider the objective function

min $C = 11x + 8y$

The slope for the function is calculated as in the previous example:

$$y = \frac{11}{8}x + \frac{\text{minimum}}{11}$$

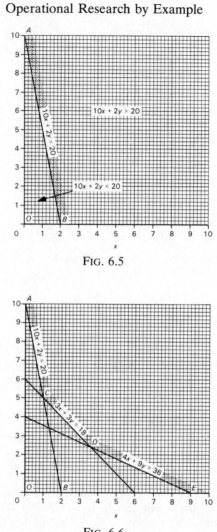

FIG. 6.5

FIG. 6.6

$$\therefore \qquad a \text{ (the slope)} = -\frac{11}{8}$$

This is plotted in Figure 6.7. The line can be seen as a locus of points which give the same cost.

To obtain the minimum value of the function, which is the minimum cost, the line must be as near to zero as possible, but still satisfy the

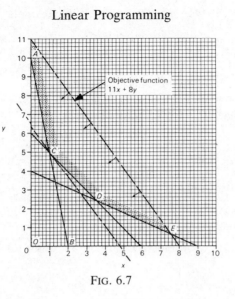

FIG. 6.7

restricting equations $10x + 2y \geq 20$, $3x + 3y \geq 18$ and $4x + 9y \geq 36$. The nearest point the cost function touches to zero and still contains a point on the perimeter $ACDE$ without going into the non-feasible region is at C. From point $C, x = 1$ and $y = 5$. Substituting these values of x and y into the algebraic statement of our problem, we obtain the following answers:

$$\text{Min } C = 11x + 8y$$
$$\text{Min } C = (11)\,(1) + (8)\,(5)$$
$$\text{Min } C = 11 + 40$$
$$\text{Min } C = £51$$

Thus the nutrients will be supplied at a minimal cost of £51 if the mix is 100 lb of ingredient A with 500 lb of ingredient B.

The amount of nutrients to be used in producing ingredients A and B will be

Nutrient 1	$(10)\,(1) + (2)\,(5) = 20$ lb
Nutrient 2	$(3)\,(1) + (3)\,(5) = 18$ lb
Nutrient 3	$(4)\,(1) + (9)\,(5) = 49$ lb

The simplex method

In the previous example only two variables were involved, but many practical industrial examples are more complex and include many variables and constraints. Each additional variable increases the number of dimensions of the solution area and each additional constraint will increase the number of corners of the solution area.

With three or more variables it is difficult to draw and interpret a solid geometric figure which could be formed from the model. Without having to draw or visualise these geometric figures, a method of solution is possible using the *simplex method* invented by Dantzig.

It would be appropriate to revise some basic algebra which would assist in understanding the simplex procedure. A method of solving equations is as follows:

$$7 = 3x + 4y \tag{1}$$
$$14 = 2x + 5y \tag{2}$$

Multiplying (1) by 5 and (2) by 4 we obtain:

$$35 = 15x + 20y \tag{3}$$
$$56 = 8x + 20y \tag{4}$$

Subtracting (4) from (3) and substituting this result for (1) at (5):

$$-21 = 7x + 0y \tag{5}$$
$$14 = 2x + 5y \tag{2}$$

Dividing (5) by 7 to obtain (6):

$$-3 = 1x + 0y \tag{6}$$
$$14 = 2x + 5y \tag{2}$$

Multiplying (6) by 2 and subtracting from (2) to obtain (7):

$$-3 = 1x + 0y \tag{6}$$
$$20 = 0x + 5y \tag{7}$$

Dividing (7) by 5 to obtain (8):

$$-3 = 1x + 0y \tag{6}$$
$$4 = 0x + 1y \tag{8}$$

By this method of solution we have a succession of row operations of the following types:

  (i) multiplying or dividing all elements of a row by some constant;
 (ii) replacing a row by the sum of that row and a multiple of some other row eventually gives a table with ones and zeros in appropriate positions from which the solution to the original 'model' can be read off.

If the constants and variables are used as column headings it is possible to carry through the same operations with only the coefficients entered. A series of tables are given from (5) onwards. A full equation can be obtained by entering in the appropriate symbol for the constant (c) and variables (x and y).

Taking (6) as an example, -3 1 0 with the attached coefficients becomes $-3 = 1x + 0y$. With the appropriate symbols at the head of columns we can write the following tables:

	c	x	y
see (6)	-3	1	0
see (7)	20	0	5
see (6)	-3	1	0
see (8)	4	0	1

Slack variables
Brief mention has been made of equations involving inequalities. In linear programming it is necessary to change the inequalities to equalities. An inequality such as $3x + 4y \leq 7$ gives a certain freedom explicit in the expression. To remove this freedom a new variable is entered to take up the 'slack' in the inequality. Calling the slack A, the equation can now be written thus:

$$3x + 4y + A = 7$$

The value of the slack will depend upon the values of x and y.

Example 6.3 Mathematically the problem is to maximise profit $(P) = 6x + 9y$, where x and y are subject to the following constraints, (P) is in £'s, x and y in units of production.

$$3x + 4y \leq 7$$
$$2x + 5y \leq 14$$
$$x \geq 0$$
$$y \geq 0$$

Convert the inequalities to equations by the addition of 'slack variables'. These measure the unused resource with which the constraint is concerned. Using A and B as slack variables respectively the constraints convert to:

$$3x + 4y + A = 7$$
$$2x + 5y + B = 14$$

where $A = 0$ and $B = 0$.
   The objective function is now:

$$6x + 9y + OA + OB = \max \textit{profit } (P)$$

We can now prepare our first simplex table by repeating the variables from each line at the top of the columns, arranging the coefficients under the respective headings:

6	9	0	0

x	y	A	B	
3	4	1	0	7
2	5	0	1	14

-6	-9	0	0	0

Above each column enter the unit profit of the variable in that column. Each unit of x will earn 6 and of y 9. All the remainder will produce zero towards profits. For methodological reasons these profits will be entered as negative values, interpreting this as the amount lost if the variable is not entered into the basis. It can be seen that the bottom row is merely the negative of the top row.

We now have:

P		-6	-9	0	0	
		x	y	A	B	
A	0	3	4	1	0	7
B	0	2	5	0	1	14
Z		-6	-9	0	0	0

We now evaluate our first feasible solution. The contribution of each slack variable is zero, and as we propose producing zero our expected profit will also be zero. Line Z shows the effect of producing zero. From this it appears sensible to introduce as much of y as possible to increase profit. There will be a limit to which x can be introduced. This was shown in the algebraic method and will depend on the first component to be used up. To find this limit divide each of the constants on the right of the table by the coefficient of the incoming variable on that line, provided the coefficient is greater than zero:

Line	Constant		Coefficient of y	
A	7	$\div$	4	$= 1\frac{3}{4}$
B	14	$\div$	5	$= 2\frac{4}{5}$

The results of the calculation are placed adjacent to the constants. The smallest figure, which in this case in $1\frac{3}{4}$, is chosen as the limiting value which prevents any variable from becoming negative. The column bringing in the chosen variable is called the *pivot column* and the row with the smallest positive calculation the *pivot row*. The intersection of the row and column, denoted ☐, is called *the pivot*. Our first complete table looks as follows:

		6	9	0	0	
P						
		x	y	A	B	
A	0	3	④	1	0	7
B	0	2	5	0	1	14
Z		−6	−9	0	0	0

Pivot row →

↑
Pivot
column

We need to substitute y for A and enter the amount per unit profit in place of zero in the table (see below). A new line y is calculated by taking row A from the above table and dividing by *the pivot*, 4. Line y in the new table will therefore result from the following calculation $-\frac{3}{4}, \frac{4}{4}, \frac{1}{4}, \frac{0}{4}, \frac{7}{4}$:

P		6	9	0	0	
		x	y	A	B	
y	−9	$\frac{3}{4}$	1	$\frac{1}{4}$	0	$\frac{7}{4}$
B						
Z						

Further cells can be filled in by the following procedure:

$$\frac{\text{New cell}}{\text{number}} = \frac{\text{Old cell}}{\text{number}} - \frac{\left(\begin{array}{c}\text{Corresponding number}\\ \text{in } pivot \text{ row}\end{array}\right) \times \left(\begin{array}{c}\text{Corresponding number}\\ \text{in } pivot \text{ column}\end{array}\right)}{The \ pivot}$$

Calculating a new B row we obtain:

$$\begin{array}{l}\text{New cell number}\\ \text{under } x \text{ column}\end{array} = 2 - \left(\frac{3 \times 5}{4}\right) = 2 - \frac{15}{4} = -1\frac{3}{4}$$

$$\begin{array}{l}\text{New cell number}\\ \text{under } y \text{ column}\end{array} = 5 - \left(\frac{4 \times 5}{4}\right) = 5 - \frac{20}{4} = 0$$

New cell number
under A column $= 0 - \left(\dfrac{1 \times 5}{4}\right) = 0 - \tfrac{5}{4} = -1\tfrac{1}{4}$

New cell number
under B column $= 1 - \left(\dfrac{0 \times 5}{4}\right) = 1 - 0 = 1$

New cell number
under F column $= 14 - \left(\dfrac{7 \times 5}{4}\right) = 14 - \tfrac{35}{4} = 5\tfrac{1}{4}$

Calculating a new Z row we obtain:

New cell number
under x column $= -6 - \left(\dfrac{3 \times -9}{4}\right) = -6 + \tfrac{27}{4} = \tfrac{3}{4}$

New cell number
under y column $= -9 - \left(\dfrac{4 \times 9}{4}\right) = -9 + 9 = 0$

New cell number
under A column $= 0 - \left(\dfrac{1 \times -9}{4}\right) = 0 + \tfrac{9}{4} = \tfrac{9}{4}$

New cell number
under B row $= 0 - \left(\dfrac{0 \times -9}{4}\right) = 0 - 0 = 0$

New cell number
under F row $= 0 - \left(\dfrac{7 \times -9}{4}\right) = 0 + \tfrac{63}{4} = 15\tfrac{3}{4}$

The new table is thus:

P		6	9	0	0	
		x	y	A	B	
y	-9	$\tfrac{3}{4}$	1	$\tfrac{1}{4}$	0	$1\tfrac{3}{4}$
B	0	$-1\tfrac{3}{4}$	0	$-1\tfrac{1}{4}$	1	$5\tfrac{1}{4}$
Z		$\tfrac{3}{4}$	0	$\tfrac{9}{4}$	0	$15\tfrac{3}{4}$

The Z row contains all positive numbers and therefore the solution is an optimum. If any negative had been entered under the variable and slack variable columns, the procedure would have been repeated until all numbers were positive. The solution obtained can be read off from the table. Only variable y was introduced, and following row y alone to the end column it suggests $1\tfrac{3}{4}$ be produced and the Z row shows a profit of £15.75.

A simple problem has been used to illustrate the method and before attempting a more complex one, the rules for the simplex method as well as a guide to interpreting the final table will be summarised.

Rules for solution by the simplex technique

(1) Write the restrictions in the form of 'inequations' using the signs

$\geq$ means equal to or greater than
$\leq$ means equal to or less than

(2) Convert the inequations into equations by adding a different non-negative variable (called *slack*) to each.
(3) Set up a table of the coefficients of the restrictions.
(4) Write the negatives of the profit in the bottom Z row.
(5) To maximise, select the column with the largest negative value in the Z row and call it the *pivot column*.
(6) Divide the elements in the F column by the corresponding elements in the pivot column. Call the row giving the smallest *positive* value of this division the *pivot row*. The element at the intersection of the pivot column and pivot row is called *the pivot*.
(7) Divide each element in the pivot row by the pivot.
(8) For each row (other than the pivot row) calculate, using the formula:

$$\frac{\text{New}}{\text{number}} = \frac{\text{Old}}{\text{number}} - \frac{\left(\begin{array}{c}\text{Corresponding}\\ \text{number of}\\ \text{pivot row}\end{array}\right) \times \left(\begin{array}{c}\text{Corresponding}\\ \text{number of}\\ \text{pivot column}\end{array}\right)}{\text{The pivot}}$$

All the entries in the pivot column (except the pivot element) will now be zero.

(9) If all the elements in the Z row are non-negative, the optimum solution has been reached; otherwise repeat the procedure commencing at Step 5.
(10) The answer is obtained by selecting (for each row) the variable which occurs in that row and equating it to the number in the F column. The maximum or minimum is shown in the Z row and F column.

Interpretation of the final table

(11) All variables not introduced under our P column are equal to zero.
(12) The number in the Z row under the F column is the value of the objective function for the solution.
(13) A negative number in the Z row under the variables and slack variable columns indicates that there would be an increase in the objective function if one unit of that variable at the head of the column were introduced into the solution.

(14) A positive number in Z row under the variables columns represents the reduction in the objective function if one unit of the variable at the head of the column were introduced into the solution.

(15) A positive number in the Z row under the slack variable columns can be considered as 'opportunity profit', or that amount of increase possible in the objective function if one more unit of the variable heading the column concerned were made available, i.e. if the restraint of the problem could be relaxed by one unit.

(16) The remaining numbers in the body of the table represent the marginal rate of exchange between the variable in the row and column at the particular solution represented in the F column.

  (i) A positive rate of exchange indicates the decrease in the variable in that row that results with the addition of one unit of the variable in that column.

  (ii) A negative rate of exchange indicates the increase in the variable in that row that results with the addition of one unit of that variable in that column.

An example in using the simplex method, together with the interpretation of the final table, follows.

Example 6.4 A company produces three products A, B and C. Each product has to pass through a drilling, a milling and a grinding process. During the next month the hours available in these three departments are as follows:

    Drilling Department   3000 hours
    Milling Department   2000 hours
    Grinding Department   500 hours

Product A takes 10 hours, 5 hours and 1 hour respectively in these departments and has a profit contribution of £10. Product B takes 5 hours, 10 hours and 1 hour respectively and has a profit of £15. Product C takes 2 hours, 4 hours and 2 hours respectively and has a profit of £20. The company wishes to maximise production within the constraints given. A full interpretation of the final table was expected. Construct the 'model' of the problem.

    Let A be the number of units of product A to be produced
    „ B „   „   „ B „
    „ C „   „   „ C „

    Maximise $10A + 15B + 20C$ (objective function)

subject to $10A + 5B + 2C \leq 3000$ (Drilling Department constraint)
$5A + 10B + 4C \leq 2000$ (Milling Department constraint)
$1A + 1B + 2C \leq 500$ (Grinding Department constraint)
A, B and $C \geq 0$

Applying 'slack variables' to obtain equalities we obtain:

$$10A + 5B + 2C + S_1 \qquad\qquad\qquad = 3000$$
$$5A + 10B + 4C + S_2 \qquad\qquad = 2000$$
$$1A + 1B + 2C + S_3 \qquad = 500$$
$$10A + 15B + 20C + 0S_1 + 0S_2 + 0S_3 = maximum$$

We set out our first table as follows:

P		10	15	20	0	0	0		
		A	B	C	S_1	S_2	S_3	F	
S_1	0	10	5	2	1	0	0	3000	
S_2	0	5	10	4	0	1	0	2000	Pivot
S_3	0	1	1	[2]	0	0	1	500	←—row
Z		−10	−15	−20	0	0	0	0	

↑
Pivot
column

Column C has the largest negative value and becomes the *pivot column* and we therefore introduce variable C into the solution. Next, determine which variable will be replaced by C. This will depend on which of the three equations restricts C to the smallest amount:

$$\frac{3000}{2}, \frac{2000}{4}, \frac{500}{2}$$

The smallest positive ratio of the three equations is 500/2 (row S_3). Row S_3 now becomes the *pivot row* and [2] at the intersection of the pivot row and pivot column, becomes *the pivot*.

To form a new table S_3 is replaced by C. The new row C is formed by dividing the S_3 row from the above Table through by the pivot [2] . The remaining rows are formed by using the formula:

$$\frac{\text{New}}{\text{number}} = \frac{\text{Old}}{\text{number}} - \frac{\left(\begin{array}{c}\text{Corresponding}\\\text{number in}\\\text{pivot row}\end{array}\right) \times \left(\begin{array}{c}\text{Corresponding}\\\text{number in}\\\text{pivot column}\end{array}\right)}{\text{The pivot}}$$

The new row C becomes 20, $\frac{1}{2}$, $\frac{1}{2}$, 1, 0, 0, $\frac{1}{2}$, 250. Using the formula above, the remaining three rows are formed thus:

New S_1 row

$$10 - \frac{(1 \times 2)}{2} = 9$$

$$5 - \frac{(1 \times 2)}{2} = 4$$

$$2 - \frac{(2 \times 2)}{2} = 0$$

$$1 - \frac{(0 \times 2)}{2} = 1$$

$$0 - \frac{(0 \times 2)}{2} = 0$$

$$0 - \frac{(1 \times 2)}{2} = -1$$

$$3000 - \frac{(500 \times 2)}{2} = 2500$$

New S_2 row

$$5 - \frac{(1 \times 4)}{2} = 3$$

$$10 - \frac{(1 \times 4)}{2} = 8$$

$$4 - \frac{(2 \times 4)}{2} = 0$$

$$0 - \frac{(0 \times 4)}{2} = 0$$

$$1 - \frac{(0 \times 4)}{2} = 1$$

$$0 - \frac{(1 \times 4)}{2} = -2$$

$$2000 - \frac{(500 \times 4)}{2} = 1000$$

New Z row

$$-10 - \frac{(1 \times -20)}{2} = 0$$

$$-15 - \frac{(1 \times -20)}{2} = -5$$

$$-20 - \frac{(2 \times -20)}{2} = 0$$

$$0 - \frac{(0 \times -20)}{2} = 0$$

$$0 - \frac{(0 \times -20)}{2} = 0$$

$$0 - \frac{(1 \times -20)}{2} = 10$$

$$0 - \frac{(500 \times -20)}{2} = 5000$$

P		10	15	20	0	0	0	
		A	B	C	S_1	S_2	S_3	F
S_1	0	9	4	0	1	0	−1	2500
S_2	0	3	[8]	0	0	1	−2	1000
C	20	$\frac{1}{2}$	$\frac{1}{2}$	1	0	0	$\frac{1}{2}$	250
Z	0	Z	−5	0	0	0	10	5000

Pivot row → (points to S_2 row)

↑
Pivot column

Following our previous procedure, we need to produce a new table as there is still a negative amount in the above table, -5, under the variable column B, row Z.

To determine which variable will be replaced by B the smallest positive ratio of the following equations is chosen:

$$\frac{2500}{4}, \quad \frac{1000}{8}, \quad \frac{250}{\frac{1}{2}}$$

The smallest positive figure is given by 1000/8 (row S_2).

Row S_2 now becomes the *pivot row* and column B the *pivot column*, with $\boxed{8}$ being the *pivot*.

To form a new table S_2 is replaced by B. The new row B is formed by dividing the S_2 row from the previous table through by the pivot $\boxed{8}$. The new row B becomes $\frac{3}{8}$, 1, 0, 0, $\frac{1}{8}$, $-\frac{1}{4}$, 125. Using the formula again the remaining three rows are formed, and the final table derived, as follows:

New S_1 row	New C row	New Z row
$9 - \dfrac{(3 \times 4)}{8} = 7\frac{1}{2}$	$\dfrac{1}{2} - \dfrac{(3 \times \frac{1}{2})}{8} = \frac{5}{16}$	$0 - \dfrac{(3 \times -5)}{8} = 1\frac{7}{8}$
$4 - \dfrac{(8 \times 4)}{8} = 0$	$\dfrac{1}{2} - \dfrac{(8 \times \frac{1}{2})}{8} = 0$	$-5 - \dfrac{(8 \times -5)}{8} = 0$
$0 - \dfrac{(0 \times 4)}{8} = 0$	$1 - \dfrac{(0 \times \frac{1}{2})}{8} = 1$	$0 - \dfrac{(0 \times -5)}{8} = 0$
$1 - \dfrac{(0 \times 4)}{8} = 1$	$0 - \dfrac{(0 \times \frac{1}{2})}{8} = 0$	$0 - \dfrac{(0 \times -5)}{8} = 0$
$0 - \dfrac{(1 \times 4)}{8} = -\frac{1}{2}$	$0 - \dfrac{(1 \times \frac{1}{2})}{8} = -\frac{1}{16}$	$0 - \dfrac{(1 \times -5)}{8} = \frac{5}{8}$
$-1 - \dfrac{(-2 \times 4)}{8} = 0$	$\dfrac{1}{2} - \dfrac{(-2 \times \frac{1}{2})}{8} = \frac{5}{8}$	$10 - \dfrac{(-2 \times -5)}{8} = 8\frac{3}{4}$
$2500 - \dfrac{(1000 \times 4)}{8} = 2000$	$250 - \dfrac{(1000 \times \frac{1}{2})}{8} = 187\frac{1}{2}$	$5000 - \dfrac{(1000 \times -5)}{8} = 5625$

P		10	15	20	0	0	0	
		A	B	C	S_1	S_2	S_3	F
S_1	0	$7\frac{1}{2}$	0	0	1	$-\frac{1}{2}$	0	2000
B	15	$\frac{3}{8}$	1	0	0	$\frac{1}{8}$	$-\frac{1}{4}$	125
C	20	$\frac{5}{16}$	0	1	0	$-\frac{1}{16}$	$\frac{5}{8}$	$187\frac{1}{2}$
Z		$1\frac{7}{8}$	0	0	0	$\frac{5}{8}$	$8\frac{3}{4}$	5625

There are no negative values in the Z row and thus we have reached the optimum solution. An interpretation of the final table is important and will be discussed fully.

Under column F we have 2000 for the S_1 row, which is a slack of 2000 hours of drilling not being utilised. Row B indicates that we will produce 125 units of B and row C $187\frac{1}{2}$ units of C. Row Z gives the total profit of £5625. This profit can be arrived at in two ways:

(i) Under column S_2, row Z this indicates that each unit of S_2 brings in a marginal contribution of £0.625 and under column S, row Z each unit of S_3 makes a marginal contribution of £8.75. Thus (2000 hours $\times$ 0.625) + (500 hours $\times$ 8.75) = £5625.

(ii) By producing 125 units of B at a profit of £15 each and $187\frac{1}{2}$ of C at £20 each, the overall result is £5625.

Rows B and C, by the very fact that these were introduced into the solution, inform us only that these will be produced, *not* that A will be produced. Column B signifies that bringing in 1 unit of B would have no effect of S_1, reduces B by 1 and has no effect on C. The reasoning applies to column C. Columns S_2 and S_3 only require explanation as only B and C are to be manufactured. Column S_2 implies that the introduction of 1 extra unit of B would decrease the slack, S_1 by $\frac{1}{2}$, it would increase production of B by $\frac{1}{8}$ and decrease production of C by $\frac{1}{16}$ and have a net effect on contribution of $+£\frac{5}{8}$ The same reasoning applies to column S_3.

It must be stressed that only the basic rudiments of the techniques of problem formulation and the simplex method have been covered but references at the end of the chapter will enable the student to study the development of the technique further.

In one particular type of problem, that of *distribution*, matching a product demand at various locations and a supply of product at several warehouses, it is possible to determine which warehouses should despatch how much product to which customer, so that the total distribution costs are at a minimum. As an extension of what has been discussed here, the transportation method will be considered in the next chapter.

Exercises 6

6.1   Fishers Ltd can produce two types of products, Fishol and Fiship. Net contribution of each product (i.e. price less direct expenses) is £10 per unit. The production team are currently considering what to produce during the following month.

To make one unit of Fishol, the company will have to use 20 lb of material *ACO* and 10 man-hours of skilled labour. On the other hand, to manufacture one unit of Fiship, the firm will need 10 lb of material *ACO*, 20 man-hours of skilled labour and 10 man-hours of semi-skilled labour.

The production team consider that the maximum number of these resources that can be obtained during this period are 800 lb of material *ACO*, 700 man-hours of skilled labour and 300 man-hours of semi-skilled labour.

You are required to use the linear programming technique (graphical method) to find the best production plan for the company and to calculate the net contribution that this will bring to the firm.

6.2   A company manufactures two types of electrical motors *A* and *B* subject to the following conditions:

(i) Both require time on the spot-welding machine which has a capacity of 3000 units of *A* per week, or 1500 units of *B* per week, or some *pro rata* combination of the two.

(ii) *A* requires 4 min. inspection time per unit and *B* requires 3 min. inspection time per unit and there is a total of 100 hours of inspection time available per week.

(iii) *A* also requires time on the spot-welding machine which can handle 1000 units per week.

(iv) The company has a contract to supply a minimum of 1000 units of *B* per week.

(v) The contribution to fixed costs of product *A* is 50p per unit and that of product *B* is 25p per unit.

1   Determine graphically the proportions of *A* and *B* the company must produce per week to maximise contribution to fixed costs.

2   What extra profit would have been produced if the contract referred to in section (iv) had not been signed?

6.3   A firm manufactures two sizes of electrical switches. The profit realised on the switches is 7p and 5p per large and small switch respectively. If all switches were large, the firm's transport department could handle a maximum of 3000 per day. If all were small, it could cope with 4500 per day. Any in-between combination is a possible maximum. The electrical contacts used are the same for the large switches as for the small and 4000 are available per day. Of the copper wire and screws, up to 2400 are available each day for the large switch and as many as are required for the small. Switches require the same amount of labour whatever their size, and to prevent work or discontent it is company policy to make at least 2000 switches of either size per day.

Using the *simplex method* discover how many switches of each kind make the maximum profit and calculate this profit. Interpret your final table.

6.4 A manufacturing department produces two products *A* and *B*. Both products are produced on the same automatic machines but the time taken on each machine varies thus:

	Product A Machine min. per unit	Product B Machine min. per unit	Total machine min. available
Machine *X*	2	6	66
Machine *Y*	8	4	120
Machine *Z*	4	8	96

The expected profit on product *A* is 16p and is 12p for product *B*.

You are required to calculate the number of units of products *A* and *B* the department should produce in order to maximise profit.

Bibliography (to Chapters 6–8)
Linear Programming and Extensions

J. Abadie (ed.), *Non-Linear Programming* (Amsterdam: North-Holland, 1967).

E. L. Arnoff and S. S. Sengupta, 'Mathematical Programming', in *Progress in Operations Research*, ed. R. L. Ackoff (New York: Wiley, 1961) vol. 1, pp. 106–210.

E. M. L. Beale, *Mathematical Programming in Practice* (London: Pitman, 1968).

J. N. Boles, 'Linear Programming and Farm Management Analysis', *Journal of Farm Economics*, vol. 37, no. 1, Feb 1955.

A. Charnes, 'Optimality and Degeneracy in Linear Programming', *Econometrica*, vol. 20, 1952, pp. 160ff.

A. Charnes and W. W. Cooper, *An Introduction to Linear Programming* (New York: Wiley, 1953).

W. W. Cooper and A. Charnes, 'The Stepping Stone Method of Explaining Linear Programming Calculations in Transportation Problems', *Management Science*, vol. 1, no. 1, Oct 1954.

G. Dantzig, 'Maximization of a Linear Function of Variables Subject to Linear Inequalities', in *Activity Analysis of Production and Allocation*, ed. T. C. Koopmans (New York: Wiley, 1951).

G. Dantzig, 'Computational Algorithm of the Revised Simplex Method', RAND Memorandum RM–1266, 1953.

G. Dantzig, *Linear Programming and Extensions* (Princeton University Press, 1963).

G. Dantizig, A. Orden and P. Wolfe, 'The Generalized Simplex Method for Minimizing a Linear Form under Linear Inequality Restraints', Rand Memorandum RM-1264, 1954.

R. Dorfman, *Application of Linear Programming to the Theory of the Firm*, (University of California Press, 1951).

R. Dorfman, 'Mathematical or "Linear" Programming: A Non-mathematical Exposition', *American Economic Review*, vol. 43, no. 5, Dec 1953.

R. Dorfman, P. A. Samuelson and R. M. Solow, *Linear Programming and Economic Analysis* (New York: McGraw-Hill, 1958).

R. O. Ferguson, 'Linear Programming', American Machinist Special Report No. 389, Apr 1955.

W. W. Garvin, *Introduction to Linear Programming* (New York: McGraw-Hill, 1960).

S. I. Gass, *Linear Programming – Methods and Applications* (New York: McGraw-Hill, 1958).

G. Hadley, *Linear Programming* (Reading, Mass.: Addison-Wesley, 1962).

G. Hadley, *Non-linear and Dynamic Programming* (Reading, Mass.: Addison-Wesley, 1964).

K. B. Haley, *Mathematical Programming for Business and Industry* (London: Macmillan, 1967).

A. Henderson and R. Schlaiffer, 'Mathematical Programming', *Harvard Business Review*, May–June 1954.

F. L. Hitchcock, 'The Distribution of a Product from Several Sources to Numerous Localities', *Journal of Mathematical Physics*, vol. 20, 1941.

S. Karlin, *Mathematical Methods and Theory of Games, Programming and Economics*, 2 vols (Reading, Mass.: Addison-Wesley, 1959).

T. C. Koopmans, *Activity Analysis of Production and Allocation* (New York: Wiley, 1951).

J. F. McCloskey and J. M. Coppinger, *Operations Research for Management* (Baltimore: Johns Hopkins Press) – see especially 'The Travelling Salesman Problem'.

R. W. Metzger, *Mathematical Programming* (New York: Wiley, 1963).

D. W. Moffett, *Applying Linear Programming to Inventory Planning in a Seasonal Market*, ASME Paper 56–MGT–1, Jan 1956.

N. W. Remfield, 'VAM: Short-cut to Mathematical Programming', *Tooling and Production*, vol. 23, no. 1, Apr 1957.

V. Riley and S. I. Gass, *Linear Programming and Associated Techniques: A Comprehensive Bibliography on Linear, Non-Linear and Dynamic Programming* (Baltimore: Johns Hopkins Press, 1958).

M. E. Salveson, 'An Introduction to Mathematical Methods in Scheduling and Programming', *Technical Review 11*, University of California, Industrial Logistics Research Project, July 1953.

H. T. Schwan and J. Wilkinson, 'Linear Programming – What Can It Do', *Chemical Engineering*, Aug. 1956.

G. H. Symonds, 'Mathematical Programming as an Aid to Decision Making', *Advanced Management*, May 1955.

G. H. Symonds, *Linear Programming: The Solution of Refinery Problems* (Esso Standard Oil Co., 1955).

S. Valda, *Mathematical Programming* (Reading, Mass.: Addison-Wesley, 1961).

J. Wilkinson, 'Better Management = Management + Industrial Engineering + Linear Programming', *Journal of Industrial Engineering*, Jan–Feb 1956.

N. Williams, *Linear and Non-Linear Programming in Industry* (London: Pitman, 1967).

7

The Transportation Method

The *transportation technique* is a further extension of linear programming and it is a special one which can only be used to solve a particular type of problem, for example when it is necessary to minimise the cost or maximise the profit of distributing goods from a number of M despatch points to a number of N receiving points. For a problem to be solved this way we require the following basic rules:

   (i) the amount of goods available for each source and the amounts required at each destination must be known;

  (ii) the total amounts despatched must equal the total amounts received;

 (iii) the cost of transporting each unit of goods from each source to each destination must also be known.

A basic feasible solution satisfies the capacities and requirements of the sources and destinations by the use of '$M + N - 1$' rates. A simple example covering the above rules will be undertaken.

Example 7.1 A company has 3 factories and 3 warehouses. Altogether the factories manufacture 30 units of a given commodity divided among them as follows:

Factory A	13 units
Factory B	11 units
Factory C	6 units
Total	30 units

The 3 warehouses require units in the following quantities:

Warehouse X	7 units
Warehouse Y	9 units
Warehouse Z	14 units
Total	30 units

The cost (in £s) for transporting one unit from any one source A, B or C to any other destination X, Y or Z is given in the following table.

From factories

		A	B	C
To warehouses	X	7	6	2
	Y	3	8	4
	Z	2	6	4

The 3 basic rules are satisfied, and the first step in the solution is to fill on a blank chart an allocation of units which is a basic feasible solution (see Table 7.1). For convenience the costs are placed in a separate square, e.g. [7], and obviously will not change throughout the problem. Notice that the largest allocation possible, without violating the restrictions given, has been placed in the top left-hand corner. This is known as the *north-west corner method* – assuming the top of the paper is North the reason for this is obvious. The amount of allocation to square *XA* is 7. Since Factory *A* has a total of 13 available, this leaves 6 units; allocate these 6 to *YA*. The requirements of *Y* are 9; therefore take the remaining 3 from *B*, entering 3 in cell *YB*. By the same reasoning allocate 8 to cell *ZB* and so on until the allocations are complete. It is not essential to put the maximum amount possible in the top left-hand corner but this method enables a first basic solution to be obtained with ease.

TABLE 7.1

From factories

		A	B	C	Total required
To warehouses	X	7 [7]	[6]	[2]	7
	Y	6 [3]	3 [8]	[4]	9
	Z	[2]	8 [6]	6 [4]	14
	Total available	13	11	6	30

The total cost of the first feasible solution is £163:

$$(7 \times 7) + (6 \times 3) + (3 \times 8) + (8 \times 6) + (6 \times 4)$$
$$49 \quad + \quad 18 \quad + \quad 24 \quad + \quad 48 \quad + \quad 24 \quad = £163$$

To try and improve further on this first feasible solution it is now assumed that the cost of transportation is made up of two parts: a cost of despatch and a cost of reception which are not true costs but are referred to as 'shadow costs'. Blank spaces have been allocated beneath the three factories and adjacent to the three warehouses in Table 7.1 to take in these 'shadow costs'. It is assumed that the cost in the north-west corner at X is 0. According to the total cost in square XA (i.e. 7) the cost of sending from A must be 7. Continue calculating despatch and reception costs only where an allocation has been made. Total costs for square XA is 3 and knowing that despatch costs for A is 7, reception cost at Y must be:

Reception costs at Y + despatch costs at A = total transportation cost YA
Reception costs at Y + 7 = 3
∴ Reception costs at $Y = 3 - 7 = -4$

Having obtained reception costs at Y, calculate despatch at B:

Reception costs at Y + despatch costs at B = total transportation cost YB
-4 + despatch costs at $B = 8$
∴ Despatch costs at $B = 8 + 4 = 12$

Having obtained despatch costs at B, calculate reception costs at Z:

Reception costs at Z + despatch costs at B = total transportation cost ZB
Reception costs at Z + 12 = 6
∴ Reception costs at $Z = 6 - 12 = -6$

Having obtained reception costs at Z, calculate the final despatch cost at C:

Reception costs at Z + despatch costs at C = total transportation cost ZC
-6 + despatch costs at $C = 4$
∴ Despatch costs at $C = 4 + 6 = 10$

These completed shadow costs are shown in Table 7.2. We now consider the unused squares, i.e. where no allocations have been made in Table 7.1. To test whether an improvement can be made on the first feasible solution we proceed as follows. The sum of the despatch and reception costs is obtained and where this exceeds the true costs it is possible for a saving in

TABLE 7.2

From factories

	A	B	C	Total required
	7	12	10	
To warehouses X 0	$7-3$ |7	|6	$+3$ |2	7
Y -4	$6+3$ |3	$3-3$ |8	|4	9
Z -6	|2	$8-3$ |6	$6-3$ |4	14
Total available	13	11	6	30

costs to be made provided we make an allocation in the square being considered:

$$
\begin{aligned}
\text{Square } XB \quad & 12 + 0 - 6 = 6 \\
\text{Square } XC \quad & 10 + 0 - 2 = 8 \\
\text{Square } YC \quad & 10 + (-4) - 4 = 2 \\
\text{Square } ZA \quad & 7 + (-6) - 2 = 1
\end{aligned}
$$

It is to our advantage to take the square with the highest positive figure, although other positive figures may be taken, as this square will show the greatest saving in cost. We select square XC for allocation.

We wish to allocate as much as possible to square XC without violating the despatch and reception totals. The goods to be transferred to square XC must come from either XA or ZC. If 1 unit is transferred from ZC to XC, then XA must be decreased by 1 unit to keep the row totals correct. Similarly, to maintain the correct row and column totals squares YA and ZB must be increased by 1 and square YB must be reduced by 1.

A figure greater than 0 is allocated to square XC so that all the quantities in the squares where allocations have been made are positive or zero. We must also have only $M + N - 1$ allocations. The only figure to satisfy these requirements is 3. The allocations shown in Table 7.2 are adjusted by 3 and a new table is formed (Table 7.3):

Total costs

$$(4 \times 7) + (9 \times 3) + (11 \times 6) + (3 \times 4) + (3 \times 2)$$
$$28 \quad + \quad 27 \quad + \quad 66 \quad + \quad 12 \quad + \quad 6 \quad = £139$$

This shows an improvement of £24 over the first feasible solution.

With the new allocations as shown in Table 7.3, new despatch and reception shadow costs are obtained as previously, commencing with reception costs at X of 0:

Reception costs at X + despatch costs at A = total transportation costs XA
0 + despatch costs at $A = 7$
∴ despatch costs at $A = 7$

With practice the remaining shadow costs can be calculated mentally and are shown complete in Table 7.3.

Each of the four blank squares in Table 7.3 require inspection to test whether an improvement in the solution can be made. If the true costs for these squares is either equal to or exceeds the sum of the despatch and

TABLE 7.3

From factories

			A	B	C	Total required
			7	4	2	
Tolwarehouses	X	0	4 −3 [7]	[6]	3 +3 [2]	7
	Y	−4	9 [3]	[8]	[4]	9
	Z	2	+3 [2]	11 [6]	3 −3 [4]	14
	Total available		13	11	6	30

reception costs, an optimum solution has been found and no further calculations are necessary. Testing the squares in Table 7.3.

Square XB $4+0 - 6 = -2$
Square YB $4+(-4) - 8 = -8$
Square YC $2+(-4) - 4 = -6$
Square ZA $7 + 2 - 2 = 5$

Choose square ZA for allocation. 3 is the maximum amount we can allocate to this square, so that we have $M + N - 1$ allocations; all quantities in
the squares where allocations have been made in Table 7.3 are positive or
zero and reception and despatch totals are not violated. New allocations
are shown in Table 7.4:

Total costs

$(1 \times 7) + (9 \times 3) + (3 \times 2) + (11 \times 6) + (6 \times 2)$
$\;\;\;\;7\;\;\;\; + \;\;\;27\;\;\; + \;\;\;\;6\;\;\; + \;\;\;\;66\;\;\; + \;\;\;\;12\;\;\;\; = £118$

This shows an improvement of £21 over the previous solution.

Commencing with zero costs at X, despatch and reception costs are
calculated as previously. Testing blank squares in Table 7.4 for a possible
improvement:

Square XB $11 + 0 - 6 = 5$
Square YB $11 + (-4) - 8 = -1$
Square YC $2 + (-4) - 8 = -10$
Square ZC $2 + (-5) - 4 = -7$

Consider square XB for allocation. The maximum number we can allocate
without violating the rules is 1. Adjustments in allocations are shown in
Table 7.4, and a new table is formed (Table 7.5).

Develop new shadow costs as previously and these are shown in Table
7.5. Consider blank squares for possible allocation:

Square XA $2 + 0 - 7 = -5$
Square YB $1 + 6 - 8 = -1$
Square YC $1 + 2 - 4 = -1$
Square ZC $0 + 2 - 4 = -2$

Figures in this case are all negative, so the solution in Table 7.5 is therefore
the optimum. If a zero had been calculated for one of the squares, then
an alternative solution of equal cost which uses that particular square is
possible.

TABLE 7.4

From factories

		A	B	C	Total required
		7	11	2	
To warehouses	X 0	1 −1 ⌐7	+1 ⌐6	6 ⌐2	7
	Y −4	9 ⌐3	⌐8	⌐4	9
	Z −5	3 +1 ⌐2	11 −1 ⌐6	⌐4	14
	Total available	13	11	6	30

TABLE 7.5

From factories

		A	B	C	Total required
		2	6	2	
To warehouses	X 0	⌐7	1 ⌐6	6 ⌐2	7
	Y 1	9 ⌐3	⌐8	⌐4	9
	Z 0	4 ⌐2	10 ⌐6	⌐4	14
	Total available	13	11	6	30

The solution is therefore as follows:

Final costs

$$(1 \times 6) + (6 \times 2) + (9 \times 3) + (4 \times 2) + (10 \times 6)$$
$$6 + 12 + 27 + 8 + 60 = £113$$

Despatch 1 unit from factory B to warehouse X
Despatch 6 units from factory C to warehouse X
Despatch 9 units from factory Z to warehouse Y
Despatch 4 units from factory A to warehouse Z
Despatch 10 units from factory B to warehouse Z

To use the transportation method it is necessary for the amount despatched and received to balance. This situation is very unlikely in practice and therefore a 'dummy' despatch or receiving row or column is introduced. The 'dummy' row or column will then be allotted the necessary amount to ensure the required balance. Zero costs are then allocated to those squares. An example using both the north-west corner method and the use of a dummy will now be discussed.

Example 7.2 The Machine Oil Supplies Ltd have two warehouses containing special machine oil. The company supply the oil to three large machine-tool manufacturers, Brit Tool, Carbon Tool and Numerical Industries. The distances between the two warehouses and the delivery points of their customers is as follows:

Distances to the nearest mile

		Customers	
Warehouses	Brit Tool	Carbon Tool	Numerical Industries
I	10	11	7
II	6	5	11

At warehouses I and II there are 900 and 600 gallons respectively. Brit Tool require 700, Carbon Tool 400 and Numerical Industries 300 gallons respectively.

Assuming costs of transportation of one gallon to be proportional to mileage, how should the Machine Oil Supplies Ltd organise its service to minimise costs and what is that minimum cost? Obtain the first basic feasible solution by the north-west corner method.

To balance supply and demand the use of a dummy is necessary. We require M rows + N columns allocations, which is $4 + 2 - 1 = 5$ allocations.

Table 7.6 is set out with a dummy column and the maximum allocation of 700 is made in the north-west corner. Reception and despatch quantities are balanced. Note that 100 is required in the dummy column to

TABLE 7.6

		Brit Tool		Carbon Tool		Numerical Industries		Dummy	Total available
Warehouses	I	700	10	200	11		7	0	900
	II		6	200	5	300	11	100 0	600
	Total required	700		400		300		100	1500

complete the balance. The cost for the first feasible solution is as follows:

$$(700 \times 10) + (200 \times 11) + (200 \times 5) + (300 \times 11) + (100 \times 0)$$
$$7000 \quad + \quad 2200 \quad + \quad 1000 \quad + \quad 3300 \quad + \quad 0 \quad = £13500$$

Reception and despatch costs can be calculated mentally commencing with 0 at warehouse I. These are shown in Table 7.7. To obtain the square in which to make an allocation to give the greatest saving we calculate as shown in the previous problem:

$$\begin{aligned}
\text{Warehouse I to Numerical Industries} \quad &17 + 0 - 7 = 10 \\
\text{Warehouse I to Dummy} \quad &6 + 0 - 0 = 6 \\
\text{Warehouse II to Brit Tool} \quad &10 + (-6) - 6 = -2
\end{aligned}$$

Warehouse I to Numerical Industries has the greater potential, having the largest positive figure.

TABLE 7.7

			Brit Tool		Carbon Tool		Numerical Industries		Dummy	Total available
			10		11		17		6	
Warehouses	I	0	700	10	200–200	11	+200	7	0	900
	II	6		6	200 + 200	5	300–200	11	100 0	600
	Total required		700		400		300		100	1500

The largest amount to be entered in square Warehouse I to Numerical Industries is 200 units. Table 7.7 shows the squares to be adjusted by this figure. Table 7.8 is then formed.

Cost =
$(700 \times 10) + (400 \times 5) + (200 \times 7) + (100 \times 11)$
$\quad 7000 \quad + \quad 2000 \quad + \quad 1400 \quad + \quad 1100 \quad = £11500$

New reception and despatch 'shadow costs' are calculated for Table 7.8. Test blank squares for any improvement in the solution:

Warehouse I to Carbon Tool $1 + 0 - 11 = -10$
Warehouse I to Dummy $-4 + 0 - 0 = -4$
Warehouse II to Brit Tool $10 + 4 - 6 = 8$

Warehouse II to Brit Tool gives the only positive figure and an allocation will be made to this square. The largest transferable amount possible, to leave $M + N - 1$ allocations and to leave one of these allocations zero and the remainder a positive amount, is 100 units. Table 7.9 is thus is formed.

Cost =
$(600 \times 10) + (100 \times 6) + (400 \times 5) + (300 \times 7)$
$\quad 6000 \quad + \quad 600 \quad + \quad 2000 \quad + \quad 2100 \quad = £10700$

New reception and despatch costs are formed for Table 7.9. Test each blank square for a possible improvement to the solution:

Warehouse I to Carbon Tool $9 + 0 - 11 = -2$
Warehouse I to Dummy $4 + 0 - 0 = 4$
Warehouse II to Numerical Industries $7 + (-4) - 11 = -8$

TABLE 7.8

		Brit Tool		Carbon Tool		Numerical Industries		Dummy	Total available
		10		1		7		−4	
I	0	700 −100	10		11	200 +100	7	0	900
II	4	+100	6	400	5	100 −100	11	100 0	600
	Total required	700		400		300		100	1500

Warehouses

TABLE 7.9

Warehouses		Brit Tool	Carbon Tool	Numerical Industries	Dummy	Total available
		10	9	7	4	
I	0	600 $^{-100}$ \[10\]	\[11\]	300 \[7\]	$^{+100}$ \[0\]	900
II	−4	100 $^{+100}$ \[6\]	400 \[5\]	\[11\]	100 $^{-100}$ \[0\]	600
Total required		700	400	300	100	1500

Improvement is possible by allocating to square Warehouse I to Dummy. The largest amount possible is 100 units, which leaves $M + N - 1$ allocations and a positive allocation of units. Table 7.10 is thus formed.

Calculate new reception and despatch costs for Table 7.10. Test blank squares for possible improvement to the solution:

Warehouse I to Carbon Tool $9 + 0 - 11 = -2$
Warehouse II to Numerical Industries $7 + (-4) - 11 = -8$
Warehouse II to Dummy $0 + (-4) - 0 = -4$

All calculations are negative, and thus no improvement can be made to the solution and the final allocations are as in Table 7.10. Note that warehouse I will be the one that does not send the total amount, only 800 of the 900 gallons available, and warehouse II supplies its entire stock of 600 gallons:

Total cost =
$(500 \times 10) + (300 \times 7) + (200 \times 6) + (400 \times 5)$
$5000 \quad + \quad 2100 \quad + \quad 1200 \quad + \quad 1200 \quad = £10300$

TABLE 7.10

Warehouses		Brit Tool	Carbon Tool	Numerical Industries	Dummy	Total available
		10	9	7	0	
I	0	500 \[10\]	\[11\]	300 \[7\]	100 \[0\]	900
II	−4	200 \[6\]	400 \[5\]	\[11\]	\[0\]	600
Total required		700	400	300	100	1500

It is possible that either one or the other of the warehouses may *not* be left with excess stock. This could have been allowed for in the first feasible solution by making the total cost in the dummy column for that warehouse which is not to have excess a very high figure, denoted usually by $\boxed{M}$. This would ensure that this particular square would not automatically be considered for an allocation.

Vogels's approximation method (V.A.M.). Even by a simple example already discussed, the arithmetic necessary to arrive at a conclusion can be tiresome. It is possible to reduce this considerably by using V.A.M. and a problem using this method, together with the necessary procedure, follows.

Example 7.3 For many years a farmers' co-operative have been hiring two large farms and three types of harvesters, which, though made by different manufacturers, do the same type of work. They are known as Senior 1, 2 and 3. Weekly repair costs on these machines are heavy but statistically they are related to the work undertaken by particular machines on four farms. The average weekly repair costs for each machine for particular farms is shown in the following table:

Weekly repair costs per harvester

	Senior 1	Senior 2	Senior 3
Farm A	16	13	15
Farm B	20	29	25
Farm C	40	38	42
Farm D	37	49	45

The Farmers' co-operative have six of each type of harvester available for hire, and the current monthly requirements by each farm is as follows:

> Farm A = 3 machines
> Farm B = 5 machines
> Farm C = 8 machines
> Farm D = 2 machines

Show the allocation of harvester to farms which will meet the co-operative's requirements and which will also minimise the repair costs incurred by the co-operative.

Set up the table according to the *north-west corner method*, but without any allocations:

Farms

		A	B	C	D	Available
	Senior 1	$\lceil 16$	$\lceil 20$	$\lceil 40$	$\lceil 37$	6
Type of harvester	Senior 2	$\lceil 13$	$\lceil 20$	$\lceil 38$	$\lceil 49$	6
	Senior 3	$\lceil 15$	$\lceil 25$	$\lceil 42$	$\lceil 45$	6
	Required	3	5	8	2	18

We shall adopt a step-by-step method for V.A.M.

Step 1
Determine the difference between the two lowest distribution costs for
each row and each column. Enter these figures alongside the rows and
columns, e.g. for farm A the two lowest figures in the column are 13 and
15; thus the difference is 2. Repeat the same procedure for the remaining
columns. In the row for harvester Senior 1 the two lowest figures are 16
and 20; thus the difference is 4. Repeat for the remaining rows.

Step 2
Select the row or column with the greatest difference. In this case it is the
row for harvester Senior 2, with 16.

Step 3
Assign the largest possible allocation within the restriction of those units
available and required to the lowest-cost square in the row or column
selected. The lowest-cost square in the row selected is 13 under column
farm A. The maximum amount we can allocate is 3.

Step 4
Cross out any row or column that is satisfied. A cross in the squares would
suffice. Thus farm A is satisfied and the two remaining squares bearing a
cross will not be considered further.

Step 5
Recalculate as step 1, except for the rows and columns that have been
satisfied.

In step 2 if two or more rows and columns have the same figure, choose
the square for allocation in step 3 that has the lowest cost. Should the costs
be the same, choosing any of the squares with that cost for allocation.

The completed allocation is shown in the following table:

Farms

		A	B	C	D	Available
	Senior 1	× [16]	5 [20]	× [40]	1 [37]	6 4̶17
Type of harvester	Senior 2	3 [13]	× [29]	3 [38]	× [49]	6 1̶6̶ 9̶ 11
	Senior 3	× [15]	× [25]	5 [42]	1 [45]	6 1̶0̶ 1̶7̶ 3
	Required	3	5	8	2	18
		2̶	5	2	8	

The solution is to:

allocate 5 Harvester Senior 1s to customer B at cost 5×20 = £100

allocate 1 Harvester Senior 1 to customer D at cost $1 \times 37 = $ £37

allocate 3 Harvester Senior 2s to customer A at cost 3×13 = £39

allocate 3 Harvester Senior 2s to customer C at cost 3×38 = £114

allocate 5 Harvester Senior 3s to customer C at cost 5×42 = £210

allocate 1 Harvester Senior 3 to customer D at cost $1 \times 45 = $ £45

∴   Total cost = £545

Towards the completion of the procedure the allocations obviously satisfy the restriction, which again will reduce the amount of arithmetic necessary. Although V.A.M. will not guarantee the optimum solution, it avoids considerable work at the beginning of the problem and it can be tested for optimality by using the procedure adopted for the north-west corner method.

An example combining the use of V.A.M., the necessity of using a dummy and testing for optimality by the procedure used for the north-west corner method seems appropriate at this stage.

Example 7.4 An organisation that has four factories in Great Britain supplies four main distribution centres with garden sheds in special containers. The number of special containers required by each distribution centre is as follows, with code names Delta 1–4 (the factories were coded Feeders 1–4):

Delta 1   10 containers
Delta 2   12 containers
Delta 3   14 containers
Delta 4   16 containers

The four factories could supply special containers as follows:

Feeder 1   8 containers
Feeder 2   12 containers
Feeder 3   15 containers
Feeder 4   16 containers

Transportation costs in £s per container, from factory to the distribution centres, are given below:

Distribution centres

Factories	Delta 1	Delta 2	Delta 3	Delta 4
Feeder 1	7	3	12	9
Feeder 2	8	11	3	21
Feeder 3	6	15	10	20
Feeder 4	10	3	8	3

Determine the optimum allocation procedure which will minimise costs and obtain the weekly cost for this procedure.

The first solution can be found by using V.A.M. A dummy is necessary to balance supply and demand:

Distribution centres

Factories

	Delta 1	Delta 2	Delta 3	Delta 4	Availability	
Feeder 1	× 7	2 3	× 12	6 9	8	4444
Feeder 2	× 8	× 11	12 3	× 21	12	55555
Feeder 3	3 6	10 15	2 10	× 20	15	44444
Feeder 4	× 10	× 3	× 8	10 3	10	00
Dummy	0	× 0	× 0	× 0	7	0
Demand	10	12	14	16	52	

0	3	3	3
1	0	3	6
1	8	7	11
1	8	7	—
2	4	7	—

Total cost at this stage

$$= (3 \times 6) + (2 \times 3) + (10 \times 15) + (12 \times 3) + (2 \times 10) + (6 \times 9)$$
$$+ (10 \times 3)$$
$$= 18 + 6 + 150 + 36 + 20 + 54 + 30 = £314$$

Using this as a first feasible solution, test for optimality by the north-west corner procedure:

Distribution centres

Factories

	Delta 1 -12	Delta 2 -3	Delta 3 -8	Delta 4 9	Availability
Feeder 1 0	7	②+6 3	12	⑥−6 9	8
Feeder 2 11	8	11	⑫ 3	21	12
Feeder 3 18	③+6 6	⑩−6 15	② 10	20	15
Feeder 4 −6	10	3	8	⑩ 3	15
Dummy 12	⑦−6 0	0	0	+6 0	7
Demand	10	12	14	16	52

To find which square to make the maximum possible allocation we calculate reception costs plus despatch costs minus the actual cost, as previously:

F_1 = Feeder 1, etc. D_1 = Delta 1, etc.

Square	$F_1 D_1$	$12 + 0 - 7$	= negative
,,	$F_1 D_3$	$8 + 0 - 12$	= negative
,,	$F_2 D_1$	$12 + 11 - 8$	= negative
,,	$F_2 D_2$	$3 + 11 - 11$	= negative
,,	$F_2 D_4$	$9 + 11 - 21$	= negative
,,	$F_3 D_4$	$9 + 18 - 20 = 7$	

$$
\begin{array}{lll}
,, & F_4D_1 & 12 - 6 - 10 = negative \\
,, & F_4D_2 & 3 - 6 - 3 = negative \\
,, & F_4D_3 & 8 - 6 - 8 = negative \\
,, & \text{Dummy } D_2 & 3 + 12 - 0 = 9 \\
,, & \text{Dummy } D_3 & 8 + 12 - 0 = 4 \\
,, & \text{Dummy } D_4 & 9 + 12 - 0 = 21 \\
\end{array}
$$

The last square receives allocation as it has the highest positive figure:

Distribution centres

Factories

	Delta 1 −6	Delta 2 3	Delta 3 −2	Delta 4 −6	Availability
Feeder 1 0	7	⑧ 3	12	9	8
Feeder 2 5	8	11	⑫ 3	21	12
Feeder 3 12	⑨+1 6	④−1 15	② 10	20	15
Feeder 4 9	10	3	8	⑩ 3	10
Dummy 6	①−1 0	+1 0	0	⑥ 0	7
Demand	10	12	14	16	52

Present cost

$$
\begin{aligned}
&= (9 \times 6) + (8 \times 3) + (4 \times 15) + (12 \times 3) + (2 \times 10) + (10 \times 3) \\
&\quad\ \ 54 \ \ + \ \ 24 \ \ + \ \ 60 \ \ + \ \ 36 \ \ + \ \ 20 \ \ + \ \ 30 \\
&= £224
\end{aligned}
$$

Considering only squares that give a positive figure we have

$$
\begin{array}{lll}
\text{Square} & F_4D_2 & 3 + 9 - 3 = 9 \\
,, & \text{Dummy } D_2 & 6 + 3 - 0 = 9 \\
,, & \text{Dummy } D_3 & 6 - 2 - 0 = 4 \\
\end{array}
$$

We have two identical figures; therefore there is an alternative solution. Square Dummy − D_2 is chosen, this having the lowest cost and we can proceed to calculate and test whether it is an optimum solution:

Distribution centres

Factories

	Delta 1 -6	Delta 2 3	Delta 3 -2	Delta 4 3	Availability
Feeder 1　0	7	⑧　3	12	9	8
Feeder 2　5	8	11	⑫　3	21	12
Feeder 3　12	⑩　6	③　15	②　10	20	15
Feeder 4　-3	10	$+1$　3	8	⑩ -1　3	10
Dummy　-3	0	① -1　0	0	⑥ $+1$　0	7
Demand	10	12	14	16	52

The present costs

$$= (10 \times 6) + (8 \times 3) + (3 \times 15) + (12 \times 3) + (2 \times 10) + (10 \times 3)$$
$$\quad\; 60 \quad + \quad 24 \quad + \quad 45 \quad + \quad 36 \quad + \quad 20 \quad + \quad 30$$
$$= £215$$

The despatch and reception costs are calculated as previously and blank squares are tested for possible improvement to the above solution:

$$
\begin{array}{lll}
\text{Square } F_1D_1 & -6 + 0 - 7 & = -13 \\
\text{,,}\quad F_1D_3 & -2 + 0 - 12 & = -14 \\
\text{,,}\quad F_1D_4 & 3 + 0 - 9 & = -6 \\
\text{,,}\quad F_2D_1 & -6 + 5 - 8 & = -9 \\
\text{,,}\quad F_2D_2 & 3 + 5 - 11 & = -3 \\
\text{,,}\quad F_2D_4 & 3 + 5 - 21 & = -13 \\
\text{,,}\quad F_3D_4 & 3 + 12 - 20 & = -5 \\
\text{,,}\quad F_4D_1 & -6 + (-3) - 10 & = -19 \\
\text{,,}\quad F_4D_2 & 3 + (-3) - 3 & = -3 \\
\text{,,}\quad F_4D_3 & -2 + (-3) - 8 & = -13 \\
\text{,,}\quad \text{Dummy } D_1 & -6 + (-3) - 0 & = -9 \\
\text{,,}\quad \text{Dummy } D_3 & -2 + (-3) - 0 & = -5 \\
\end{array}
$$

All figures are negative, so £215 is the lowest cost and the solution shown in the above table is the optimum one. An alternative solution exists and had square F_4D_2 been chosen for the allocation, the adjustment of 1 unit as shown in the above table would have been the correct procedure, following the north-west corner methodology, and a new table would have been formed thus:

Distribution centres

Factories

	Delta 1	Delta 2	Delta 3	Delta 4	Availability
Feeder 1	7	⑧ 3	12	9	8
Feeder 2	8	11	⑫ 3	21	12
Feeder 3	⑩ 6	③ 15	② 10	20	15
Feeder 4	10	① 3	8	⑨ 3	10
Dummy	0	0	0	⑦ 0	7
Demand	10	12	14	16	52

The total costs would have been as in the previous solution, i.e.

$$(10 \times 6) + (8 \times 3) + (3 \times 15) + (1 \times 3) + (12 \times 3) + (2 \times 10) + (9 \times 3)$$
$$60 \quad + \quad 24 \quad + \quad 45 \quad + \quad 3 \quad + \quad 36 \quad + \quad 20 \quad + \quad 27$$

$$= £215$$

Exercises 7

7.1 A large manufacturing organisation has four departments A_1, B_1, C_1 and D_1 producing special car components which are despatched to three centres R_1, R_2 and R_3 within the company. The parts are transported by small electric trucks. The requirements of the centres are constant as is the production by the four departments, and these are as follows (the parts are supplied in standard containers):

Production Department A_1 = 70 containers
Production Department B_1 = 30 containers
Production Department C_1 = 50 containers
Production Department D_1 = 50 containers

Requirement Centre R_1 =   40 containers
Requirement Centre R_2 = 100 containers
Requirement Centre R_3 =   60 containers

The Costs Department supplied the necessary transportation costs
(p) per container, which were as follows:

A_1 to R_1 =4p A_1 to R_2 = 4p A_1 to R_3 =3p
B_1 to R_1 = 6p B_1 to R_2 = 5p B_1 to R_3 =0   (because of close
C_1 to R_1 =4p C_1 to R_2 = 2p C_1 to R_3 =3p   proximity)
D_1 to R_1 =8p D_1 to R_2 = 2p D_1 to R_3 = 5p

Determine the best allocation pattern and the minimum costs.

7.2   A Latin American country has four mines which are producing a
valuable ore and all four are financed by the U.K. Government.
They are Decca, producing 14000 tons, Polydor 12000 tons, Alvis
9000 tons and Regent 5000 tons. Before the ore leaves each mine
it goes through 3 special processes, denoted 1, 2 and 3, each
having a capacity of 15000 tons. The cost per ton in cruzeiros from
the mines to each process is as follows:

From Decca (D) to Process 1 =   80 crs
From Decca (D) to Process 2 =   60 crs
From Decca (D) to Process 3 = 135 crs
From Alvis (A) to Process 1 = 130 crs
From Alvis (A) to Process 2 =   95 crs
From Alvis (A) to Process 3 = 110 crs
From Polydor (P) to Process 1 =   75 crs
From Polydor (P) to Process 2 =   85 crs
From Polydor (P) to Process 3 = 100 crs
From Regent (R) to Process 1 = 150 crs
From Regent (R) to Process 2 =   90 crs
From Regent (R) to Process 3 = 130 crs

(i) By using the north-west corner method make a basic feasible solution to the above problem.
(ii) Show the optimum transportation plan to give minimum costs, and state these costs.

Bibliography

See pp. 118–20 for Bibliography to Chapters 6–8.

8

Assignment

In Chapters 6 and 7, which covered the areas to which the graphical and simplex methods could be applied as well as the transportation method, we were basically looking at the problems of allocation. Whenever there are a number of activities to be performed, but limitations on either the amount of resources or the way they can be spent prevent the performance of each separate activity in the most effective way, then in such cases we allot the resources available in a way that will optimise the total effectiveness.

There is a particular specialised group that could be called *assignment problems*. This group comprises problems where we are given a method of effectiveness, showing what happens when we associate each of a number of 'origins' with each of the *same* number of destinations. The 'origin' is to be associated with one and one only 'destination', and the objective is to make the association in such a way as to maximise or minimise the total effectiveness.

The number of possible ways of allocating the resources available to the activities can be finite or infinite. With problems having a finite number of choices it is possible to enumerate all the possible choices, but in practical problems it is a too lengthy a process. (To give a simple example, there are 15! different ways of allocating 15 contracts to 15 contractors, each receiving one contract.)

Assignment techniques

Problems in this area can be solved by the transportation method, by considering each facility as a despatch point with only one unit of goods available and the receiving point requiring one unit. However, an alternative and generally easier method of solution is by the assignment technique.

We are endeavouring to assign n number of items to n number of trays in such a way that the over-all result from the assignment is optimised. For example, a company has 6 people available for 6 appointments which require filling: what would be the best assignment for the company? The same company has a fleet of 20 lorries, each requiring loads for transportation. The lorries are in 20 different cities, which we will call A–T, and they are required to move to 20 other different locations 1–19. Knowing the different mileages involved, how should we assign the lorries to give the minimum mileage? One can see the magnitude of the task by having to consider 20! alternatives. We will use an example for choosing the optimum assignment.

Example 8.1 A company has 5 people for 5 appointments. The men differ in efficiency and the appointments in their requirements. A grading is given for each man for each task. The company has a system of grading of 1–100 which it uses for such occasions. The lower the grade, the higher the efficiency. How should the appointments be allocated to give the over-all lowest grade (highest efficiency)?

Employees

		1	2	3	4	5
	I	9	27	18	11	12
	II	14	29	5	27	30
Appointments	III	38	19	18	15	40
	IV	19	26	24	10	20
	V	50	40	32	17	6

We will proceed with a systematic method of solving this simple example. Choose the smallest number in the first row I and subtract this amount from all other figures in that row, with the following result:

0	18	9	2	3
14	29	5	27	30
38	19	18	15	40
19	26	24	10	20
50	40	32	17	6

We then proceed to repeat the process for all other rows, i.e. take the lowest figure from all other figures in each row. This gives the following:

0	18	9	2	3
9	24	0	22	25
23	4	3	0	25
9	16	14	0	10
44	36	26	11	0

Then proceed by taking the lowest number from each column and reducing all figures in that column by that amount:

0	14	9	2	3
9	20	0	22	25
23	0	3	0	10
44	32	26	11	0

(1) Examine each row to find those having one single zero, mark that particular zero $\boxed{0}$ to denote an assignment. All other zeros in that particular *column* can be crossed out, i.e. ∅.

(2) When the rows have been examined check each column for those having single zeros, mark the zero as before for any assignment, crossing out all other zeros in the *rows*.

(3) Repeat 1 and 2 until the situation occurs where there are:

  (i) no zeros left that are unmarked; or
  (ii) that zeros remaining unmarked consist of at least two in each row or column.

If we get the situation (i) then we have a maximal assignment; otherwise if (ii) exists, then a basis of trial and/or error is necessary to obtain the maximal assignment. A complex algorithm is necessary for larger matrices if outcome (ii) is not completed by trial and error, but for many situations this is satisfactory.
    Thus we construct a final table:

$\boxed{0}$	14	9	2	3
9	20	$\boxed{0}$	22	25
23	$\boxed{0}$	3	∅	25
9	12	14	$\boxed{0}$	10
44	32	26	11	$\boxed{0}$

Answer:

Give Appointment I to 1, II to 3, III to 2, IV to 4, V to 5.

Although the solution to this problem is obtained easily, further steps are often required in problems of more complexity to obtain the optimum solution. Steps already taken and further analysis is shown in the next example.

Example 8.2   6 lorries A, B, C, D, E, F, are required at 6 depots I, II, III, IV, V and VI, with the mileage between their present positions and depots known. Our problem is to designate where each lorry should travel to enable a minimum mileage to be achieved. The data covering the problem are as follows:

To

	I	II	III	IV	V	VI
A	47	78	45	58	31	57
B	28	35	55	71	87	56
C	33	45	66	57	38	38
D	51	56	54	58	43	49
E	35	46	45	32	36	39
F	88	46	46	66	57	36

From (rows A–F)

Step 1

Subtract the smallest figure of each row from all figures of the row:

To

	I	II	III	IV	V	VI
A	16	47	14	27	0	26
B	0	7	27	43	59	28
C	0	12	33	24	5	5
D	8	13	11	15	0	6
E	3	14	13	0	4	7
F	52	10	10	30	21	0

From (rows A–F)

Step 2

Subtract the smallest figure of each column from all other figures of the columns. Proceed to check rows with a single zero and marking $\boxed{0}$, crossing out all other zeros in the column and repeat for columns with a single zero, crossing out the remaining zero in the row. We are now left with the table below

To

	I	II	III	IV	V	VI
A	16	40	4	27	$\boxed{0}$	26
B	$\emptyset$	$\boxed{0}$	17	43	59	28
C	$\boxed{0}$	5	23	24	5	5
D	8	6	1	15	$\boxed{0}$	6
E	3	7	3	$\boxed{0}$	4	7
F	32	3	$\boxed{0}$	30	21	$\emptyset$

From (rows A–F)

This does not give the complete assignment and we proceed (without proof) so that an optimum assignment can be achieved.

Step 3

Draw the minimum number of lines to cover all zeros:

	To					
	I	II	III	IV	V	VI
A	1|6	4|0	4	2|7	|0	26
B	|0	|0	17	4|3	5|9	28
C (From)	|0	5	23	2|4	|5	5
D	|8	6	1	1|5	|0	6
E	|3	7	3	|0	|4	7
F	3|2	3	0	3|0	2|1	0

Step 4

Subtract the smallest figure not covered by any line from the remaining figures not covered by any line. Then add this same figure to any figure at the intersection of lines. We would thus obtain the final matrix:

	To					
	I	II	III	IV	V	VI
A	16	40	3	27	[0]	25
B	∅	[0]	16	43	59	27
C (From)	[0]	5	22	24	5	4
D	8	6	[0]	15	∅	5
E	3	7	2	[0]	4	6
F	53	4	∅	31	22	[0]

Repeat step 2 to see if an optimum assignment exists; if so, the procedure ends at this point, otherwise continue with step 3 until a complete solution exists.

Answer

Lorry *A* to V, *B* to II, *C* to I, *D* to III, *E* to IV, *F* to VI.

As in the transportation method shown previously, it may be necessary to use a dummy row or column. In assignment problems an $n \times n$ matrix is required and the following problem shows the necessity of using a dummy to enable the procedure to be used.

Example 8.3 A firm wishes to build 5 warehouses and 6 possible sites are available. How should they be allocated? The cost (in £000s) of building the warehouses on different sites is given in the following matrix.

Warehouses

Sites	1	2	3	4	5
A	18	15	22	25	21
B	9	11	10	15	8
C	12	10	14	16	17
D	9	10	10	21	20
E	14	18	26	26	24
F	14	19	23	20	25

Introduce a dummy warehouse. Apply step 2, then step 3, which is to draw the minimum number of lines to cover all zeros.

Warehouses

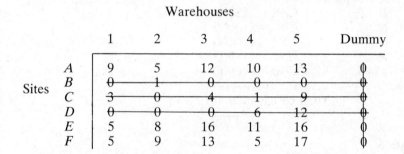

Sites	1	2	3	4	5	Dummy
A	9	5	12	10	13	0
B	0	1	0	0	0	0
C	3	0	4	1	9	0
D	0	0	0	6	12	0
E	5	8	16	11	16	0
F	5	9	13	5	17	0

We apply step 4, which is to subtract the smallest figure not covered by any line from the remaining figures *not* covered by any line. Add this same figure to any figure at the intersection of lines.

Warehouses

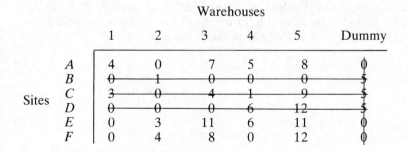

Sites	1	2	3	4	5	Dummy
A	4	0	7	5	8	0
B	0	1	0	0	0	5
C	3	0	4	1	9	5
D	0	0	0	6	12	5
E	0	3	11	6	11	0
F	0	4	8	0	12	0

Observe a column or row with a single zero and work this for an assignment, in this case column 5. Cancel all remaining zeros in that column and row. Proceed with this method until only 6 assignments, in this problem, have been made. The final table will be thus:

Warehouses

	1	2	3	4	5	Dummy
A	4	0	8	5	8	[0]
B	0	1	0	0	[0]	5
C	3	[0]	4	1	9	5
D	0	0	[0]	6	12	5
E	[0]	3	11	6	11	0
F	0	4	8	[0]	12	0

Sites (label spans rows C and D)

Answer

A – unused
B – 5   Cost = £8000
C – 2   Cost = £10000
D – 3   Cost = £10000
E – 1   Cost = £14000
F – 4   Cost = £20000

Total cost = £62000

Exercises 8

8.1 A plant-hire company is to service 6 sites with equipment. The equipment consists of 6 tractors of the same type and size, each being on 6 different sites. The tractors are required at different sites and the objective is to transport the tractors so that the minimum mileage of travel is achieved. From which of 6 sites A, B, C, D, E and F would it be advisable to transport the tractors to which sites 1, 2, 3, 4, 5 and 6 so that the minimal mileage results?

Mileage chart
From sites

	A	B	C	D	E	F
1	51	82	49	62	35	61
2	32	39	59	75	91	60
3	37	49	70	61	42	42
4	55	60	58	62	47	53
5	39	50	49	36	40	43
6	92	50	50	70	61	40

To sites (rows 3, 4 labelled)

8.2 Five doctors form a group practice and they wish to allocate one of five densely populated areas to each doctor so that the travelling time from the doctors' homes to the central point of each area is at a minimum for the group. The average time in minutes was calculated for each doctor to the central point of each area and these are as follows:

Doctors' residence

	1	2	3	4	5
A	21	24	30	20	29
B	24	29	27	38	22
C	34	25	17	26	29
D	31	39	38	25	38
E	31	35	21	29	27

Areas

Bibliography

See pp. 118–20 for Bibliography to Chapters 6–8.

9

Replacement

We all experience the problems of replacement and try to establish the best time to renew our car, refrigerator and some other such item. We may not always be rational over this replacement, taking into account what would be the best time financially for us to replace and quite often these are left until a break-down occurs. After such a break-down we often then consider, when faced with the bill for replaced parts and maintenance, that we ought to have had some organised plan perhaps based on previous experience which may have saved this outlay of money.

The problem of replacement falls into two areas:

(i) articles that deteriorate with time, such as cars and machinery; and
(ii) articles that come into the category of sudden failure, such as radio valves, car and street lighting.

In both areas to be discussed the keeping and collection of historical data will become apparent. This aspect can be overlooked when considering examples of this type, due to the data being given to the student to solve the problem. In many areas of industry the keeping of data in failure rates and actual maintenance costs could save considerable money over time and enable realistic replacement policies based on reliable figures to be presented.

In considering the area of sudden failure, while the individual failures may be unpredictable, the statistical characteristics of the *group* is often stable, and this is of great importance to us.

Example 9.1 An example covering 100 machines of a particular kind will be taken to introduce the problems of sudden failure. Each machine costs £2 to repair if the repair is performed on an individual basis. If all machines are serviced at the same time, the cost is £100, which is £1 per machine. The data available on failures or mortality rates for the particular machines were as follows:

Month	4	5	6	7	8	9
Percentage failing by month ending	0	15	35	65	90	100

The machines are repaired as and when they break down. The company also service simultaneously all the 100 machines at regular intervals irrespective of their condition. Because of the heavy costs incurred by the company for repairs a decision covering group repair must be made.

It has been company policy to group repair at 6-monthly intervals and a comparison with this procedure is required together with the effect of group repair greater than 6 months. It is assumed that break-downs within a month are evenly spaced throughout the month.

We first compute the probability that a machine fails in successive months. Let f_1 denote the probability that a machine which was new when installed fails during the nth month of its life. This probability is the difference between those surviving at the beginning of the nth month and the proportion surviving at the end of the nth month. We can compute a table thus:

Month (n)	Average life of machine failing in that month (x)	f	fx
5	4.5	$0.15 = f_1$	0.675
6	5.5	$0.20 = f_2$	1.100
7	6.5	$0.30 = f_3$	1.950
8	7.5	$0.25 = f_4$	1.875
9	8.5	$0.10 = f_5$	0.850
			$\Sigma fx = 6.450$

From the table it can be seen that the probability of a machine installed at time zero failing in month 5 is 0.15 and that no machine survives after month 9. However, the probability of a machine installed at time zero failing in the 9th month, denoted f_5, is 0.10.

From our table, by totalling the column fx we obtain the average time between failures, which in this example is 6.45. Thus with no mass servicing the average number of failures per month is

$$\frac{100}{6.45} = 15 \text{ machines}$$

The cost of repair on an individual basis is £2 and therefore the cost of those failures is $15 \times £2 = £30$ per month.

By making assumptions we can compute the number of repairs due to failure in successive months under a policy of no group repair. We assume:

(i) that machines failing during a month are repaired just before the end of that month; and

(ii) that the actual percentage of failure during a month for a sub-population of machines with the same age is the same as the expected percentage of failures during the month for that sub-population.

Let x denote the number of repairs made at the end of the nth month. If all 100 machines are new initially we can obtain:

$$x_1 = 100$$
$$x_2 = 0$$
$$x_3 = 0$$
$$x_4 = 0$$
$$x_5 = f_1x_1 = 15$$
$$x_6 = f_2x_1 + f_1x_2 = 20 + 0 = 20$$
$$x_7 = f_3x_1 + f_2x_2 + f_1x_3 = 30 + 0 + 0 = 30$$
$$x_8 = f_4x_1 + f_3x_2 + f_2x_3 + f_1x_4 = 25 + 0 + 0 + 0 = 25$$
$$x_9 = f_5x_1 + f_4x_2 + f_3x_3 + f_2x_4 + f_1x_5 = 10 + 0 + 0 + 0 + 2 = 12$$

It will be noticed that the number of machines failing each month increases until month 7 and then starts decreasing. Further calculations on the basis shown will later start to increase and it will continue to oscillate until finally it will settle down to a 'steady state' in which the proportion of machines failing each month is the reciprocal of their calculated average life.

If all the machines were replaced at the end of the first month the cost would be £100, and this is also true for months 2, 3 and 4. In considering month 5 the cost would be £100 plus the cost of replacing 15 failures during the month. A table showing the necessary calculations and average monthly costs follows:

Interval between group replacement (months)	Resulting average cost per month (£)
1	$100 \div 1 = 100$
2	$100 \div 2 = 50$
3	$100 \div 3 = 33\frac{1}{3}$
4	$100 \div 4 = 25$
5	$(100 + 30) \div 5 = 26$
6	$(100 + 70) \div 6 = 28$
7	$(100 + 130) \div 7 = 31$

By comparing these policies we find that the cheapest would be to replace the group at month 4 costing an average monthly figure of £25; and the cost of replacing at 6-monthly intervals would be £28.

When considering methods of assessing the correct period to replace items that deteriorate over time, there are basically 3 that require reviewing:

  (i) the returns possible over the first n years of the item's life,
  (ii) the break-even data; and
  (iii) the discounted cash flow (D.C.F.).

The first method usually covers periods of up to 10 years, but in the case of large plants and complex developments the periods can be larger. Figures 9.1 and 9.2 show the distribution of returns of two projects over an 8-year period, the sum of the return having the same total. It can be seen that the return for project I accrues over the first 3 years and for project II over the last 3. Unfortunately, it does not assess the difference between the distributions over the period nor takes into consideration any savings beyond the specified period.

To remedy the problem the method of 'break-even' was introduced. Using the previous two projects as examples with developments cost of £6,000,000 and knowing the returns, then in Figure 9.1 the break-even point would be after approximately 2 years, in Figure 9.2 after

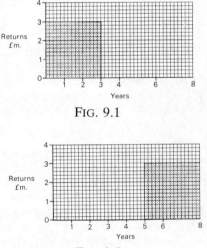

FIG. 9.1

FIG. 9.2

approximately 7 years, which does give a form of comparison. However, it still does not meet with the requirement of evaluating how much one investment is better than another over their whole lives.

A method is required to cover this difficulty of bringing in the concept of time into the analysis of returns. Discounted cash flow techniques assist greatly in this direction and will be discussed later in the chapter.

Many examinations include questions on replacement which emphasise the use of the 'average cost per year basis', and we now consider this.

Example 9.2   To purchase a new car the cost is £1800 and it can be sold at the end of the year for the figures shown below:

End of year	1	2	3	4	5	6
Price (£)	1500	1330	1200	1000	600	100

Running costs are estimated to be:

Year	1	2	3	4	5	6
Costs (£)	150	170	200	250	350	550

The economic life of the car is required together with the minimum average annual cost.

If a small business needs the car for a fixed 5-year period and at the beginning of this period has a 2-year-old car which is of the same type, state the replacement policy which should be adopted.

We can develop a table covering the 6-year period. Column B, commencing with the cost of the new car at £1800, shows the amount recoverable if the car was sold. Column C shows the running costs and column D is the depreciation, which is the difference between the amount that could have been received in the previous and current year. Column E is the sum of C and D and totals the amount lost by keeping the car from one year to the next plus running costs. Column F is the cumulative costs of column E. To obtain the average annual costs we divide column F by the number of years being considered, thus denoted by column G:

Year	B	C	D	E = (C + D)	F	G
0	1800					
1	1500	150	300	450	450	450
2	1330	170	170	340	790	395
3	1200	200	130	330	1120	373
4	1000	250	200	450	1570	392
5	600	350	400	750	2320	464
6	100	550	500	1050	3370	561

The economic life of the car is 3 years at a minimum average cost of £373, ignoring compound interest.

We need now to consider the situation regarding the 2-year-old car using the same basic procedure just completed. We know that we can receive £1330 for the 2-year-old car which will now be year 0 in the following table:

Year	B	C	D	E = (C + D)	F
0	1330	170			
1	1200	200	130	330	330
2	1000	250	200	450	780
3	600	350	400	750	1530
4	100	550	500	1050	2580

Reviewing a policy over the 4-year period we can see that if we keep the 2-year-old car zero years and buy a new one for a full 5 years the total cost will be £0 + £2320 = £2320 and if we keep the 2-year-old car for 1 year and buy a new one for a full 4 years, this results in the total cost of £330 + £1570 = £1900, and so on, resulting in the following complete policies:

2-year-old car kept for 0 years and buy new one for full 5 years
Total cost   £0 + £2320 + £2320

2-year-old car kept for 1 year, then buy new one for 4 years
Total cost   £330 + £1570 + £1900

2-year-old car kept for 2 years, then buy new one for 3 years
Total cost   £780 + £1120 = £1900

2-year-old car kept for 3 years then buy new one for 2 years
Total cost   £1530 + £790 = £2320

2-year-old car kept for 4 years, then buy new one for 1 year
Total cost   £2580 + £450 = £3030

Therefore, we have a choice of policies: either keep the 2-year-old car a further year and buy new for 4 years, or keep for 2 years and purchase for 3 years, the cost over the 5-year period being £1900 in each case.

Discounted cash flow

The basis of discounted cash flow (D.C.F.) is to estimate the effective life of the project and to estimate the total net cash to be expended or received each year. We must then value it in present-day terms in order to compare it with the amount of today's proposed investment and to take into account the cost of borrowing money.

The following table show the method of calculation for the present value of £1 at 10 per cent after the number of years stated. The values of K can be obtained from the tables on page 214.

The basic concept is that £1 in the future has less value than in the present. If £1, therefore, is invested at 4 per cent today, it would produce approximately £1.50 in ten years time. It follows that the present value of £1.50 in ten years time is £1 at 4 per cent interest.

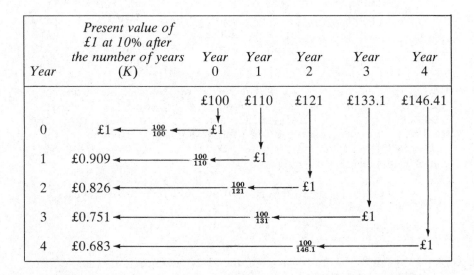

Year	Present value of £1 at 10% after the number of years (K)	Year 0	Year 1	Year 2	Year 3	Year 4
		£100	£110	£121	£133.1	£146.41
0	£1 ← $\frac{100}{100}$ ← £1					
1	£0.909 ← $\frac{100}{110}$ ← £1					
2	£0.826 ← $\frac{100}{121}$ ← £1					
3	£0.751 ← $\frac{100}{131}$ ← £1					
4	£0.683 ← $\frac{100}{146.1}$ ← £1					

Application of this principle enables cash in and out to be brought to today's value regardless of the actual date in which the cash payment or receipt would arise.

One definition of present worth is 'what the present value would be of

a future value some years away'. The following symbols will be used for
D.C.F. calculations:

P = sum of money at the present time
i = interest rate per interest period
n = number of interest periods
S = sum of money in x number of years
C = cost savings

If S is given and we wish to find P the formula is

$$P = S \frac{1}{(1 + i)^n}$$

Example 9.3 The present value of £133.10 in three years time at 10
per cent interest is

$$P = 133.10 \times \frac{1}{(1 + \frac{1}{10})^3}$$

$$= 133.10 \times 0.7513$$
$$= £100$$

Knowing the value of S and i it is possible to obtain the values for the
calculation $1/(1 + i)^n$ from present-value tables (see Table 7, p. 214);
thus a single multiplication calculation will give the required value of P.

By a straightforward transposition of the previous formula we can
obtain the *compound interest*. Given P and knowing the interest rate we
have the following:

$$S = P(1 + i)^n$$

Example.   £100 invested at 10 per cent a year for three years:

$$S = 100(1 + \frac{1}{10})^3$$
$$= 100 + 33.10$$
$$= £133.10$$

As an extension of the previous examples on replacement, consideration
of D.C.F. in arriving at a policy will be given via the following problem.

Example 9.4 A company is considering the replacement of a special
press. The initial capital would be £10000 and the estimated maintenance costs gained from past experience for an 8-year period is given

in the following table:

Year	1	2	3	4	5	6	7	8
Maintenance cost (£)	290	480	925	1275	2470	4100	6000	7750

Assuming an interest rate of 10 per cent, use a present-worth value as a basis for cost comparison and obtain the best time for replacement. What other factors could influence a decision for replacement?

The table is formed for the 8-year period with the capital cost of £10000 in column (2). Column (3) is formed from the given maintenance costs. The cumulative maintenance from 3 is found in column (4). The capital cost of £10000 plus the cumulative maintenance costs is given in column (5). The values of K are obtained from present-worth D.C.F. tables and are read off against the appropriate year and percentage interest of 10 per cent.

(1)	(2)	(3)	(4)	(5)	(6)	(7)	(8)
						Present-worth total	Present worth of average
	Capital cost	Mainten-ance cost	Cumulative mainten-ance cost	Total cost to end of		cost	cost/year
Year	(£)	(£)	(£)	year	K	(£)	(£)
1	10000	290	290	10290	0.909	9360	9360
2		480	770	10770	0.826	8900	4450
3		925	1695	11695	0.751	8770	2923
4		1275	2970	12970	0.683	8850	2212
5		2470	5440	15440	0.621	9600	1920
6		4100	9540	19540	0.564	10980	1830
7		6000	15540	25540	0.531	13550	1936
8		7750	23290	32290	0.467	15550	1944

From column 8 it can be seen that the best replacement policy would be to replace in the sixth year of life (present worth of £1830).

Exercises 9

9.1 A company specialising in small pressings wishes to purchase a press in the near future. From records of maintenance from similar machines, estimated costs have been collected. While it is not necessary that a new machine be bought, because of economic factors estimates of the selling and purchasing prices of the press from new to 5 years' old have been obtained:

Year end		0	1	2	3	4	5
Maintenance costs (£)		—	48	61	77	96	124
Selling price	(£)	—	840	720	610	520	450
Purchase price	(£)	1000	930	790	670	570	470

What would be the best replacement policy?

9.2 Calculate the mean life of the items in the following table:

Life effectiveness (months)	Probability of failure
1	0.05
2	0.10
3	0.20
4	0.25
5	0.20
6	0.20

The cost of replacing items that fail individually is £1 per item. When replaced on a group basis the cost is 25p per item.

Would a policy of replacing on a group basis be more economical than replacing individually as they fail? Consider the periods of 1 month and 2 months for replacement.

9.3 A special electronic machine has a part that is subject to failure and must be replaced immediately when this occurs. A batch of 50 such machines are used in a factory. The cost of individual replacement is £5 per item and for group replacement £100 for all 50 machines. Group replacement can only be carried out at the end of the month.

Records are kept of previous failure rates and from these figures the probability of failure for 50 parts over 5 months is:

5 will fail during the 1st month
10 „   „   „   „ 2nd month
15 „   „   „   „ 3rd month
15 „   „   „   „ 4th month
 5 „   „   „   „ 5th month

What replacement policy should be adopted over an 8-month period?

9.4 An organisation manufacturing plastic mouldings is considering the replacement for two moulding machines. Capital for machine X initially is £18000 and for machine Y is £20000. For a 6-year period the estimated maintenance costs were established and are presented in the following table:

Moulding machine X

Year	1	2	3	4	5	6
Maintenance cost (£)	1200	1400	1900	2200	5000	8000

Moulding machine Y

Year	1	2	3	4	5	6
Maintenance cost (£)	260	420	900	1200	2500	3500

The department concerned with replacement has stated that it would be advisable, regarding cost, to replace machine X after 4 years and machine Y after 3 years.

Assuming interest rates of 10 per cent, use a present-worth value as a basis for cost comparison and comment on the policy suggested by the department responsible for machine replacement.

Bibliography

R. L. Ackoff (ed.), *Progress in Operations Research*, vol. 1 (New York: Wiley, 1961).

R. L. Ackoff and M. W. Sasieni, *Fundamentals of Operations Research* (New York: Wiley, 1968).

A. A. Alchian, 'Economic Replacement Policy', RAND Corporation Report R–22, Apr 1952; reprinted as RM–2153, Apr 1958.

American Management Association, *Tested Approaches to Capital Equipment Replacement*, a Special Report.

R. Bellman, 'Equipment Replacement Policy', *Journal of Social, Industrial and Applied Mathematics*, Sep 1955.

D. R. Cox, *Renewal Theory* (London: Methuen, 1962).

B. V. Dean, 'Replacement Theory', in *Progress in Operations Research*, vol. 1, ed. R. L. Ackoff (New York: Wiley, 1961) pp. 327–362.

J. Dean, *Capital Budgeting* (Columbia University Press, 1951).

A. Kaufmann, *Methods and Models of Operations Research* (Englewood Cliffs, N.J.: Prentice-Hall, 1963).

J. J. McCall, 'Maintenance Policies for Stochastically Failing Equipment: A Survey', *Management Science*, vol. 11, 1965, pp. 493–534.

W. Mendenhall, 'A Bibliography on Life Testing and Related Topics', *Biometrica*, vol. 45, 1958, pp. 521–43.

G. L. Preinreich, 'The Economic Life of Industrial Equipment', *Econometrica*, vol. 8, no. 1, 1940.

W. L. Smith, 'Renewal Theory and its Ramifications', *Journal of the Royal Statistical Society*, Series B, vol. 20, no. 2, 1958.

B. Terborgh, *Dynamic Equipment Policy* (New York: McGraw-Hill, 1949).

10

Network Control

These techniques are particular applications of planning and control, having special application for non-routine operations such as projects in design, in product development, in construction and in maintenance. The more complex the operations or project, the more useful network control can be. A project is analysed into its component activities. The optimum relative scheduling of each is decided; as the actual work proceeds, failures to meet completion dates can be forecast and corrections made in good time; it is an essential part of the technique that any 'change of plan' decisions are made with the costs of the changes clearly determined in advance.

Various terms have come into popular usage for the systems of control based on the 'network' concept and some of them have the force virtually of brand-names, in the sense of being associated with the widely known names such as:

(1) Critical Path Scheduling (C.P.S.)
(2) The Critical Path Method (C.P.M.)
(3) Programme Evaluation and Review Technique (PERT)
(4) Resource Allocation in Multi-project Scheduling (RAMPS)

Differences in these systems tend to be marginal; the third one (PERT), for example, uses a three-estimate formula in planning the expected times, and this will be described later in the chapter. The fourth method concentrates attention on the planning and control of the distribution of resources rather than primarily on the time progress of the activities. The common terminology employed are *Critical Path Planning*, *Network Analysis* and *Network Control*.

The application of network control has increased considerably over the past few years; apart from the technical fields successful applications have been made for advertising campaigns, for launching new products, for removals to new premises and for the control of systems design progress in data-processing applications.

An important factor of the technique is often overlooked in popular presentations, namely the integrated combination of planning and control. Frequently advocates of these network systems will be found emphasising their value in 'planning' by reason of the systematic and

FIG. 10.1

detailed logical and sequential analysis that is required for the formulation of the network. This value is certainly there and is usually of great benefit, both in the preparation of the project and in subsequent supervision. Yet a greater value lies in the control medium which this analysis provides when the centres of responsibility and the expected times are allocated, and the subsequent comparisons are made so that pointers to management action can be discovered. These points are expanded later in the problems to be discussed.

The project is subjected to detailed logical analysis so as to divide it up into activities and events. Activities are operations, jobs, processing, or other occurrences, and they necessarily consume time; they also use up resources, e.g. manpower, equipment time, etc. An activity is denoted by an arrow. Each 'activity' begins from and ends in an 'event', is usually denoted by a circle. An 'event' is a specific situation or occurrence which indicates a point in time but does not consume time. For convenience of reference particularly significant events can be identified as milestones.

The network is built up in a series of events and activities in a logical sequence, usually flowing from left to right (see Figure 10.1). The centre 'event' forms the completion of activity A and commencement of activity B. As it stands the network communicates that 'activity B' is dependent on 'activity A'. To signify that 'activity A' is independent of 'activity B', see the diagram in Figure 10.2. The 'event' adjacent to the arrow is called the 'head event', and the other the 'tail event'. The activities are numbered with the head number being larger than the tail and the time for the activity entered in the arrow (see Figure 10.3). From this network we communicate that there are 3 activities 1–5, 1–3 and 3–5. Activity 1–5 is independent of 1–3 and 3–5, but activity 3–5 is dependent on activity 1–3.

'Dummies' are used to assist in the logic of the network; however, a dummy is a 'non-existing' activity with zero time. To avoid, for example,

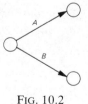

FIG. 10.2

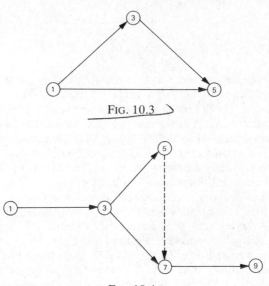

Fig. 10.3

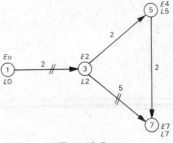

Fig. 10.4

2 activities having the same head and tail number, a dummy can be
inserted which does not affect the logic or timing. A dummy is denoted
by a dotted arrow (see Figure 10.4). This network signifies that activities
3–7 and 3–5 are independent of each other but dependent on 1–3.
Activity 7–9 is dependent on 3–7, 3–5, and 1–3.

  Before attempting a problem, the analysis of the network requires
explanation. A simple example will satisfy our needs with 4 activities
(see Figure 10.5). Alongside the 'events', E denotes *earliest*, and L
denotes *latest*. Commencing at time zero at 'event' (1), we work our way
through the network, which basically flows from left to right. At each
head event we denote the earliest time of arrival, which to event

Fig. 10.5

(3) = 2, and to event (5) = 2 + 2 a total of 4. The earliest time we can expect to complete the project at event (7) will be the *longest path* through the network, which is 7. Thus we know that the *critical* activities are 1–3 and 3–7, giving the 7 time units. Working our way back to the start of the network we note the *latest* time we can afford to be at the 'events' to enable us to complete the project in the 7 time units. At event (5) it will be 5, at event (3) it will be 2 and we do not wish to start later than zero at (1).

The *critical path* is 1–3–7 shown by ⫫. It will be noticed that activities on the critical path must start and finish between the times at the head and tail events and that there is no excess time available. This excess time is called *float* and a definition of an activity on the critical path could be 'an activity which has zero *float*'.

Three kinds of float are usually calculated: *total* (*T*), *free* (*F*) and *independent float* (*I*).

Total float (T)

This figure gives an indication of the amount of float available in the network, but by using up this amount of time on one activity it could affect the total float available on other activities:

$$
\begin{matrix}
\text{Latest time of} & \text{Earliest time} & \text{Duration time} \\
= \text{the head event} - \text{of the tail event} - \text{of the activity} \\
\text{(L.T.H.E.)} & \text{(E.T.T.E.)} & (D)
\end{matrix}
$$

Free float (F)

This is the time available that can be used up on the activity, and would not affect the earliest starting time of the activity following. This is provided the activity commences at the earliest start time:

$$
\begin{matrix}
\text{Earliest start time} & \text{Earliest start time} & \text{Duration time} \\
F = \text{of the head event} - \text{of the tail event} - \text{of the activity} \\
\text{(E.T.H.E.)} & \text{(E.T.T.E.)} & (D)
\end{matrix}
$$

Independent float (I)

This is the amount of time that can be used up on the activity without affecting any other activities, the start or the finishing time:

$$
\begin{matrix}
\text{Earliest time of} & \text{Latest time of} & \text{Duration time} \\
I = \text{the head event} - \text{the tail event} - \text{of the activity} \\
\text{(E.T.H.E.)} & \text{(L.T.T.E.)} & (D)
\end{matrix}
$$

Calculations of float activities 1–3 and 3–7 would give zero for all 3 floats, due to these being critical activities. Taking activity 3–5 as an example, the 3 float figures are calculated:

$$T = \text{L.T.H.E.} - \text{E.T.T.E.} - D$$
$$= \quad 5 \quad - \quad 2 \quad - 2 = 1 \text{ time unit}$$

$$F = \text{E.T.H.E.} - \text{E.T.T.E.} - D$$
$$= \quad 4 \quad - \quad 2 \quad - 2 = 0 \text{ time units}$$

$$I = \text{E.T.H.E.} - \text{L.T.T.E.} - D$$
$$= \quad 4 \quad - \quad 2 \quad - 2 = 0 \text{ time units}$$

Considerable practice is necessary to become proficient in network analysis and to understand the building of logic diagrams forming the networks together with their analysis.

Example 10.1 The network shown in Figure 10.6 covers the assembly of machined parts:

(i) Establish the different routes through the network and evaluate the total project time.
(ii) Develop a table, showing for each of the activities the *earliest* start/finish and the *latest* start/finish.
(iii) Calculate the *total*, *free* and *independent* floats in the network.

The activity duration times are given in weeks.

	Total time
Routes through the network	(weeks)
1–2–4–6–7–8	16
1–2–3–4–6–7–8	15
1–3–4–6–7–8	12
1–2–3–5–6–7–8	24*
1–2–3–5–7–8	17
1–3–5–7–8	14
1–3–5–6–7–8	21

*The critical path = 1–2–3–5–6–7–8 = 24

Listing the activities and calculating the earliest start/finish and latest start/finish for *each* individual activity and the 3 floats we should arrive

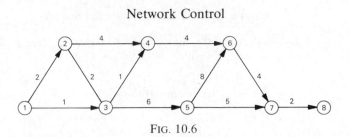

FIG. 10.6

at the following table:

Activity	Duration	Earliest Start	Earliest Finish	Latest Start	Latest Finish	T	F	I
1–2	2	0	2	0	2	0	0	0
1–3	1	0	1	3	4	3	3	3
2–3	2	2	2	4	4	0	0	0
2–4	4	2	6	10	14	8	0	0
3–4	1	4	5	13	14	9	1	1
3–5	6	4	4	10	10	0	0	0
4–6	4	6	10	14	18	8	8	0
5–6	8	10	10	18	18	0	0	0
5–7	5	10	15	17	22	7	7	7
6–7	4	18	18	22	22	0	0	0
7–8	2	22	22	24	24	0	0	0

In PERT provision is made for 3 estimates of expected activity times to be submitted. The calculation is based on the normal curve and a weighting factor is given to 'the most likely' time or 'normal time'. In requesting 3 estimates it is primarily a matter of psychological value, especially in projects where there is little guidance from previous experience. It is felt that a more realistic 'expected time' can be assessed if some recognition is given at the estimating stage to the possibility of unforeseeable occurrences which could either hinder or promote progress. The three estimates invited are:

most likely or 'normal' (*m*)–the best possible realistic assessment of the required duration without allowing for unforseeable contingencies;
pessimistic (p)–the longer duration that would be required if possible contingencies are allowed for;
optimistic (a)–the shortest duration within which the activity could be accomplished if all circumstances worked out favourably.

A formula is used to calculate the 'planned' expected time (t_e) as the position on a beta curve giving 0.50 probability:

$$t_e = \frac{a + 4m + p}{6}, \qquad variance = \left(\frac{p - a}{6}\right)^2$$

The use of the 3 time estimates, especially if they are used in the revision of estimates at the updating reviews, makes the availability of a computer service the more valuable.

Example 10.2   An example in using PERT is from a company which has an old generator which has to be removed and then replaced by the later model. This procedure has been performed many times and a careful collection of data has been maintained. The removal time of the generator is as follows:

Generator removal

Time (hours)	1	2	3	4	5	6	
Frequency	3	18	11	9	7	2	Total 50

The engineers responsible estimate the times for fitting the new generator (which has not been done before) and these are as follows:

Most optimistic time	$(a) =$	2 hours
Most likely time	$(m) =$	6 hours
Most pessimistic time	$(p) =$	13 hours

A time estimate is required to the nearest hour for the completion of both jobs, using a 0.95 confidence level.

Calculating the *standard deviation*:

Duration (hours)		Frequency	
x	f	fx	fx^2
1	3	3	3
2	18	36	72
3	11	33	99
4	9	36	144
5	7	35	175
6	2	12	72
	$\Sigma f = 50$	$\Sigma fx = 155$	$\Sigma fx^2 = 565$

Generator removal:

$$\text{Mean } \bar{x}_1 = \frac{\Sigma fx}{\Sigma f} = \frac{155}{50} = 3.1$$

Variance:

$$(\sigma x_1)^2 = \frac{\Sigma fx^2}{\Sigma f} - \bar{x}_1^2$$

$$= \frac{565}{50} - 3.1^2$$

$$= 11.3 - 9.61$$

$$= 1.69$$

Generator fitting:

$$\text{Mean } \bar{x}_2 = \frac{a + 4m + p}{6} = \frac{2 + 24 + 13}{6} = 6.5$$

Variance:

$$(\sigma x_2)^2 = \left(\frac{13 - 2}{6}\right)^2 = 1.83^2 = 3.34$$

The combined mean for removal and fitting

$$= \bar{x}_1 + \bar{x}_2 = 3.1 + 6.5 = 9.6$$

The combined variances

$$(\sigma x_1)^2 + (\sigma x_2)^2 = 1.69 + 3.34 = 5.03$$

$\therefore$ Standard deviation for removal and fitting combined $= \sqrt{5.03} = 2.23$

Using normal curve tables (see Table 8, p. 220):

$$-Z = \frac{x - \bar{x}}{\sigma}$$

$$= 1.645 = \frac{x - 9.6}{2.23}$$

$\therefore$ $\quad (2.23 \times 1.645) + 9.6$

$$= 3.66 + 9.6$$

$$= 13.26$$

Therefore, time estimate to complete both jobs $\simeq 13\frac{1}{4}$ hours.

Example 10.3 A problem, putting together all the stages developed so far in this chapter, consists of a small project having six activities:

Estimation of duration (days)

Activities	Optimistic	Most likely	Pessimistic
1–2	3	7	9
1–3	3	4	7
2–4	2	4	6
3–5	1	3	4
2–5	6	8	9
4–5	5	7	9

The network is required together with the critical path. A list of total float, mean duration and standard deviation is also required.

The scheduled date for event 5 has been given as 19 days. What is the probability of this being achieved? If event 4 is delayed by 2 days, what is the probability of the project being completed on time?

We first draw the network (see Figure 10.7). From the network we find the critical path to be 1–2–4–5, totalling 18 days.

For activity 1–2, which has an expected duration time of 7 days, the mean time is calculated:

$$\bar{x} = \frac{a + 4m + p}{6} = \frac{3 + 28 + 9}{6} \simeq 6.6$$

and the variance

$$\sigma^2 = \left(\frac{p - a}{6}\right)^2 = \left(\frac{9 - 3}{6}\right)^2 = 1$$

and

$$\sigma = \sqrt{1} = 1$$

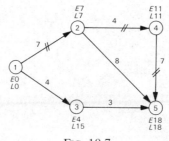

FIG. 10.7

The remaining calculations follow the same procedure for each activity in the network:

Activities	Expected duration time (days)	Standard deviation	Variance	Total float
1–2	7	1	1	0*
1–3	4	0.66	0.44	11
2–4	4	0.66	0.44	0*
3–5	3	0.5	0.25	11
2–5	8	0.5	0.25	3
4–5	7	0.66	0.44	0*

*on the critical path.

The scheduled dated for event 5 has been given as 19 days and the probability of achieving this is calculated using activities on the critical path 1–2–4–5:

Activities	Variance
1–2	1.00
2–4	0.44
4–5	0.44
Total	1.88

$$\therefore \sigma = \sqrt{1.88} \simeq 1.37$$

Probability

$$= \frac{19 - 18}{1.37} = \frac{1}{1.37} = 0.73.$$

Thus the probability of achieving the date scheduled for event 5 is $1.00 - 0.233 = 76.7$ per cent.

With event 4 possibility being delayed by 2 days and with this event being critical the mean completion time will be $18 + 2 = 20$ days.

The axis value in the standard normal distribution $= (19 - 20)/1.37 = -0.73$.

$\therefore$ probability that the scheduled date for completion will be achieved is 23.3 per cent.

No consideration has been given to costs in the analysis of projects. This must be included if an optimum plan is to be obtained.

Example 10.4 The network shown in Figure 10.8 has 6 activities and each of the activities uses resources which costs £90 per week. An additional indirect cost of £200 for every week the project is in progress is chargeable.

The total project cost consists of   33 weeks × £200 =   6600
         (Activity *A*)   19 weeks ×   90 =   1710
         (Activity *B*)   11 weeks ×   90 =   990
         (Activity *C*)   3 weeks ×   90 =   270
         (Activity *D*)   11 weeks ×   90 =   990
         (Activity *E*)   3 weeks ×   90 =   270
         (Activity *F*)   3 weeks ×   90 =   270

                                          £11100

It is found possible to reduce the times on each activity but at a cost and these are calculated to be:

Activity	Cost (per week saved)
A	125
B	75
C	60
D	180
E	250
F	400

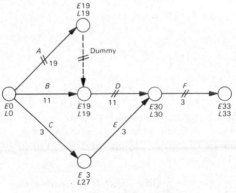

FIG. 10.8

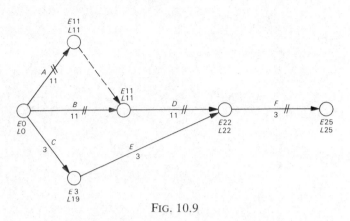

FIG. 10.9

Commencing with the lowest cost per week, activity C at £60 per week, we find that as this activity is not on a critical path, no reduction in the over-all project time would be possible. This is also applies to the next highest, activity B at £75 per week. When reviewing activity A at £125 per week, this being on the critical path enables us to consider this for reduction. The maximum amount we can reduce this activity is by 8 weeks because the remaining activities would still ensure an over-all project time of 25 weeks (see Figure 10.9).

The next highest cost is activity D at £180 per week, and the maximum amount of weeks it can be reduced is 10, which will reduce the over-all project time to 15 weeks (see Figure 10.10).

Our final reduction is achieved by considering both activities A and B at £125 and £75 per week respectively. These are the lowest costs we can consider on the critical paths. Both A and B can be reduced by 6

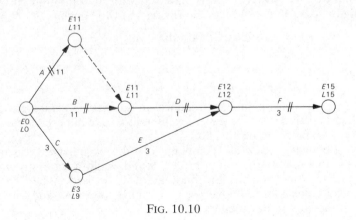

FIG. 10.10

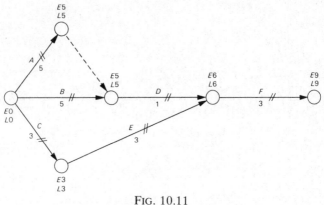

FIG. 10.11

weeks, giving an over-all final project time of 9 weeks (see Figure 10.11).

A survey of these reductions gives:

	Reducing	by	Cost	Saving	Balance	Project duration
(1)	Activity A	8 weeks	8 × 125	8 × 200	£600	25
(2)	Activity D	10 weeks	10 × 180	10 × 200	£200	15
(3)	Activity A	5 weeks	5 × 125	5 × 200	£375	9
	Activity B	5 weeks	5 × 75	5 × 200	£625	9
				Total	£1800	

The final over-all project time is 9 weeks, with the optimum cost being the original cost of £11100 less the saving of £1800 giving

$$£11100 - £1800 = £9300 \text{ total cost}$$

Exercises 10

10.1 A company is planning to launch an advertising campaign for the introduction of a new car. They intend to make full use of television, newspapers and poster display.

Following careful planning of the campaign a suitable photograph of the car must be found while a carefully worded article to accompany the photograph is devised. When both are ready blocks of the advertisement will be prepared and forwarded to the chosen newspapers.

A suitable poster is to be designed to give the necessary impact, but again the Managing Director must give approval before any printing is carried out. Posters will be sent to U.K. distributors. A special poster for overseas distributors will be designed; these posters will be sent out before those for the U.K.

After planning the campaign a television contract will be negotiated and a commercial then made.

Before any advertising is carried out the campaign advertising agency will plan a special day for launching the campaign so that television, newspaper and poster advertising is carried out at the same time.

(i) Draw the network and show the critical path.
(ii) State the over-all project time.
(iii) What would the effect be on the project time if the printing of the poster was 1 week late?
(iv) The car photograph was found later to have taken 6 weeks instead of the 2 already planned. Would this affect the over-all project time?

Activities	Duration (weeks)
Plan campaign	3
Write newspaper article	1
Forward advert to newspaper	1
Plan advertising launch date	2
Sign television contract	2
Make television commercial	3
Design overseas poster	2
Print poster	1
Forward poster to U.K. distributors	2
Forward poster to overseas distributors	3
Managing Director approves poster	1
Obtain car photograph	2
Design U.K. poster	3
Prepare blocks for newspaper	2
Managing Director approves newspaper article	1

10.2 Plantex Ltd are to expand their horticultural business, and this will require the following activities to be carried out. The present manager has stated that all activities must be carried out in the order given. However, the owner considers that many activities could be carried out at the same time.

The ground owned by Plantex Ltd, adjacent to the present site, has an old manor house which requires demolition, the site cleared and roses planted ready for budding and the ground open to the public.

Activities	Duration (weeks)
Clear site	6
Analyse soil	2
Plough ground	1
Fertilise soil	1
Obtain rose stock	2
Plant rose stock	2
Bud roses	3
Plan entrance to site	2
Obtain planning permission for entrance	4
Construct entrance	3
Obtain trees	2
Plant trees around site	3
Advertise for office staff	1
Interview staff	1
Rose field open to the public	1

Planning is to be done after site clearance. You are invited to plan the network and state a date when you consider the rose field could be open to the public. What would be the effect if the budding of stock takes an extra 1 week?

Bibliography

A. Battersby, *Network Analysis for Planning and Scheduling* (London: Macmillan, 1967).

C. Berge, *The Theory of Graphs and its Applications*, trans. A. Diog (London: Methuen, 1962).

R. G. Busacker and T. L. Saaty, *Finite Graphs and Networks* (New York: McGraw-Hill, 1965).

A. Fletcher and G. Clarke, *Management and Mathematics* (London: Business Publications, 1964).

L. R. Ford Jr and D. R. Fulkerson, *Flows in Networks* (Princeton University Press, 1962).

A. Kaufmann, *Graphs, Dynamic Programming and Finite Games*, trans. H. C. Sneyd (New York: Academic Press, 1967).

J. G. Kemey, A. Scheleifer Jr, J. L. Snell and G. L. Thompson, *Finite Mathematics with Business Applications* (Englewood Cliffs, N.J.: Prentice-Hall, 1962).

J. F. Muth and G. L. Thompson (eds.), *Industrial Scheduling* (Englewood Cliffs, N.J.: Prentice-Hall, 1963).

G. Thornley (ed.), *Critical Path Analysis in Practice* (London: Tavistock, 1968).

H. S. Woodgate, *Planning by Network* (London: Business Publications, 1967).

Answers, Hints and Solutions to Exercises

Exercises 2, pages 23–4

2.1 (i) Adapt Figure 2.1. Draw the time scale as before, 1 horizontal line for Clerk A, 1 for B. Number workers consecutively, showing service time for each. (ii) Repeat outlines, but show breaks as data require.

2.2 (i) 30.6 min. (ii) 53.3 per cent.

2.3 (ii) 1.29. (iii) (a) decrease of 0.075/hr, (b) increase of 0.1481/hr.

2.4 (i) approx. 79 days. (ii) approx. 7 days.

2.5 Follow general method of Example 2.3. Select reasonably wide limits, e.g. 9 min. to 15 min., and show proportion within these limits is comparatively small. Variability would decrease.

2.6 Self-service rate 40/hr, traffic intensity 0.75. Average 2.25 people queueing, 3 in system, measured over whole time. Based on time that queues occur, queue length averages 4. Pump not being used on average 25 per cent of time. On the average customer queues for $4\frac{1}{2}$ min. before pump is free.

2.7 (i) (a) Decrease of 62.5 per cent. (b) Decrease of 58.3 per cent. (c) Increase of 16.7 per cent. (ii) In theory as the calculations are based on average arrival rates and service times, we could devise a particular situation where a large number of clerks were inadequate for a very short time. In practice the probability would be so low as to be ignored.

2.9 (ii) 32 min. 57 sec.

2.10 (i) 1.27 hr. (ii) 39 min.

Exercises 3, pages 46–8

3.1 (i) Simulate 6 days' purchases and, independently, 6 days' demands. (iii) Consider balance of plus and minus values in (1), as well as arithmetic means of purchases and of demand.

3.2 Simulate 10 arrival times, number the customers and mark these times on a scale. Draw parallel lines to correspond with this scale to show activity at check-out A and at check-out B, customer going to vacant check-out or shorter queue. Analyse the graph values to give average queueing times, lengths, times when check-out unused, etc.

3.3 Follow general method of Example 3.6, using Table 6 on p. 212.

3.4 Draw a time-scale of about 12 min., marked in $\frac{1}{4}$ min. intervals, with a line for fitter A and one for fitter B. Simulate separately demand times for each of the 4 machines. Relate these chronologically to the lines for A and B. Estimate in unit time such values as: extent each fitter is occupied; extent to which they are both occupied; times when machines are running, not running, awaiting service, being serviced. Consider how situation would be affected by increasing number of fitters or number of machines.

3.5 Draw a graph and follow the general method of Example 3.7.

Exercises 4, pages 80–4

4.1 (i) (b) 2471 m. calls, (c) 2472.4 m. calls. (ii) for (i) (b) -76.1 m. calls, for (i) (c) 2 m. calls. Both lines are a fairly good fit, but the second, as expected, is the better.

4.2 (ii) 1.08, or 8 per cent increase for each year on the year before. (iii) 241.9 (000s kWh). (ii) is only an average, and the separate rates vary, e.g. compare 1964–5 rate with 1973–4.

4.3 (i) Trend values, 3rd quarter 1965, 98.45, others in order are 93.90, 93.21, 92.75, 93.61, 96.70, 99.25, 102.85. (ii) Data inadequate to establish a trend, which falls and rises over 3 years. Seasonal pattern not strong. Moving average covers only two years' run.

4.4 1964 value is £4299 (000s); others in order are, same units, 4270, 4359, 4567, 4894, 5338, 5902, 6583, 7383, 8301, 9338. Some help, but price changes may affect sales of products in different ways. We have to assume that the pen/refill ratio is reasonably constant, whereas sales of pens without refills may be increasing more quickly than the other type.

4.5 Starting with Jan 1965 percentage yield (%) = 8.12, 8.44, 9.772, 9.091, 9.386, 9.659, 10.095, 10.449, 9.662, 8.994, 8.429, 8.150, 7.998, 7.795, 7.681, 7.629, 7.514, 7.289, 7.114, 7.408, 7.772, 7.923, 8.117, 8.154, 8.065. Starting with Jan 1965 errors (%) = -0.8, -0.83, 0.202, -0.739, -0.684, -1.091, -0.885, 1.969, 1.672, 1.414, 0.699, 0.38, 0.508, 0.285, 0.131, 0.289, 0.564, 0.439, -0.386, -0.912, -0.378, -0.487, -0.093, 0.224, 0.135. In this example total differences = + 1.626 per cent with $-$ and errors almost equal in numbers, suggesting that this is a better fit than in the text example. But $\alpha = 0.4$ is rather high, and if the forecast follows the original data too closely, the smoothing effect is reduced.

4.6 (i) $\dfrac{250}{100} \times \dfrac{50}{100} \times \dfrac{80}{100} = 1$, i.e. successive applications of the 3 indices over a year leaves the trend unchanged. (ii) 1970 – 1st 4-month period is 250 per cent up on the trend, so that the trend is $\dfrac{100}{250} \times \dfrac{200}{1} = 80$ (000s). Applying the other indices gives a linear trend, 75, 60, 55, etc. (000s). 1973 trend figures are 25, 20 and 15, giving forecasts of 62.5, 10 and 12 (000s).

Exercises 5, pages 95–6

5.1 (i) (a) £1667,   (b) £1000,   (c) £333.   (ii) (a) £1765/day,   (b) £1963/day. Under (i) stock declines in a straight line, but in (ii) the decline is by a convex curve above the straight line.

5.2 No – average costs are £84 (old) and £87.575 and £92.76 new.

5.3 141 units. Size is proportional to $\sqrt{}$ (order cost), e.g. if order cost goes up 4 times, size goes up twice.

5.4 To minimise average costs, order 95 at a time. i.e. about 21 times a year.

5.5 (i) Minimum level should be 254 units. (ii) (a) No, (b) No. In each case we can only be 95 per cent certain.

Exercises 6, pages 117–18

6.1 Let x_1 = number of units Fishol produced
Let x_2 = number of units Fiship produced

Restrictions

$$(1) \qquad 20x_1 + 10x_2 = 800 \qquad \text{(material, } ACO\text{)}$$
$$\text{when} \qquad x_1 = 0, x_2 = 80$$
$$x_2 = 0, x_1 = 40$$

$$(2) \qquad 10x_1 + 20x_2 = 700 \qquad \text{(skilled labour)}$$
$$\text{when} \qquad x_1 = 0 \ x_2 = 35$$
$$x_2 = 0 \ x_1 = 70$$

(3) $10x_2 = 300$ (semi-skilled labour)
                  $x_2 = 30$

Objective function

$$10x_1 + 10x_2 = \text{(say) } 400 \qquad \text{(maximise)}$$

when $x_1 = 0, x_2 = 40$
          $x_2 = 0, x_1 = 40$

From Figure A.1 the last point touched entering a non-feasible region is *C*. Best plan reading off the graph is produce:

    30 units of Fishol, and
    20 units of Fiship

Net contribution $= (10 \times 30) + (10 \times 20) = 300 + 200 = £500$

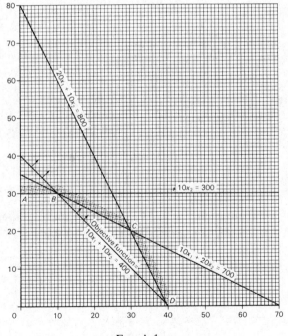

FIG. A.1

6.2 Let A = number of A products produced per week
Let B = number of B products produced per week

Restrictions

(1) $A + 2B \leq 3000$ (spot-welding restriction)
       when $A = 0, B = 1500$
              $B = 0, A = 3000$

(2) $4A + 3B \leq 6000$ (time restriction)
       when $A = 0, B = 2000$
              $B = 0, A = 1500$

(3) $A \leq 1000$ (production restriction)

(4) $B \geq 1000$ (contract restriction)

Objective function

       $0.5A + 0.25B$ = (say) 1000   (maximise)
       when $A = 0, B = 4000$
              $B = 0, A = 2000$

1 From Figure A.2 the farthest point reached on the feasible region is
  where $A = 750$ and $B = 1000$, i.e. at a. Maximum = (0.5×750) +
  $(0.25 \times 1000) = 375 + 250 = £625$.
2 From Figure A.2 the farthest point reached in the new feasible region
  is where $A = 1000$ and $B = 667$, i.e. at b. Maximum = (0.5×1000) +
  $(0.25 \times 667) = 500 + 167 = £667$,   an   increase   in   profit   of
  $667 - 625 = £42$.

6.3 Let x = number of small electrical switches produced per day
Let y = number of large electrical switches produced per day

Restrictions

       $\frac{2}{3}x + 1y = 3000$ (transport)
       $1x + 1y = 4000$ (electrical contacts)
              $1y = 2400$ (copper wire and screws)
       $1x + 1y = 2000$ (labour)

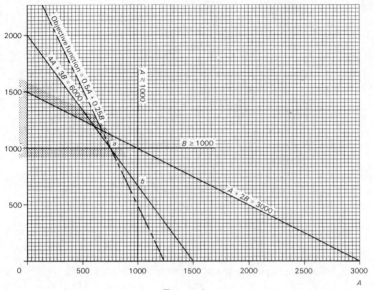

FIG. A.2

Objective function

$$5x + 7y = \text{maximum}$$

Equation for table

$$2x + 3y + a = 9000$$
$$x + y + b = 4000$$
$$y + c = 2400$$
$$x + y = d + 2000$$

Profit = $5x + 7y$

1st table

x	y	a	b	c	d	Quantity
2	3	1	0	0	0	9000
1	1	0	1	0	0	4000
0	1	0	0	1	0	2400
−1	−1	0	0	0	1	−2000
−5	−7	0	0	0	0	0

Either x or y could be brought in. Here x is chosen:

2nd table

x	y	a	b	c	d	Quantity
0	1	1	−2	0	0	1000
1	1	0	1	0	0	4000
0	1	0	0	1	0	2400
0	0	0	1	0	1	2000
0	−2	0	5	0	0	20000

3rd table

x	y	a	b	c	d	Quantity
0	1	1	−2	−	0	1000
1	0	−1	3	0	0	3000
0	0	−1	2	1	0	1400
0	0	0	1	0	1	2000
0	0	2	1	0	0	22000

Interpreting the final table: manufacture 3000 small electrical switches, and 1000 large electrical switches, giving 1400 copper wire and screws, profit £220 and labour utilisation equal to the minimum agreed.

6.4 Let x_1 = number of products A produced per hour
Let x_2 = number of products B produced per hour

Restrictions

$$2x_1 + 6x_2 \leq 66 \text{ (machine } X)$$
$$8x_1 + 4x_2 \leq 120 \text{ (machine } Y)$$
$$4x_1 + 8x_2 \leq 96 \text{ (machine } Z)$$

Objective function

$$16x_1 + 12x_2 = \text{maximum}$$

Equations for table

$$2x_1 + 6x_2 + x_3 = 66$$
$$8x_1 + 4x_2 + x_4 = 120$$
$$4x_1 + 8x_2 + x_5 = 96$$

Profit $= 16x_1 + 12x_2$

1st table

x_1	x_2	x_3	x_4	x_5	Quantity
2	6	1	0	0	66
8	4	0	1	0	120
4	8	0	0	1	96
-16	-12	0	0	0	0

Either x_1 or x_2, can be introduced. Here x_1 is chosen:

2nd table

x_1	x_2	x_3	x_4	x_5	Quantity
0	5	1	$-\frac{1}{4}$	0	36
1	$\frac{1}{3}$	0	$\frac{1}{3}$	0	15
0	6	0	$-\frac{1}{2}$	1	36
0	-8	0	2	0	

3rd table

x_1	x_2	x_3	x_4	x_5	Quantity
0	0	1	$\frac{1}{6}$	$-\frac{5}{6}$	6
1	0	0	$\frac{1}{12}$	$-\frac{1}{12}$	12
0	1	0	$-\frac{1}{12}$	$\frac{1}{6}$	6
0	0	0	$\frac{4}{12}$	$\frac{8}{12}$	

The required number to produce is 12 of Product *A* and 6 of Product *B*.

Exercises 7, pages 139–41

7.1

Centres

Factories

	R_1 4	R_2 4	R_3 5	
A_1 0	(40) 4	(30) 4	3	70
B_1 1	6	−10 (30) 5	+10 0	30
C_1 −2	4	+10 (40) 2	−10 (10) 3	50
D_1 0	8	2	(50) 5	50
	40	100	60	

Squares		
	A_1R_3	$5 + 0 - 3 = 2$
	B_1R_1	$4 + 1 - 6 = -1$
	B_1R_3	$5 + 1 - 0 = 6$
	C_1R_1	$4 + (-2) - 4 = -2$
	D_1R_1	$4 + 0 - 8 = -4$
	D_1R_2	$4 + 0 - 2 = 2$

The square B_1R_3 receives allocation as it has the highest figure:

Centres

		R_1 4	R_2 4	R_3 -1	
A_1 0		(40) \ 4	(30) \ 4	3	70
B_1 1		6	-20 (20) \ 5	$+20$ (10) \ 0	30
C_1 -2		4	(50) \ 2	3	50
D_1 6		8	$+20$ 2	-20 (50) \ 5	50
		40	100	60	

Factories (label at left of C_1 row)

Squares		
A_1R_3	$0 + (-1) - 3$	$= -4$
B_1R_1	$1 + 4 - 6$	$= -1$
C_1R_1	$-2 + 4 - 4$	$= -2$
C_1R_3	$-2 + (-1) - 3$	$= -6$
D_1R_1	$6 + 4 - 8$	$= 2$
D_1R_2	$6 + 4 - 2$	$= 8$

The square D_1R_2 receives attention as it has the highest figure:

Centres

	R_1 4	R_2 4	R_3 7	
A_1 0	⑷⓪ 4	③⓪ −30 4	+30 3	70
B_1 −7	6	5	③⓪ 0	30
C_1 −2	4	⑤⓪ 2	3	50
D_1 −2	8	②⓪ +30 2	③⓪ −30 5	50
	40	100	60	

Factories (row label at left)

Squares

A_1R_3	$0 + 7 - 3 = 4$
B_1R_1	$-7 + 4 - 6 = -9$
B_1R_2	$-7 + 4 - 5 = -8$
C_1R_1	$-2 + 4 - 4 = -2$
C_1R_3	$-2 + 7 - 3 = 2$
D_1R_1	$-2 + 4 - 8 = -6$

The square A_1R_3 now receives attention:

Centres

		R_1 4	R_2 4	R_3 3	
A_1	0	(40) 4	(0) 4	(30) 3	70
B_1	-3	6	5	(30) 0	30
C_1	-2	4	(50) 2	3	50
D_4	-2	8	(50) 2	5	50
		40	100	60	

Squares
$$
\begin{aligned}
B_1R_1 \quad & -3+4-6=-5 \\
B_1R_2 \quad & -3+4-5=-4 \\
C_1R_1 \quad & -2+4-4=-2 \\
C_1R_3 \quad & -2+3-3=-2 \\
D_1R_1 \quad & -2+4-8=-6 \\
D_1R_3 \quad & -2+3-5=-4
\end{aligned}
$$

The rates which will produce the minimum costs and the amounts to be transported are:

A_1 to R_1 — 40 units
A_1 to R_3 — 30 units
B_1 to R_3 — 30 units
C_1 to R_2 — 50 units
D_1 to R_2 — 50 units

Calculations give negative figures, thus an optimum solution.

7.2 (i) A dummy mine must be added, to enable the mine production to balance the special processes capacity:

1st table

	Decca 80	Polydor 75	Alvis 85	Regent 105	Dummy −25	
Process 1 0	−1000 (14000) [80]	+1000 (1000) [75]	[130]	[150]	[0]	15000
Process 2 10	+1000 [60]	−1000 (11000) [85]	(4000) [95]	[90]	[0]	15000
Process 3 25	[135]	[100]	(5000) [110]	(5000) [130]	(5000) [0]	15000
	14000	12000	9000	5000	5000	45000 / 45000

Squares	P1A	$85 + 0 - 130$	$= -45$	
	P1R	$105 + 0 - 150$	$= -45$	
	P1 Dummy	$-25 + 0 - 0$	$= -25$	
	P2D	$10 + 80 - 60$	$= +30$	(highest number)
	P2R	$10 + 105 - 90$	$= +25$	
	P2 Dummy	$10 - 25 + 0$	$= -15$	
	P3D	$25 + 80 - 135$	$= -30$	
	P3P	$25 + 75 - 100$	$= 0$	

2nd table

	D 80	P 75	A 115	R 135	Dummy 5	
Process 1 0	(13000) 80	(2000) 75	130	150	0	15000
Process 2 −20	(1000) 60	(1000) 85	−4000 (4000) 95	+4000 90	0	15000
Process 3 −5	135	100	+4000 (5000) 110	−4000 (5000) 130	(5000) 0	15000
	14000	12000	9000	5000	5000	45000 / 45000

Squares	P1A	$115 + 0 - 130$	$= -15$	
	P1R	$135 + 0 - 150$	$= -15$	
	P1 Dummy	$5 + 0 - 0$	$= + 5$	
	P2P	$-20 + 75 - 80$	$= -30$	
	P2R	$-20 + 135 - 90$	$= +25$	(highest number)
	P2 Dummy	$-20 + 5 - 0$	$= -15$	
	P3D	$-5 + 80 - 135$	$= -60$	
	P3P	$-5 + 75 - 100$	$= -30$	

3rd table

	D 80	P 75	A 90	R 110	Dummy −20	
Process 1 0	(3000) 80	(12000) 75	130	150	0	15000
Process 2 −20	(11000) 60	85	95	(4000) 90	0	15000
Process 3 20	135	100	(9000) 110	(1000) 130	(5000) 0	15000
	14000	12000	9000	5000	5000	45000 / 45000

Squares

P1A	90 + 0 − 130	=	−40
P1R	110 + 0 − 150	=	−40
P1 Dummy	−20 + 0 − 0	=	−20
P2P	75 − 20 − 85	=	−30
P2A	90 − 20 − 95	=	−25
P3 Dummy	20 − 20 − 0	=	0
P3D	80 + 20 − 135	=	−35
P3P	75 + 20 − 100	=	− 5

All figures are zero or negative; thus this is an optimum solution.

(ii) The optimum plan is as follows:

From	to	Quantity	Cost/unit	Total cost	Cruzieros (crs)
Decca	Process	1	3000	80	240000
Decca	Process	2	11000	60	660000
Polydor	Process	1	12000	75	900000
Regent	Process	2	4000	90	360000
Alvis	Process	3	9000	110	990000
Regent	Process	3	1000	130	130000
					3280000

To the extent shown in the dummy the capacity of process 3 is not fully utilised, i.e. 5000 tons.

Exercises 8, pages 148–49

8.1 *Step 1* Subtract the smallest element of each row from all elements of the row:

From sites

		A	B	C	D	E	F
	1	16	47	14	27	0	26
	2	0	7	27	43	59	28
To sites	3	0	12	33	24	5	5
	4	8	13	11	15	0	6
	5	3	14	13	0	4	7
	6	52	10	10	30	21	0

Step 2 Subtract the minimum element of each column from all other elements of the column:

From sites

		A	B	C	D	E	F
	1	16	40	4	27	0	26
	2	0	0	17	43	59	28
To sites	3	0	4	23	24	5	5
	4	8	6	1	15	0	6
	5	3	7	3	0	4	7
	6	52	3	0	30	21	0

Step 3 Draw the minimum number of lines to cover all zeros:

From sites

		A	B	C	D	E	F
	1	16	40	4	27	0	26
	2	0	0	17	43	59	28
To sites	3	0	4	23	24	5	5
	4	8	6	1	15	0	6
	5	3	7	3	0	4	7
	6	52	3	0	30	2	0

Step 4 Subtract the smallest element not covered by any line from the remaining elements not covered by any line:

From sites

		A	B	C	D	E	F
	1	16	40	3	27	[0]	25
	2	0	[0]	16	43	59	27
To sites	3	[0]	4	22	24	5	4
	4	8	6	[0]	15	0	5
	5	3	7	2	[0]	4	6
	6	53	4	0	31	22	[0]

The maximum assignment shown is $\boxed{0}$; from sites

A–3 at 37 miles
B–2 at 39 miles
C–4 at 58 miles
D–5 at 36 miles
E–1 at 35 miles
F–6 at 40 miles

Total mileage = 245.

8.2 *Step 1* Subtract the smallest element of each row from all elements in that row:

	1	2	3	4	5
A	1	4	10	0	9
B	2	7	5	16	0
C	17	8	0	9	12
D	6	14	13	0	13
E	10	14	0	8	6

Step 2 Subtract the smallest element of each column from all other elements of the column:

	1	2	3	4	5
A	0	0	10	0	9
B	1	3	5	16	0
C	16	4	0	9	12
D	5	10	13	0	13
E	0	10	0	8	6

Step 3 Draw the minimum number of lines to cover all zeros:

	1	2	3	4	5
A	0	0	10	0	9
B	1	3	5	16	0
C	16	4	0	9	12
D	5	10	13	0	13
E	9	10	0	8	6

Step 4 Subtract the smallest element not covered by any line from the remaining elements not covered by any line. Add this amount to the elements where the lines intersect:

	1	2	3	4	5
A	[0]	⊠	14	4	9
B	1	3	9	20	[0]
C	12	[0]	⊠	9	8
D	1	6	13	[0]	9
E	5	6	[0]	8	2

Maximum assignment shown is [0] :

Doctor Residence 1 to area *A* at 21 min.
Doctor Residence 2 to area *C* at 25 min.
Doctor Residence 3 to area *E* at 21 min.
Doctor Residence 4 to area *D* at 25 min.
Doctor Residence 5 to area *B* at 22 min.

Exercises 9, pages 158–60

9.1

Maintenance totals
Year-end of sale

Year of purchase		1	2	3	4	5
	0	48	109	186	282	406
	1		61	138	234	358
	2			77	173	297
	3				96	220
	4					124

Depreciation totals
Year-end of sale

Year of purchase		1	2	3	4	5
	0	160	280	390	480	550
	1		210	320	410	480
	2			180	270	340
	3				150	220
	4					120

Total cost
Year-end of sale

		1	2	3	4	5
	0	208	389	576	762	956
	1		271	458	644	838
Year of purchase	2			257	443	637
	3				246	440
	4					244

Average costs
Year-end of sale

		1	2	3	4	5
	0	208	194	192	(190)	191
	1		271	229	214	209
Year of purchase	2			257	221	212
	3				246	220
	4					244

The best policy would be to buy a new press and replace after 4 years.

9.2 Calculating the mean life:

Month (m)	Probability of failure (p)	mp
1	$0.05 = p_1$	0.05
2	$0.10 = p_2$	0.20
3	0.20	0.60
4	0.25	1.00
5	0.20	1.00
6	0.20	1.20
	Total	4.05

Mean life = 4.05 months.

Taking a batch of 100, the average number of failures per month

$$= \frac{100}{4.05} \simeq 24$$

Cost of a steady-state replacement = 24 × £1 = £24 per month. The cost of individual replacement in the *first month* with probability of failure at 5 per cent = $100 \times \frac{1}{20}$ = 5.5 at £1 = £5 plus replacement of all at the end of the month = 100 at £0.25 = £25.

$$\text{Total cost} = £25 + £5 = £30$$

We require the failures for *month 2*. Let $f_0 = 100$ items:

Replacements at month 1 $f_1 = p_1 f_0 = 0.05 \times 100 = 5$
Replacements at month 2 $f_2 = p_2 f_0 + p_1 f_1 = (0.10 \times 100)$
$$+ (0.05 \times 5) = 10 + 0.25 \simeq 11$$
(next nearest whole number)

Therefore, total for 2 months = 5 + 11 = 16.
Total cost for a two-month policy is

$$\frac{11 + 24}{2} = \frac{35}{2} = £17.50/\text{month}$$

It would be more economical to have the 2-month policy.

9.3 Consider individual replacement. Here the failures occur at random during the month and not just at the end of the month. These must be replaced individually at the time:

Average life

(p_1) $0.10 \times \frac{1}{2}$ $= 0.05$
(p_2) $0.20 \times 1\frac{1}{2} = 0.30$
(p_3) $0.30 \times 2\frac{1}{2} = 0.75$
(p_4) $0.30 \times 3\frac{1}{2} = 1.05$
(p_5) $0.10 \times 4\frac{1}{2} = 0.45$
                      ————
              Total 2.60
                      ————

Average life = 2.6 months.

The average cost/month is

$$\frac{50 \times 5}{2.6} = \frac{250}{2.6} \simeq £96$$

To consider group replacement and the number which is replaced during a period of 8 months:

$f_0 = 50$ *Cumulative*
$f_1 = f_0 p_1 = 50 \times 0.10$ 5
$f_2 = f_0 p_2 + f_1 p_1 = 10 + 1$ 16
$f_3 = f_0 p_3 + f_1 p_2 + f_2 p_1 = 15 + 1 + 1$ 33
$f_4 = f_0 p_3 + f_1 p_3 + f_2 p_2 + f_3 p_1 = 15 + 2 + 2 + 2$ 51
$f_5 = f_0 p_5 + f_1 p_4 + f_2 p_3 + f_3 p_2 + f_4 p_1 = 5 + 2 + 3 + 2 + 2$ 65
$f_6 = \quad\quad f_1 p_5 + f_2 p_4 + f_3 p_3 + f_4 p_2 + f_5 p_1 = 1 + 3 + 5 + 4 + 2$ 80
$f_7 = \quad\quad\quad\quad f_2 p_5 + f_3 p_4 + f_4 p_3 + f_5 p_2 + f_6 p_1$ 97
$f_8 = \quad\quad\quad\quad\quad f_3 p_5 + f_4 p_4 + f_5 p_3 + f_6 p_2 + f_7 p_1$ 117

Cost of group replacement:

Interval months	Individual cost	Total cost	Total cost per month
1	$5 \times 5 = 25$	125	125
2	$16 \times 5 = 80$	180	90
3	$33 \times 5 = 165$	265	88
4	$51 \times 5 = 255$	355	89
5	$65 \times 5 = 325$	425	85
6	$80 \times 5 = 400$	500	83
7	$97 \times 5 = 485$	585	84
8	$117 \times 5 = 585$	685	86

Group policy would be to group replace during the sixth month.

Machine tool X

Year	Capital cost (£)	Maintenance cost (£)	Cumulative maintenance cost (£)	Total cost to end of year	K	Present worth total cost (£)	Present worth of average cost/year (£)
1	18000	1200	1200	19200	0.909	17450	17450
2		1400	2600	20600	0.826	17000	8500
3		1900	4500	22500	0.751	16900	5633
4		2200	6700	24700	0.683	16850	4215
5		5000	11700	29700	0.621	18450	3690
6		8000	19700	37700	0.564	21250	3541

Machine tool Y

Year	Capital cost (£)	Mainten- ance cost (£)	Cumulative mainten- ance cost (£)	Total cost to end of year	K	Present worth total cost (£)	Present worth of average cosy/year (£)
1	20000	260	260	20260	0.909	18400	18400
2		420	680	20680	0.826	17050	8525
3		900	1580	21580	0.751	16180	5395
4		1200	2780	22780	0.683	15500	3872
5		2500	5280	25280	0.621	15700	3140
6		3500	8780	28780	0.564	16200	2700

Consider only the 6-year period, machine tool X and also machine tool Y should be replaced after the 6-year period. A possible review of mainten- ance costs and estimate of the seventh year costs would be worth while and should be investigated.

Exercises 10, pages 174–6

10.1 See Figure A.3:

Key to network	Activity	Duration (weeks)
1–2	Plan campaign	3
2–3	Obtain car photograph	2
2–7	Write article for newspaper	1
2–6	Design poster for U.K.	3
2–4	Design poster for overseas	2
2–5	Sign television contract	2
3–7	Dummy	0
4–6	Dummy	0
5–13	Television commercial	3
6–8	Managing Director approval of poster	1
7–11	Prepare blocks	2
11–12	Managing Director approves news- paper article	1
8–9	Print poster	1
9–10	Forward posters to overseas distributor	3
10–13	Forward posters to U.K. distributor	2
12–13	Forward photograph and article to newspaper	1
13–14	Launch date planned	2

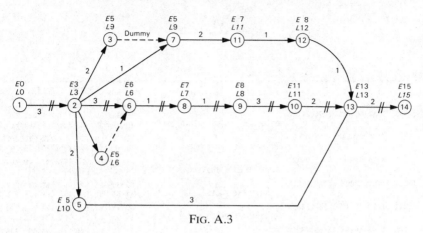

FIG. A.3

(i) Critical path 1–2–6–8–9–10–13–14.
(ii) Over-all project date = 15 weeks.
(iii) The over-all project time would be increased by 1 week unless other activities on the critical path can be increased by a total of 1 week.
(iv) No. Providing the time is not exceeded, the over-all project time would not be affected.

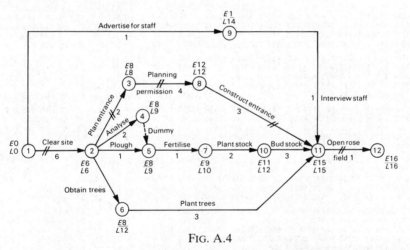

FIG. A.4

10.2 See Figure A.4. If budding takes an extra week, the over-all project time would not be affected, providing it is commenced after 11 weeks and the opening of the rose field commences immediately on completion and takes 1 week.

Tables

TABLE 1 Logarithms

	0	1	2	3	4	5	6	7	8	9	Mean Differences								
											1	2	3	4	5	6	7	8	9
10	00000	00432	00860	01284	01703						42	85	127	170	212	254	297	339	381
						02119	02531	02938	03342	03743	40	81	121	162	202	242	283	323	264
11	04139	04532	04922	05308	05690						37	77	116	154	193	232	270	309	348
						06070	06446	06819	07188	07555	37	74	111	148	185	222	259	296	333
12	07918	08279	08636	08991	09342						36	71	106	142	177	213	248	284	319
						09691	10037	10380	10721	11059	34	68	102	136	170	204	238	272	307
13	11394	11727	12057	12385	12710						33	66	98	131	164	197	229	262	295
						13033	13354	13672	13988	14301	32	63	95	126	158	190	221	253	284
14	14613	14922	15229	15534	15836						30	61	91	122	152	183	213	244	274
						16137	16435	16732	17026	17319	29	59	88	118	147	177	206	236	265
15	17609	17898	18184	18469	18752						28	57	85	114	142	171	199	228	256
						19033	19312	19590	19866	20140	28	55	83	110	138	165	193	221	248
16	20412	20683	20951	21219	21484						27	53	80	107	134	160	187	214	240
						21748	22011	22272	22531	22789	26	52	78	104	130	156	182	208	233
17	23045	23300	23553	23805	24055						26	50	76	101	126	151	176	201	227
						24304	24551	24797	25042	25285	25	49	73	98	122	147	171	196	220
18	25527	25768	26007	26245	26482						24	48	71	95	119	143	167	190	214
						26717	26951	27184	27416	27646	23	46	69	93	116	139	162	185	208
19	27875	28103	28330	28556	28780						23	45	68	90	113	135	158	180	203
						29003	29226	29447	29667	29885	22	44	66	88	110	132	154	176	198
20	30103	30320	30535	30750	30963	31175	31387	31597	31806	32015	21	43	64	85	106	127	148	170	190
21	32222	32428	32634	32838	33041	33244	33445	33646	33846	34044	20	41	61	81	101	121	141	162	182
22	34342	34439	34635	34830	35025	35218	35411	35603	35793	35984	20	39	58	77	97	116	135	154	174
23	36173	36361	36549	36736	36922	37107	37291	37475	37658	37840	19	37	56	74	93	111	130	148	167
24	38021	38202	38382	38561	38739	38917	39094	39270	39445	39620	18	35	53	71	89	106	124	142	159
25	39794	39967	40140	40312	40483	40654	40824	40993	41162	41330	17	34	51	68	85	102	119	136	153
26	41497	41664	41830	41996	42160	42325	42488	42651	42813	42975	16	33	49	66	82	98	115	131	148
27	43136	43297	43457	43616	43775	43933	44091	44248	44404	44560	16	32	47	63	79	95	111	126	142
28	44716	44871	45025	45179	45332	45484	45637	45788	45939	46090	15	30	46	61	76	91	107	122	137
29	46240	46389	46538	46687	46835	46982	47129	47276	47422	47567	15	29	44	59	74	88	103	118	132
30	47712	47857	48001	48144	48287	48430	48572	48714	48855	48996	14	29	43	57	72	86	100	114	129
31	49136	49276	49415	49554	49693	49831	49969	50106	50243	50379	14	28	41	55	69	83	97	110	124
32	50515	50650	50786	50920	51054	51188	51322	51455	51587	51720	13	27	40	54	67	80	94	107	121
33	51851	51983	52114	52244	52375	52504	52634	52763	52892	53020	13	26	39	52	65	78	91	104	117
34	53148	53275	53403	53529	53656	53782	53908	54033	54158	54283	13	25	38	50	63	76	88	101	113
35	54407	54531	54654	54777	54900	55023	55145	55267	55388	55509	12	24	37	49	61	73	85	98	110
36	55630	55751	55871	55991	56110	56229	56348	56467	56585	56703	12	24	36	48	60	71	83	95	107
37	56820	56937	57054	57171	57287	57403	57519	57634	57749	57864	12	23	35	46	58	70	81	93	104
38	57978	58092	58206	58320	58433	58546	58659	58771	58883	58995	11	23	34	45	57	68	79	90	102
39	59106	59218	59329	59439	59550	59660	59770	59879	59988	60097	11	22	33	44	55	66	77	88	99
40	60206	60314	60423	60531	60638	60746	60853	60959	61066	61172	11	21	32	43	54	64	75	86	97
41	61278	61384	61490	61595	61700	61805	61909	62014	62118	62221	10	21	31	42	53	63	74	84	95
42	62325	62428	62531	62634	62737	62839	62941	63043	63144	63246	10	20	31	41	51	61	71	82	92
43	63347	63448	63548	63649	63749	63849	63949	64048	64147	64246	10	20	30	40	50	60	70	80	90
44	64345	64444	64542	64640	64738	64836	64933	65031	65128	65225	10	20	29	39	49	59	68	78	88
45	65321	65418	65514	65610	65706	65801	65896	65992	66087	66181	10	19	29	38	48	57	67	76	86
46	66276	66370	66464	66558	66652	66745	66839	66932	67025	67117	9	19	28	37	47	56	65	74	84
47	67210	67302	67394	67486	67578	67669	67761	67852	67943	68034	9	18	27	36	46	55	64	73	82
48	68124	68215	68305	68395	68485	68574	68664	68753	68842	68931	9	18	27	36	45	53	63	72	81
49	69020	69108	69197	69285	69373	69461	69548	69636	69723	69810	9	18	26	35	44	53	62	70	79

TABLE 1 (contd)

	0	1	2	3	4	5	6	7	8	9	Mean Differences								
											1	2	3	4	5	6	7	8	9
50	69897	69984	70070	70157	70243	70329	70415	70501	70586	70672	9	17	26	34	43	52	60	69	77
51	70757	70842	70927	71012	71096	71181	71265	71349	71433	71517	8	17	25	34	42	50	59	67	76
52	71600	71684	71767	71850	71933	72016	72099	72181	72263	72346	8	17	25	33	42	50	58	66	75
53	72428	72509	72591	72673	72754	72835	72916	72997	73078	73159	8	16	24	32	41	49	57	65	73
54	73239	73320	73400	73480	73560	73640	73719	73799	73878	73957	8	16	24	32	40	48	56	64	72
55	74036	74115	74194	74273	74351	74429	74507	74586	74663	74741	8	16	23	31	39	47	55	63	70
56	74819	74896	74974	75051	75128	75205	75282	75358	75435	75511	8	15	23	31	39	46	54	62	69
57	75587	75664	75740	75815	75891	75967	76042	76118	76193	76268	8	15	23	30	38	45	53	60	68
58	76343	76418	76492	76567	76641	76716	76790	76864	76938	77012	7	15	22	30	37	44	52	59	67
59	77085	77159	77232	77305	77379	77452	77525	77597	77670	77743	7	15	22	29	37	44	51	58	66
60	77815	77887	77960	78032	78104	78176	78247	78319	78390	78462	7	14	22	29	36	43	50	58	65
61	78533	78604	78675	78746	78817	78888	78958	79029	79099	79169	7	14	21	28	36	43	50	57	64
62	79239	79309	79379	79449	79518	79588	79657	79727	79796	79865	7	14	21	28	35	41	48	55	62
63	79934	80003	80072	80140	80209	80277	80346	80414	80482	80550	7	14	20	27	34	41	48	54	61
64	80618	80686	80754	80821	80889	80956	81023	81090	81158	81224	7	13	20	27	34	40	47	54	60
65	81291	81358	81425	81491	81558	81624	81690	81757	81823	81889	7	13	20	26	33	40	46	53	59
66	81954	82020	82086	82151	82217	82282	82347	82413	82478	82543	7	13	20	26	33	39	46	52	59
67	82607	82672	82737	82802	82866	82930	82995	83059	83123	83187	6	13	19	26	32	38	45	51	58
68	83251	83315	83378	83442	83506	83569	83632	83696	83759	83822	6	13	19	25	32	38	44	50	57
69	83885	83948	84011	84073	84136	84198	84261	84323	84386	84448	6	12	19	25	31	37	43	50	56
70	84510	84572	84634	84696	84757	84819	84880	84942	85003	85065	6	12	19	25	31	37	43	50	56
71	85126	85187	85248	85309	85370	85431	85491	85552	85612	85673	6	12	18	24	31	37	43	49	55
72	85733	85794	85854	85914	85974	86034	86094	86153	86213	86273	6	12	18	24	30	36	42	48	54
73	86332	86392	86451	86510	86570	86629	86688	86747	86806	86864	6	12	18	24	30	35	41	47	53
74	86923	86982	87040	87099	87157	87216	87274	87332	87390	87448	6	12	17	23	29	35	41	46	52
75	87506	87564	87622	87679	87737	87795	87852	87910	87967	88024	6	12	17	23	29	35	41	46	52
76	88081	88138	88195	88252	88309	88366	88423	88480	88536	88593	6	11	17	23	29	34	40	46	51
77	88649	88705	88762	88818	88874	88930	88986	89042	89098	89154	6	11	17	22	28	34	39	45	50
78	89209	89265	89321	89376	89432	89487	89542	89597	89653	89708	6	11	17	22	28	33	39	44	50
79	89763	89818	89873	89927	89982	90037	90091	90146	90200	90255	6	11	17	22	28	33	39	44	50
80	90309	90363	90417	90472	90526	90580	90634	90687	90741	90795	5	11	16	22	27	32	38	43	49
81	90848	90902	90956	91009	91062	91116	91169	91222	91275	91328	5	11	16	21	27	32	37	42	48
82	91381	91434	91487	91540	91593	91645	91698	91751	91803	91855	5	11	16	21	27	32	37	42	48
83	91908	91960	92012	92064	92117	92169	92221	92273	92324	92376	5	10	16	21	26	31	36	42	47
84	92428	92480	92531	92583	92634	92686	92737	92788	92840	92891	5	10	15	20	26	31	36	41	46
85	92942	92993	93044	93095	93146	93197	93247	93298	93349	93399	5	10	15	20	26	31	36	41	46
86	93450	93500	93551	93601	93651	93702	93752	93802	93852	93902	5	10	15	20	25	30	35	40	45
87	93952	94002	94052	94101	94151	94201	94250	94300	94349	94399	5	10	15	20	25	30	35	40	45
88	94448	94498	94547	94596	94645	94694	94743	94792	94841	94890	5	10	15	20	25	29	34	39	44
89	94939	94988	95036	95085	95134	95182	95231	95279	95328	95376	5	10	15	19	24	29	34	39	44
90	95424	95472	95521	95569	95617	95665	95713	95761	95809	95856	5	10	14	19	24	29	34	38	43
91	95904	95952	95999	96047	96095	96142	96190	96237	96284	96332	5	9	14	19	24	28	33	38	42
92	96379	96426	96473	96520	96567	96614	96661	96708	96755	96802	5	9	14	19	24	28	33	38	42
93	96848	96895	96942	96988	97035	97081	97128	97174	97220	97267	5	9	14	18	23	28	32	38	42
94	97313	97359	97405	97451	97497	97543	97589	97635	97681	97727	5	9	14	18	23	28	32	37	42
95	97772	97818	97864	97909	97955	98000	98046	98091	98137	98182	5	9	14	18	23	27	32	36	41
96	98227	98272	98318	98363	98408	98453	98498	98543	98588	98632	5	9	14	18	23	27	32	36	41
97	98677	98722	98767	98811	98856	98900	98945	98989	99034	99078	4	9	13	18	22	27	31	36	40
98	99123	99167	99211	99255	99300	99344	99388	99432	99476	99520	4	9	13	18	22	26	31	35	40
99	99564	99607	99651	99695	99739	99782	99826	99870	99913	99957	4	9	13	17	22	26	31	35	39

TABLE 2   Antilogarithms

	0	1	2	3	4	5	6	7	8	9	Mean Difference								
											1	2	3	4	5	6	7	8	9
.00	10000	10023	10046	10069	10093	10116	10139	10162	10186	10209	2	5	7	9	12	14	16	19	21
.01	10233	10257	10280	10304	10328	10351	10375	10399	10423	10477	2	5	7	10	12	14	17	19	21
.02	10471	10495	10520	10544	10568	10593	10617	10641	10666	10691	2	5	7	10	12	15	17	20	22
.03	10715	10740	10765	10789	10814	10839	10864	10889	10914	10940	3	5	8	10	13	15	18	20	23
.04	10965	10990	11015	11041	11066	11092	11117	11143	11169	11194	3	5	8	10	13	15	18	20	23
.05	11220	11246	11272	11298	11324	11350	11376	11402	11429	11455	3	5	8	11	13	16	18	21	24
.06	11482	11508	11535	11561	11588	11614	11641	11668	11695	11722	3	5	8	11	13	16	19	21	24
.07	11749	11776	11803	11830	11858	11885	11912	11940	11967	11995	3	5	8	11	14	16	19	22	25
.08	12023	12050	12078	12106	12134	12162	12190	12218	12246	12274	3	6	8	11	14	17	20	22	25
.09	12303	12331	12359	12388	12417	12445	12474	12503	12531	12560	3	6	9	11	14	17	20	23	26
.10	12589	12618	12647	12677	12706	12735	12764	12794	12823	12853	3	6	9	12	15	18	21	24	26
.11	12882	12912	12942	12972	13002	13032	13062	13092	13122	13152	3	6	9	12	15	18	21	24	27
.12	13183	13213	13243	13274	13305	13335	13366	13397	13428	13459	3	6	9	12	15	18	21	25	28
.13	13490	13521	13552	13583	13614	13646	13677	13709	13740	13772	3	6	9	13	16	19	22	25	28
.14	13804	13836	13868	13900	13932	13964	13996	14028	14060	14093	3	6	10	13	16	19	22	26	29
.15	14125	14158	14191	14223	14256	14289	14322	14355	14388	14421	3	7	10	13	16	20	23	26	30
.16	14454	14488	14521	14555	14588	14622	14655	14689	14723	14757	3	7	10	13	17	20	24	27	30
.17	14791	14825	14859	14894	14928	14962	14997	15031	15066	15101	3	7	10	14	17	21	24	28	31
.18	15136	15171	15205	15241	15276	15311	15346	15382	15417	15453	4	7	11	14	18	21	25	28	32
.19	15488	15524	15560	15596	15631	15668	15704	15740	15776	15812	4	7	11	14	18	22	25	29	32
.20	15849	15885	15922	15959	15996	16032	16069	16106	16144	16181	4	7	11	15	18	22	26	30	33
.21	16218	16255	16293	16331	16368	16406	16444	16482	16520	16558	4	8	11	15	19	23	26	30	34
.22	16596	16634	16672	16711	16749	16788	16827	16866	16904	16943	4	8	12	15	19	23	27	31	35
.23	16982	17022	17061	17100	17140	17179	17219	17258	17298	17338	4	8	12	16	20	24	28	32	36
.24	17378	17418	17458	17498	17539	17579	17620	17660	17701	17742	4	8	12	16	20	24	28	32	36
.25	17783	17824	17865	17906	17947	17989	18030	18072	18113	18155	4	8	12	17	21	25	29	33	37
.26	18197	18239	18281	18323	18365	18408	18450	18493	18535	18578	4	8	13	17	21	25	30	34	38
.27	18621	18664	18707	18750	18793	18836	18880	18923	18967	19011	4	9	13	17	22	26	30	35	39
.28	19055	19099	19143	19187	19231	19275	19320	19364	19409	19454	4	9	13	18	22	26	31	35	40
.29	19498	19543	19588	19634	19679	19724	19770	19815	19861	19907	5	9	14	18	23	27	32	36	41
.30	19953	19999	20045	20091	20137	20184	20230	20277	20324	20370	5	9	14	19	23	28	32	37	42
.31	20417	20464	20512	20559	20606	20654	20701	20749	20797	20845	5	10	14	19	24	29	33	38	43
.32	20893	20941	20989	21038	21086	21135	21184	21232	21281	21330	5	10	15	19	24	29	34	39	44
.33	21380	21429	21478	21528	21577	21627	21677	21727	21777	21827	5	10	15	20	25	30	35	40	45
.34	21878	21928	21979	22029	22080	22131	22182	22233	22284	22336	5	10	15	20	25	31	36	41	46
.35	22387	22439	22491	22542	22594	22646	22699	22751	22803	22856	5	10	16	21	26	31	37	42	47
.36	22909	22961	23014	23067	23121	23174	23227	23281	23336	23388	5	11	16	21	27	32	37	43	48
.37	23442	23496	23550	23605	23659	23714	23768	23823	23878	23933	5	11	16	22	27	33	38	44	49
.38	23988	24044	24099	24155	24210	24266	24322	24378	24434	24491	6	11	17	22	28	34	39	45	50
.39	24547	24604	24660	24717	24774	24831	24889	24946	25003	25061	6	11	17	23	29	34	40	46	51
.40	25119	25177	25236	25293	25351	25410	25468	25527	25586	25645	6	12	18	23	29	35	41	47	53
.41	25704	25763	25823	25882	25942	26002	26062	26122	26182	26242	6	12	18	24	30	36	42	48	54
.42	26303	26363	26424	26485	26546	26607	26669	26730	26792	26853	6	12	18	24	31	37	43	49	55
.43	26915	26977	27040	27102	27164	27227	27290	27353	27416	27479	6	13	19	25	31	38	44	50	56
.44	27542	27606	27669	27733	27797	27861	27925	27990	28054	28119	6	13	19	26	32	39	45	51	58
.45	28184	28249	28314	28379	28445	28510	28576	28642	28708	28774	7	13	20	26	33	39	46	52	59
.46	28840	28907	28973	29040	29107	29174	29242	29309	29376	29444	7	13	20	27	34	40	47	54	60
.47	29512	29580	29648	29717	29785	29854	29923	29992	30061	30130	7	14	21	28	34	41	48	55	62
.48	30200	30269	30339	30409	30479	30549	30620	30690	30761	30832	7	14	21	28	35	42	49	56	63
.49	30903	30974	31046	31117	31189	31261	31333	31405	31477	31550	7	14	22	29	36	43	50	58	65

TABLE 2 (contd)

	0	1	2	3	4	5	6	7	8	9	Mean Differences								
											1	2	3	4	5	6	7	8	9
.50	31623	31696	31769	31842	31916	31989	32063	32137	32211	32285	7	15	22	29	37	44	52	59	66
.51	32359	32434	32509	32584	32659	32735	32809	32885	32961	33037	8	15	23	30	38	45	53	60	68
.52	33113	33189	33266	33343	33420	33497	33574	33651	33729	33806	8	15	23	31	39	46	54	62	69
.53	33884	33963	34041	34119	34198	34277	34356	34435	34514	34594	8	16	24	32	40	47	55	63	71
.54	34674	34754	34834	34914	34995	35075	35156	35237	35318	35400	8	16	24	32	40	48	56	65	73
.55	35481	35563	35645	35727	35810	35892	35975	36058	36141	36224	8	16	25	33	41	50	58	66	74
.56	36308	36392	36475	36559	36644	36728	36813	36898	36983	37068	8	17	25	34	42	51	59	68	76
.57	37154	37239	37325	37411	37497	37584	37670	37757	37844	37931	9	17	26	35	43	52	61	69	78
.58	38019	38107	38194	38282	38371	38459	38548	38637	38726	38815	9	18	27	35	44	53	62	71	80
.59	38905	38994	39084	39174	39264	39355	39446	39537	39628	39719	9	18	27	36	45	54	63	72	82
.60	39811	39902	39994	40087	40179	40272	40365	40458	40551	40644	9	19	28	37	46	56	65	74	83
.61	40738	40832	40926	41020	41115	41210	41305	41400	41495	41591	9	19	28	38	47	57	66	76	85
.62	41687	41783	41879	41976	42073	42170	42267	42364	42462	42560	10	19	29	39	49	58	68	78	87
.63	42658	42756	42855	42954	43053	43152	43251	43351	43451	43551	10	20	30	40	50	60	70	80	89
.64	43652	43752	43853	43954	44055	44157	44259	44361	44463	44566	10	20	30	41	51	61	71	81	91
.65	44668	44771	44875	44978	45082	45186	45290	45394	45499	45604	10	21	31	42	52	62	73	83	94
.66	45709	45814	45920	46026	46132	46238	46345	46452	46559	46666	11	21	32	43	53	64	75	85	96
.67	46774	46881	46989	47098	47206	47315	47424	47534	47643	47753	11	22	33	44	54	65	76	87	98
.68	47863	47973	48084	48195	48306	48417	48529	48641	48753	48865	11	22	33	45	56	67	78	89	100
.69	48978	49091	49204	49317	49431	49545	49659	49774	49888	50003	11	23	34	46	57	68	80	91	103
.70	50119	50234	50350	50466	50582	50699	50816	50933	51050	51168	12	23	35	47	58	70	82	93	105
.71	51286	51404	51523	51642	51761	51880	52000	52119	52240	52360	12	24	36	48	60	72	84	96	108
.72	52481	52602	52723	52845	52966	53088	53211	53333	53456	53580	12	24	37	49	61	73	85	98	110
.73	53703	53827	53951	54075	54200	54325	54450	54576	54702	54828	13	25	38	50	63	75	88	100	113
.74	54954	55081	55208	55336	55463	55590	55719	55847	55976	56105	13	26	38	51	64	77	90	102	115
.75	56234	56364	56494	56624	56754	56885	57016	57148	57280	57412	13	26	39	52	66	79	92	105	118
.76	57544	57677	57810	57943	58076	58210	58345	58479	58614	58749	13	27	40	54	67	80	94	107	121
.77	58884	59020	59156	59293	59429	59566	59704	59841	59979	60117	14	27	41	55	69	82	96	110	123
.78	60256	60395	60534	60674	60814	60954	61094	61235	61376	61518	14	28	42	56	70	84	98	112	126
.79	61659	61802	61944	62087	62230	62373	62517	62661	62806	62951	14	29	43	58	72	86	101	115	130
.80	63096	63241	63387	63533	63680	63826	63973	64121	64269	64417	15	29	44	59	74	88	103	118	132
.81	64565	64714	64863	65013	65163	65313	65464	65615	65766	65917	15	30	45	60	75	90	105	120	135
.82	66069	66222	66374	66527	66681	66834	66988	67143	67298	67453	15	31	46	62	77	92	108	123	139
.83	67608	67764	67920	68077	68234	68391	68549	68707	68865	69024	16	32	47	63	79	95	110	126	142
.84	69183	69343	69503	69663	69823	69984	70146	70307	70469	70632	16	32	48	64	81	97	113	129	145
.85	70795	70958	71121	71285	71450	71614	71779	71945	72111	72277	17	33	50	66	83	99	116	132	149
.86	72444	72611	72778	72946	73114	73282	73451	73621	73790	73961	17	34	51	68	85	101	118	135	152
.87	74131	74302	74473	74645	74817	74989	75162	75336	75509	75683	17	35	52	69	87	104	121	138	156
.88	75858	76033	76208	76384	76560	76736	76913	77090	77268	77446	18	35	53	71	89	107	125	142	159
.89	77625	77804	77983	78163	78343	78524	78705	78886	79068	79250	18	36	54	72	91	109	127	145	163
.90	79433	79616	79799	79983	80168	80353	80538	80724	80910	81096	19	37	56	74	93	111	130	148	167
.91	81283	81470	81658	81846	82035	82224	82414	82604	82794	82985	19	38	57	76	95	113	132	151	170
.92	83176	83368	83560	83753	83946	84140	84333	84528	84723	84918	19	39	58	78	97	116	136	155	175
.93	85114	85310	85507	85704	85901	86099	86298	86497	86696	86896	20	40	60	79	99	119	139	158	178
.94	87096	87297	87498	87700	87902	88105	88308	88512	88716	88920	20	41	61	81	102	122	142	162	183
.95	89125	89331	89536	89743	89950	90157	90365	90573	90782	90991	21	42	62	83	104	125	146	166	187
.96	91201	91411	91622	91833	92045	92257	92470	92683	92897	93111	21	42	64	85	106	127	149	170	191
.97	93325	93541	93756	93972	94189	94406	94624	94842	95060	95280	22	43	65	87	109	130	152	174	195
.98	95499	95719	95940	96161	96383	96605	96828	97051	97275	97499	22	44	67	89	111	133	155	178	200
.99	97724	97949	98175	98401	98628	98855	99083	99312	99541	99770	23	46	68	91	114	137	160	182	205

TABLE 3   Squares

	0	1	2	3	4	5	6	7	8	9	Mean Differences								
											1	2	3	4	5	6	7	8	9
1.0	1.0000	1.0201	1.0404	1.0609	1.0816	1.1025	1.1236	1.1449	1.1664	1.1881	21	42	63	84	105	126	147	168	189
1.1	1.2100	1.2321	1.2544	1.2769	1.2996	1.3225	1.3456	1.3689	1.3924	1.4161	23	46	69	92	115	138	161	184	207
1.2	1.4400	1.4641	1.4884	1.5129	1.5376	1.5625	1.5876	1.6129	1.6384	1.6641	25	50	75	100	125	150	175	200	225
1.3	1.6900	1.7161	1.7424	1.7689	1.7956	1.8225	1.8496	1.8769	1.9044	1.9321	27	54	81	108	135	162	189	216	243
1.4	1.9600	1.9881	2.0164	2.0449	2.0736	2.1025	2.1316	2.1609	2.1904	2.2201	29	58	87	116	145	174	203	232	261
1.5	2.2500	2.2801	2.3104	2.3409	2.3716	2.4025	2.4336	2.4649	2.4964	2.5281	31	62	93	124	155	186	217	248	279
1.6	2.5600	2.5921	2.6244	2.6569	2.6896	2.7225	2.7556	2.7889	2.8224	2.8561	33	66	99	132	165	198	231	264	297
1.7	2.8900	2.9241	2.9584	2.9929	3.0276	3.0625	3.0976	3.1329	3.1684	3.2041	35	70	105	140	175	210	245	280	315
1.8	3.2400	3.2761	3.3124	3.3489	3.3856	3.4225	3.4596	3.4969	3.5344	3.5721	37	74	111	148	185	222	259	296	333
1.9	3.6100	3.6481	3.6864	3.7249	3.7636	3.8025	3.8416	3.8809	3.9204	3.9601	39	78	117	156	195	234	273	312	351
2.0	4.0000	4.0401	4.0804	4.1209	4.1616	4.2025	4.2436	4.2849	4.3264	4.3681	41	82	123	164	205	246	287	328	369
2.1	4.4100	4.4521	4.4944	4.5369	4.5796	4.6225	4.6656	4.7089	4.7524	4.7961	43	86	129	172	215	258	301	344	387
2.2	4.8400	4.8841	4.9284	4.9729	5.0176	5.0625	5.1076	5.1529	5.1984	5.2441	45	90	135	180	225	270	315	360	405
2.3	5.2900	5.3361	5.3824	5.4289	5.4756	5.5225	5.5696	5.6169	5.6644	5.7121	47	94	141	188	235	282	329	376	423
2.4	5.7600	5.8081	5.8564	5.9049	5.9536	6.0025	6.0516	6.1009	6.1504	6.2001	49	98	147	196	245	294	343	392	441
2.5	6.2500	6.3001	6.3504	6.4009	6.4516	6.5025	6.5536	6.6049	6.6564	6.7081	51	102	153	204	255	306	357	408	459
2.6	6.7600	6.8121	6.8644	6.9169	6.9696	7.0225	7.0756	7.1289	7.1824	7.2361	53	106	159	212	265	318	371	424	477
2.7	7.2900	7.3441	7.3984	7.4529	7.5076	7.5625	7.6176	7.6729	7.7284	7.7841	55	110	165	220	275	330	385	440	495
2.8	7.8400	7.8961	7.9524	8.0089	8.0656	8.1225	8.1796	8.2369	8.2944	8.3521	57	114	171	228	285	342	399	456	513
2.9	8.4100	8.4681	8.5264	8.5849	8.6436	8.7025	8.7616	8.8209	8.8804	8.9401	59	118	177	236	295	354	413	472	531
3.0	9.0000	9.0601	9.1204	9.1809	9.2416	9.3025	9.3636	9.4249	9.4864	9.5481	61	122	183	244	305	366	427	488	549
3.1	9.6100	9.6721	9.7344	9.7969	9.8596	9.9225	9.9856	10.0489	10.1124	10.1761	63	125	188	251	313	376	439	502	564
3.2	10.240	10.304	10.368	10.433	10.498	10.563	10.628	10.693	10.758	10.824	7	13	20	26	33	39	46	52	59
3.3	10.890	10.956	11.022	11.089	11.156	11.223	11.290	11.357	11.424	11.492	7	13	20	27	34	40	47	54	60
3.4	11.560	11.628	11.696	11.765	11.834	11.903	11.972	12.041	12.110	12.180	7	14	21	28	35	41	48	55	62
3.5	12.250	12.320	12.390	12.461	12.532	12.603	12.674	12.745	12.816	12.888	7	15	21	28	36	43	50	57	64
3.6	12.960	13.032	13.104	13.177	13.250	13.323	13.396	13.469	13.542	13.616	7	15	22	29	37	44	51	58	66
3.7	13.690	13.764	13.838	13.913	13.988	14.063	14.138	14.213	14.288	14.364	8	15	23	30	38	45	53	60	68
3.8	14.440	14.516	14.592	14.669	14.746	14.823	14.900	14.977	15.054	15.132	8	15	23	31	39	46	54	62	69
3.9	15.210	15.288	15.366	15.445	15.524	15.603	15.682	15.761	15.840	15.920	8	16	24	32	40	47	55	63	71
4.0	16.000	16.080	16.160	16.241	16.322	16.403	16.484	16.565	16.646	16.728	8	16	24	32	41	49	57	65	73
4.1	16.810	16.892	16.974	17.057	17.140	17.223	17.306	17.389	17.472	17.556	8	17	25	33	42	50	58	66	75
4.2	17.640	17.724	17.808	17.893	17.978	18.063	18.148	18.233	18.318	18.404	9	17	26	34	43	51	60	68	77
4.3	18.490	18.576	18.662	18.749	18.836	18.923	19.010	19.097	19.184	19.272	9	17	26	35	44	52	61	70	78
4.4	19.360	19.448	19.536	19.625	19.714	19.803	19.892	19.981	20.070	20.160	9	18	27	36	45	53	62	71	80
4.5	20.250	20.340	20.430	20.521	20.612	20.703	20.794	20.885	20.976	21.068	9	18	27	36	46	55	64	73	82
4.6	21.160	21.252	21.344	21.437	21.530	21.623	21.716	21.809	21.902	21.996	9	19	28	37	47	56	65	74	84
4.7	22.090	22.184	22.278	22.373	22.468	22.563	22.658	22.753	22.848	22.944	10	19	29	38	48	57	67	76	86
4.8	23.040	23.136	23.232	23.329	23.426	23.523	23.620	23.717	23.814	23.912	10	19	29	39	49	58	68	78	87
4.9	24.010	24.108	24.206	24.305	24.404	24.503	24.602	24.701	24.800	24.900	10	20	30	40	50	59	69	79	89
5.0	25.000	25.100	25.200	25.301	25.402	25.503	25.604	25.705	25.806	25.908	10	20	30	40	51	61	71	81	91
5.1	26.010	26.112	26.214	26.317	26.420	26.523	26.626	26.729	26.832	26.936	10	21	31	41	52	62	72	82	93
5.2	27.040	27.144	27.248	27.353	27.458	27.563	27.668	27.773	27.878	27.984	11	21	32	42	53	63	74	84	95
5.3	28.090	28.196	28.302	28.409	28.516	28.623	28.730	28.837	28.944	29.052	11	21	32	43	54	64	75	86	96
5.4	29.160	29.268	29.376	29.485	29.594	29.703	29.812	29.921	30.030	30.140	11	22	33	44	55	65	76	87	98

TABLE 3 (*contd*)

	0	1	2	3	4	5	6	7	8	9	Mean Differences								
											1	2	3	4	5	6	7	8	9
5.5	30.250	30.360	30.470	30.581	30.692	30.803	30.914	31.025	31.136	31.248	11	22	33	44	56	67	78	89	100
5.6	31.360	31.472	31.584	31.697	31.810	31.923	32.036	32.149	32.262	32.376	11	23	34	45	57	68	79	90	102
5.7	32.490	32.604	32.718	32.833	32.948	33.063	33.178	33.293	33.408	33.524	12	23	35	46	58	69	81	92	104
5.8	33.640	33.756	33.872	33.989	34.106	34.223	34.340	34.457	34.574	34.692	12	23	35	47	59	70	82	94	105
5.9	34.810	34.928	35.046	35.165	35.284	35.403	35.522	35.641	35.760	35.880	12	24	36	48	60	71	83	95	107
6.0	36.000	36.120	36.240	36.361	36.482	36.603	36.724	36.845	36.966	37.088	12	24	36	48	61	73	85	97	109
6.1	37.210	37.332	37.454	37.577	37.700	37.823	37.946	38.069	38.192	38.316	12	25	37	49	62	74	86	98	111
6.2	38.440	38.564	38.688	38.813	38.938	39.063	39.188	39.313	39.438	39.564	13	25	38	50	63	75	88	100	113
6.3	39.690	39.816	39.942	40.069	40.196	40.323	40.450	40.577	40.704	40.832	13	25	38	51	64	76	89	102	114
6.4	40.960	41.088	41.216	41.345	41.474	41.603	41.732	41.861	41.990	42.120	13	26	39	52	65	77	90	103	116
6.5	42.250	42.380	42.510	42.641	42.772	42.903	43.034	43.165	43.296	43.428	13	26	39	52	66	79	92	105	118
6.6	43.560	43.692	43.824	43.957	44.090	44.223	44.356	44.489	44.622	44.756	13	27	40	53	67	80	93	106	120
6.7	44.890	45.024	45.158	45.293	45.428	45.563	45.698	45.833	45.968	46.104	14	27	41	54	68	81	95	108	122
6.8	46.240	46.376	46.512	46.649	46.786	46.923	47.060	47.197	47.334	47.472	14	27	41	55	69	82	96	110	123
6.9	47.610	47.748	47.886	48.025	48.164	48.303	48.442	48.581	48.720	48.860	14	28	42	56	70	83	97	111	125
7.0	49.000	49.140	49.280	49.421	49.562	49.703	49.844	49.985	50.126	50.268	14	28	42	56	71	85	99	113	127
7.1	50.410	50.552	50.694	50.837	50.980	51.123	51.266	51.409	51.552	51.696	14	29	43	57	72	86	100	114	129
7.2	51.840	51.984	52.128	52.273	52.418	52.563	52.708	52.853	52.998	53.144	15	29	44	58	73	87	102	116	131
7.3	53.290	53.436	53.582	53.729	53.876	54.023	54.170	54.317	54.464	54.612	15	29	44	59	74	88	103	118	132
7.4	54.760	54.908	55.056	55.205	55.354	55.503	55.652	55.801	55.950	56.100	15	30	45	60	75	89	104	119	134
7.5	56.250	56.400	56.550	56.701	56.852	57.003	57.154	57.305	57.456	57.608	15	30	45	60	76	91	106	121	136
7.6	57.760	57.912	58.064	58.217	58.370	58.523	58.676	58.829	58.982	59.136	15	31	46	61	77	92	107	122	138
7.7	59.290	59.444	59.598	59.753	59.908	60.063	60.218	60.373	60.528	60.684	16	31	47	62	78	93	109	124	140
7.8	60.840	60.996	61.152	61.309	61.466	61.623	61.780	61.937	62.094	62.252	16	31	47	63	79	94	110	126	141
7.9	62.410	62.568	62.726	62.885	63.044	63.203	63.362	63.521	63.680	63.840	16	32	48	64	80	95	111	127	143
8.0	64.000	64.160	64.320	64.481	64.642	64.803	64.964	65.125	65.286	65.448	16	32	48	64	81	97	113	129	145
8.1	65.610	65.772	65.934	66.097	66.260	66.423	66.586	66.749	66.912	67.076	16	33	49	65	82	98	114	130	147
8.2	67.240	67.404	67.568	67.733	67.898	68.063	68.228	68.393	68.558	68.724	17	33	50	66	83	99	116	132	149
8.3	68.890	69.056	69.222	69.389	69.556	69.723	69.890	70.057	70.224	70.392	17	33	50	67	84	100	117	134	150
8.4	70.560	70.728	70.896	71.065	71.234	71.403	71.572	71.741	71.910	72.080	17	34	51	68	85	101	118	135	152
8.5	72.250	72.420	72.590	72.761	72.932	73.103	73.274	73.445	73.616	73.788	17	34	51	68	86	103	120	137	154
8.6	73.960	74.132	74.304	74.477	74.650	74.823	74.996	75.169	75.342	75.516	17	35	52	69	87	104	121	138	156
8.7	75.690	75.864	76.038	76.213	76.388	76.563	76.738	76.913	77.088	77.264	18	35	53	70	88	105	123	142	158
8.8	77.440	77.616	77.792	77.969	78.146	78.323	78.500	78.677	78.854	79.032	18	35	53	71	89	106	124	140	159
8.9	79.210	79.388	79.566	79.745	79.924	80.103	80.282	80.461	80.640	80.820	18	36	54	72	90	107	125	143	161
9.0	81.000	81.180	81.360	81.541	81.722	81.903	82.084	82.265	82.446	82.628	18	36	54	72	91	109	127	145	163
9.1	82.810	82.992	83.174	83.357	83.540	83.723	83.906	84.089	84.272	84.456	18	37	55	73	92	110	128	146	165
9.2	84.640	84.824	85.008	85.193	85.378	85.563	85.748	85.933	86.118	86.304	19	37	56	74	93	111	130	148	167
9.3	86.490	86.676	86.862	87.049	87.236	87.423	87.610	87.797	87.984	88.172	19	37	56	75	94	112	131	150	168
9.4	88.360	88.548	88.736	88.925	89.114	89.303	89.492	89.681	89.870	90.060	19	38	57	76	95	113	132	151	170
9.5	90.250	90.440	90.630	90.821	91.012	91.203	91.394	91.585	91.776	91.968	19	38	57	76	96	115	134	153	172
9.6	92.160	92.352	92.544	92.737	92.930	93.123	93.316	93.509	93.702	93.896	19	39	58	77	97	116	135	154	174
9.7	94.090	94.284	94.478	94.673	94.868	95.063	95.258	95.453	95.648	95.844	20	39	59	78	98	117	137	156	176
9.8	96.040	96.236	96.432	96.629	96.826	97.023	97.220	97.417	97.614	97.812	20	39	59	79	99	118	138	158	177
9.9	98.010	98.208	98.406	98.605	98.804	99.003	99.202	99.401	99.600	99.800	20	40	60	80	100	119	139	159	179

TABLE 4　Square roots

	0	1	2	3	4	5	6	7	8	9	Mean Differences								
											1	2	3	4	5	6	7	8	9
1.0	1.0000	1.0050	1.0100	1.0149	1.0198	1.0247	1.0296	1.0344	1.0392	1.0440	5	10	15	20	24	29	34	49	44
1.1	1.0488	1.0536	1.0583	1.0630	1.0677	1.0724	1.0770	1.0817	1.0863	1.0909	5	9	14	19	23	28	33	37	42
1.2	1.0954	1.1000	1.1045	1.1091	1.1136	1.1180	1.1225	1.1269	1.1314	1.1358	4	9	13	18	22	27	31	36	40
1.3	1.1402	1.1446	1.1489	1.1533	1.1576	1.1619	1.1662	1.1705	1.1747	1.1790	4	9	13	17	22	26	30	34	39
1.4	1.1832	1.1874	1.1916	1.1958	1.2000	1.2042	1.2083	1.2124	1.2166	1.2207	4	8	13	17	21	25	29	33	37
1.5	1.2247	1.2288	1.2329	1.2369	1.2410	1.2450	1.2490	1.2530	1.2570	1.2610	4	8	12	16	20	24	28	32	36
1.6	1.2649	1.2689	1.2728	1.2767	1.2806	1.2845	1.2884	1.2923	1.2961	1.3000	4	8	12	16	19	23	27	31	35
1.7	1.3038	1.3077	1.3115	1.3153	1.3191	1.3229	1.3266	1.3304	1.3342	1.3379	4	8	11	15	19	23	27	30	34
1.8	1.3416	1.3454	1.3491	1.3528	1.3565	1.3601	1.3638	1.3675	1.3711	1.3748	4	7	11	15	18	22	26	29	33
1.9	1.3784	1.3820	1.3856	1.3892	1.3928	1.3964	1.4000	1.4036	1.4071	1.4107	4	7	11	14	18	22	25	29	32
2.0	1.4142	1.4177	1.4213	1.4248	1.4283	1.4318	1.4353	1.4387	1.4422	1.4457	4	7	11	14	18	21	24	28	31
2.1	1.4491	1.4526	1.4560	1.4595	1.4629	1.4663	1.4697	1.4731	1.4765	1.4799	3	7	10	14	17	20	24	27	31
2.2	1.4832	1.4866	1.4900	1.4933	1.4966	1.5000	1.5033	1.5067	1.5100	1.5133	3	7	10	13	17	20	24	27	30
2.3	1.5166	1.5199	1.5232	1.5264	1.5297	1.5330	1.5362	1.5395	1.5427	1.5460	3	7	10	13	16	20	23	26	29
2.4	1.5492	1.5524	1.5556	1.5588	1.5620	1.5652	1.5684	1.5716	1.5748	1.5780	3	7	10	13	16	19	22	26	29
2.5	1.5811	1.5843	1.5875	1.5906	1.5937	1.5969	1.6000	1.6031	1.6062	1.6093	3	6	9	13	16	19	22	25	28
2.6	1.6125	1.6155	1.6186	1.6217	1.6248	1.6279	1.6310	1.6340	1.6371	1.6401	3	6	9	12	15	18	22	25	28
2.7	1.6432	1.6462	1.6492	1.6523	1.6553	1.6583	1.6613	1.6643	1.6673	1.6703	3	6	9	12	15	18	21	24	27
2.8	1.6733	1.6763	1.6793	1.6823	1.6852	1.6882	1.6912	1.6941	1.6971	1.7000	3	6	9	12	15	18	20	24	27
2.9	1.7029	1.7059	1.7088	1.7117	1.7146	1.7176	1.7205	1.7234	1.7263	1.7292	3	6	9	12	15	18	20	23	26
3.0	1.7321	1.7349	1.7378	1.7407	1.7436	1.7464	1.7493	1.7521	1.7550	1.7578	3	6	9	11	14	17	20	23	26
3.1	1.7607	1.7635	1.7664	1.7692	1.7720	1.7748	1.7776	1.7804	1.7833	1.7861	3	6	9	11	14	17	20	23	25
3.2	1.7889	1.7916	1.7944	1.7972	1.8000	1.8028	1.8055	1.8083	1.8111	1.8138	3	6	8	11	14	17	19	22	25
3.3	1.8166	1.8193	1.8221	1.8248	1.8276	1.8303	1.8330	1.8358	1.8385	1.8412	3	5	8	11	14	16	19	22	25
3.4	1.8439	1.8466	1.8493	1.8520	1.8547	1.8574	1.8601	1.8628	1.8655	1.8682	3	5	8	11	13	16	19	22	24
3.5	1.8708	1.8735	1.8762	1.8788	1.8815	1.8841	1.8868	1.8894	1.8921	1.8947	3	5	8	11	13	16	19	21	24
3.6	1.8974	1.9000	1.9026	1.9053	1.9079	1.9105	1.9131	1.9157	1.9183	1.9209	3	5	8	10	13	16	18	21	24
3.7	1.9235	1.9261	1.9287	1.9313	1.9339	1.9365	1.9391	1.9416	1.9442	1.9468	3	5	8	10	13	16	18	21	23
3.8	1.9494	1.9519	1.9545	1.9570	1.9596	1.9621	1.9647	1.9672	1.9698	1.9723	3	5	8	10	13	15	18	21	23
3.9	1.9748	1.9774	1.9799	1.9824	1.9849	1.9875	1.9900	1.9925	1.9950	1.9975	3	5	8	10	13	15	18	20	23
4.0	2.0000	2.0025	2.0050	2.0075	2.0100	2.0125	2.0149	2.0174	2.0199	2.0224	2	5	7	10	12	15	17	20	22
4.1	2.0248	2.0273	2.0298	2.0322	2.0347	2.0372	2.0396	2.0421	2.0445	2.0469	2	5	7	10	12	15	17	20	22
4.2	2.0494	2.0518	2.0543	2.0567	2.0591	2.0616	2.0640	2.0664	2.0688	2.0712	2	5	7	10	12	15	17	19	22
4.3	2.0736	2.0761	2.0785	2.0809	2.0833	2.0857	2.0881	2.0905	2.0928	2.0952	2	5	7	10	12	14	17	19	22
4.4	2.0976	2.1000	2.1024	2.1048	2.1071	2.1095	2.1119	2.1142	2.1166	2.1190	2	5	7	9	12	14	17	19	21
4.5	2.1213	2.1237	2.1260	2.1284	2.1307	2.1331	2.1354	2.1378	2.1401	2.1424	2	5	7	9	12	14	16	19	21
4.6	2.1448	2.1471	2.1494	2.1517	2.1541	2.1564	2.1587	2.1610	2.1633	2.1656	2	5	7	9	12	14	16	19	21
4.7	2.1679	2.1703	2.1726	2.1749	2.1772	2.1794	2.1817	2.1840	2.1863	2.1886	2	5	7	9	12	14	16	18	21
4.8	2.1909	2.1932	2.1954	2.1977	2.2000	2.2023	2.2045	2.2068	2.2091	2.2113	2	5	7	9	11	14	16	18	20
4.9	2.2136	2.2519	2.2181	2.2204	2.2226	2.2249	2.2271	2.2293	2.2316	2.2338	2	5	7	9	11	14	16	18	20
5.0	2.2361	2.2383	2.2405	2.2428	2.2450	2.2472	2.2494	2.2517	2.2539	2.2561	2	4	7	9	11	13	16	18	20
5.1	2.2583	2.2605	2.2627	2.2650	2.2672	2.2694	2.2716	2.2738	2.2760	2.2782	2	4	7	9	11	13	15	18	20
5.2	2.2804	2.2825	2.2847	2.2869	2.2891	2.2913	2.2935	2.2956	2.2978	2.3000	2	4	7	9	11	13	15	17	20
5.3	2.3022	2.3043	2.3065	2.3087	2.3108	2.3130	2.3152	2.3173	2.3195	2.3216	2	4	6	9	11	13	15	17	19
5.4	2.3238	2.3259	2.3281	2.3302	2.3324	2.3345	2.3367	2.3388	2.3409	2.3431	2	4	6	9	11	13	15	17	19

TABLE 4 (*contd*)

	0	1	2	3	4	5	6	7	8	9	\multicolumn{9}{c}{Mean Differences}

	0	1	2	3	4	5	6	7	8	9	1	2	3	4	5	6	7	8	9
5.5	2.3452	2.3473	2.3495	2.3516	2.3537	2.3558	2.3580	2.3601	2.3622	2.3643	2	4	6	8	11	13	15	17	19
5.6	2.3664	2.3685	2.3707	2.3728	2.3749	2.3770	2.3791	2.3812	2.3833	2.3854	2	4	6	8	11	13	15	17	19
5.7	2.3875	2.3896	2.3917	2.3937	2.3958	2.3979	2.4000	2.4021	2.4042	2.4062	2	4	6	8	10	12	15	17	19
5.8	2.4083	2.4104	2.4125	2.4145	2.4166	2.4187	2.4207	2.4228	2.4249	2.4269	2	4	6	8	10	12	14	16	19
5.9	2.4290	2.4310	2.4331	2.4352	2.4372	2.4393	2.4413	2.4434	2.4454	2.4474	2	4	6	8	10	12	14	16	18
6.0	2.4495	2.4515	2.4536	2.4556	2.4576	2.4597	2.4617	2.4637	2.4658	2.4678	2	4	6	8	10	12	14	16	18
6.1	2.4698	2.4718	2.4739	2.4759	2.4779	2.4799	2.4819	2.4839	2.4860	2.4880	2	4	6	8	10	12	14	16	18
6.2	2.4900	2.4920	2.4940	2.4960	2.4980	2.5000	2.5020	2.5040	2.5060	2.5080	2	4	6	8	10	12	14	16	18
6.3	2.5100	2.5120	2.5140	2.5159	2.5179	2.5199	2.5219	2.5239	2.5259	2.5278	2	4	6	8	10	12	14	16	18
6.4	2.5298	2.5318	2.5338	2.5357	2.5377	2.5397	2.5417	2.5436	2.5456	2.5475	2	4	6	8	10	12	14	16	18
6.5	2.5495	2.5515	2.5534	2.5554	2.5573	2.5593	2.5612	2.5632	2.5652	2.5671	2	4	6	8	10	12	14	16	18
6.6	2.5690	2.5710	2.5729	2.5749	2.5768	2.5788	2.5807	2.5826	2.5846	2.5865	2	4	6	8	10	12	14	16	17
6.7	2.5884	2.5904	2.5923	2.5942	2.5962	2.5981	2.6000	2.6019	2.6038	2.6058	2	4	6	8	10	12	14	15	17
6.8	2.6077	2.6096	2.6115	2.6134	2.6153	2.6173	2.6192	2.6211	2.6230	2.6249	2	4	6	8	10	11	13	15	17
6.9	2.6268	2.6287	2.6306	2.6325	2.6344	2.6363	2.6382	2.6401	2.6420	2.6439	2	4	6	8	10	11	13	15	17
7.0	2.6458	2.6476	2.6495	2.6514	2.6533	2.6552	2.6571	2.6589	2.6608	2.6627	2	4	6	8	9	11	13	15	17
7.1	2.6646	2.6665	2.6683	2.6702	2.6721	2.6739	2.6758	2.6777	2.6796	2.6814	2	4	6	7	9	11	13	15	17
7.2	2.6833	2.6851	2.6870	2.6889	2.6907	2.6926	2.6944	2.6963	2.6981	2.7000	2	4	6	7	9	11	13	15	17
7.3	2.7019	2.7037	2.7055	2.7074	2.7092	2.7111	2.7129	2.7148	2.7166	2.7185	2	4	6	7	9	11	13	15	17
7.4	2.7203	2.7221	2.7240	2.7258	2.7276	2.7295	2.7313	2.7331	2.7350	2.7368	2	4	5	7	9	11	13	15	16
7.5	2.7386	2.7404	2.7423	2.7441	2.7459	2.7477	2.7495	2.7514	2.7532	2.7550	2	4	5	7	9	11	13	15	16
7.6	2.7568	2.7586	2.7604	2.7622	2.7641	2.7659	2.7677	2.7695	2.7713	2.7731	2	4	5	7	9	11	13	14	16
7.7	2.7749	2.7767	2.7785	2.7803	2.7821	2.7839	2.7857	2.7875	2.7893	2.7911	2	4	5	7	9	11	13	14	16
7.8	2.7928	2.7946	2.7964	2.7982	2.8000	2.8018	2.8036	2.8054	2.8071	2.8089	2	4	5	7	9	11	13	14	16
7.9	2.8107	2.8125	2.8142	2.8160	2.8178	2.8196	2.8213	2.8231	2.8249	2.8267	2	4	5	7	9	11	12	14	16
8.0	2.8284	2.8302	2.8320	2.8337	2.8355	2.8373	2.8390	2.8408	2.8425	2.8443	2	4	5	7	9	11	12	14	16
8.1	2.8460	2.8478	2.8496	2.8513	2.8531	2.8548	2.8566	2.8583	2.8601	2.8618	2	4	5	7	9	11	12	14	16
8.2	2.8636	2.8653	2.8671	2.8688	2.8705	2.8723	2.8740	2.8758	2.8775	2.8792	2	3	5	7	9	10	12	14	16
8.3	2.8810	2.8827	2.8844	2.8862	2.8879	2.8896	2.8914	2.8931	2.8948	2.8965	2	3	5	7	9	10	12	14	16
8.4	2.8983	2.9000	2.9017	2.9034	2.9052	2.9069	2.9086	2.9103	2.9120	2.9138	2	3	5	7	9	10	12	14	15
8.5	2.9155	2.9172	2.9189	2.9206	2.9223	2.9240	2.9257	2.9275	2.9292	2.9309	2	3	5	7	9	10	12	14	15
8.6	2.9326	2.9343	2.9360	2.9377	2.9394	2.9411	2.9428	2.9445	2.9462	2.9479	2	3	5	7	9	10	12	14	15
8.7	2.9496	2.9513	2.9530	2.9547	2.9563	2.9580	2.9597	2.9614	2.9631	2.9648	2	3	5	7	9	10	12	14	15
8.8	2.9665	2.9682	2.9698	2.9715	2.9732	2.9749	2.9766	2.9783	2.9799	2.9816	2	3	5	7	8	10	12	13	15
8.9	2.9833	2.9850	2.9866	2.9883	2.9900	2.9917	2.9933	2.9950	2.9967	2.9983	2	3	5	7	8	10	12	13	15
9.0	3.0000	3.0017	3.0033	3.0050	3.0067	3.0083	3.0100	3.0116	3.0133	3.0150	2	3	5	7	8	10	12	13	15
9.1	3.0166	3.0183	3.0199	3.0216	3.0232	3.0249	3.0265	3.0282	3.0299	3.0315	2	3	5	7	8	10	12	13	15
9.2	3.0332	3.0348	3.0364	3.0381	3.0397	3.0414	3.0430	3.0447	3.0463	3.0480	2	3	5	7	8	10	11	13	15
9.3	3.0496	3.0512	3.0529	3.0545	3.0561	3.0578	3.0594	3.0610	3.0627	3.0643	2	3	5	7	8	10	11	13	15
9.4	3.0659	3.0676	3.0692	3.0708	3.0725	3.0741	3.0757	3.0773	3.0790	3.0806	2	3	5	7	8	10	11	13	15
9.5	3.0822	3.0838	3.0854	3.0871	3.0887	3.0903	3.0919	3.0935	3.0952	3.0968	2	3	5	6	8	10	11	13	15
9.6	3.0984	3.1000	3.1016	3.1032	3.1048	3.1064	3.1081	3.1097	3.1113	3.1129	2	3	5	6	8	10	11	13	14
9.7	3.1145	3.1161	3.1177	3.1193	3.1209	3.1225	3.1241	3.1257	3.1273	3.1289	2	3	5	6	8	10	11	13	14
9.8	3.1305	3.1321	3.1337	3.1353	3.1369	3.1385	3.1401	3.1417	3.1432	3.1448	2	3	5	6	8	10	11	13	14
9.9	3.1464	3.1480	3.1496	3.1512	3.1528	3.1544	3.1559	3.1575	3.1591	3.1607	2	3	5	6	8	9	11	13	14

TABLE 5 Random numbers

	I	II	III	IV	V
A	28 89 65 87 08	13 50 63 04 23	25 47 57 91 13	52 62 24 19 94	91 67 48 57 10
	30 29 43 65 42	78 66 28 55 80	47 46 41 90 08	55 98 78 10 70	49 92 05 12 07
	95 74 62 60 53	51 57 32 22 27	12 72 72 27 77	44 67 32 23 13	67 95 07 76 30
	01 85 54 96 72	66 86 65 64 60	56 59 75 36 75	46 44 33 63 71	54 50 06 44 75
	10 91 46 96 86	19 83 52 47 53	65 00 51 93 51	30 80 05 19 29	56 23 27 19 03
B	05 33 18 08 51	51 78 57 26 17	34 87 96 23 95	89 99 93 39 79	11 28 94 15 52
	04 43 13 37 00	79 68 96 26 60	70 39 83 66 56	62 03 55 86 57	77 55 33 62 02
	05 85 40 25 24	73 52 93 70 50	48 21 47 74 63	17 27 27 51 26	35 96 29 00 45
	84 90 90 65 77	63 99 25 69 02	09 04 03 35 78	19 79 95 07 21	02 84 48 51 97
	28 55 53 09 48	86 28 30 02 35	71 30 32 06 47	93 74 21 86 33	49 90 21 69 74
C	89 83 40 69 80	97 96 47 59 97	56 33 24 87 36	17 18 16 90 46	75 27 28 52 13
	73 20 96 05 68	93 41 69 96 07	97 50 81 79 59	42 37 13 81 83	82 42 85 04 31
	10 89 07 76 21	40 24 74 36 42	40 33 04 46 24	35 63 02 31 61	34 59 43 36 96
	91 50 27 78 37	06 06 16 25 98	17 78 80 36 85	26 41 77 63 37	71 63 94 94 33
	03 45 44 66 88	97 81 26 03 89	39 46 67 21 17	98 10 39 33 15	61 63 00 25 92
D	89 41 58 91 63	65 99 59 97 84	90 14 79 61 55	56 16 88 87 60	32 15 99 67 43
	13 43 00 97 26	16 91 21 32 41	60 22 66 72 17	31 85 33 69 07	68 49 20 43 29
	71 71 00 51 72	62 03 89 26 32	35 27 99 18 25	78 12 03 09 70	50 93 19 35 56
	19 28 15 00 41	92 27 73 40 38	37 11 05 75 16	98 81 99 37 29	92 20 32 39 67
	56 38 30 92 30	45 51 94 69 04	00 84 14 36 37	95 66 39 01 09	21 68 40 95 79
E	39 27 52 89 11	00 81 06 28 48	12 08 05 75 26	03 35 63 05 77	13 81 20 67 58
	73 13 28 58 01	05 06 42 24 07	60 60 29 99 93	72 93 78 04 36	25 76 01 54 03
	81 60 84 51 57	12 68 46 55 89	60 09 71 87 89	70 81 10 95 91	83 79 68 20 66
	05 62 98 07 85	07 79 26 69 61	67 85 72 37 41	85 79 76 84 23	61 58 87 08 05
	62 97 16 29 18	52 16 16 23 56	62 95 80 97 63	32 25 34 03 36	48 84 60 37 65

```
F  31 13 63 21 08   16 01 92 58 21   48 79 74 73 72   08 64 80 91 38   07 28 66 61 59
   97 38 35 34 19   89 84 05 34 47   88 09 31 54 88   97 96 86 01 69   46 13 95 65 96
   32 11 78 33 82   51 99 98 44 39   12 75 10 60 36   80 66 39 94 97   42 36 31 16 59
   81 99 13 37 05   08 12 60 39 23   61 73 84 89 18   26 02 04 37 95   96 18 69 06 30
   45 74 00 03 05   69 99 47 26 52   48 06 30 00 18   03 30 28 55 59   66 10 71 44 05

G  11 84 13 69 01   88 91 28 79 50   71 42 14 96 55   98 59 96 01 36   88 77 90 45 59
   14 66 12 87 22   59 45 27 08 51   85 64 23 85 41   64 72 08 59 44   67 98 56 65 56
   40 25 67 87 82   84 27 17 30 37   48 69 49 02 58   98 02 50 58 11   95 39 06 35 63
   44 48 97 49 43   65 45 53 41 07   14 83 46 74 11   76 66 63 60 08   90 54 33 65 84
   41 94 54 06 57   48 28 01 83 84   09 11 21 91 73   97 28 44 74 06   22 30 95 69 72

H  07 12 15 58 84   93 18 31 83 45   54 52 62 29 91   53 58 54 66 05   47 19 63 92 75
   64 27 90 43 52   18 26 32 96 83   50 58 45 27 57   14 96 39 64 85   73 87 96 76 23
   80 71 86 41 03   45 62 63 40 88   35 69 34 10 94   32 22 52 04 74   69 63 21 83 41
   27 06 08 09 92   26 22 59 28 27   38 58 22 14 79   24 32 12 38 42   33 56 90 92 57
   54 68 97 20 54   33 26 74 03 30   74 22 19 13 48   30 28 01 92 49   58 61 52 27 03

I  02 92 65 68 99   05 53 15 26 70   04 69 22 64 07   04 73 25 74 82   78 35 22 21 88
   83 52 57 78 62   98 61 70 48 22   68 50 64 55 75   42 70 32 09 60   58 70 61 43 97
   82 82 76 31 33   85 13 41 38 10   16 47 61 43 77   83 27 19 70 41   34 78 77 60 25
   38 61 34 09 49   04 41 66 09 76   20 50 73 40 95   24 77 95 73 20   47 42 80 61 03
   01 01 11 88 38   03 10 16 82 24   39 58 20 12 39   82 77 02 18 88   33 11 49 15 16

J  21 66 14 38 28   54 08 18 07 04   92 17 63 36 75   33 14 11 11 78   97 30 53 62 38
   32 29 30 69 59   68 50 33 31 47   15 64 88 75 27   04 51 41 61 96   86 62 93 66 71
   04 59 21 65 47   39 90 89 86 77   46 86 86 88 86   50 09 13 24 91   54 80 67 78 66
   38 64 50 07 36   56 50 45 94 25   48 28 48 30 51   60 73 73 03 87   68 47 37 10 84
   48 33 50 83 53   59 77 64 59 90   58 92 62 50 18   93 09 45 89 06   13 26 98 86 29
```

This table is taken from table xxxiii of Fisher and Yates, *Statistical Tables for Biological, Agricultural and Medical Research*, published by Oliver & Boyd Ltd, Edinburgh, and by permission of the authors and publishers.

TABLE 6   Random standardised normal deviates

The numbers in the table constitute a 'population' of standardised normal deviates arranged in a random sequence; they may be used where a small sample (i.e. not greater than size 50 and preferably less) of normal deviates is required.

A random sample of standardised normal deviates from an infinite population (i.e. sampling with replacement) may be obtained in conjunction with a table of random numbers. Use a 3-digit random number to select a row and a column; the intersection gives a random standardised normal deviate. For example, if the random number is 861, the remainder after dividing by 500 is 361 and so the corresponding normal deviate is +0.539.

The mean of the 500 tabulated values is 0.00 and the variance is 1.00.

	0	1	2	3	4	5	6	7	8	9
00	−0.179	−0.399	−0.235	−0.098	−0.465	+1.563	−1.085	+0.860	+0.388	+0.710
01	+0.421	+1.454	+0.904	+0.437	−2.120	+1.085	−0.277	−2.170	+0.018	−0.722
02	+0.210	−0.556	+0.465	−1.812	−2.748	−0.345	−0.251	+0.622	−1.015	+0.762
03	−1.598	+0.919	−0.266	−0.999	+0.308	−0.592	+0.817	−0.454	+1.598	+0.240
04	+1.717	+1.514	−0.012	−0.852	+0.118	+0.399	−0.123	+0.432	−0.470	+0.776
05	−0.308	+0.867	−0.372	+0.697	−1.787	+0.568	−0.002	−0.133	+0.545	−0.824
06	−0.421	+0.516	−0.038	+1.200	+0.063	−0.377	−1.007	−0.334	+1.299	+0.038
07	−0.776	+0.874	−1.265	−0.580	+0.377	−0.697	−2.226	−1.299	−0.796	−0.628
08	+0.640	−0.522	+0.023	−0.393	−1.412	−2.457	−1.580	+1.160	+0.008	+0.487
09	−0.319	+0.889	+1.180	−0.404	+1.322	+0.410	+1.468	+0.235	−0.810	−1.131
10	+0.610	−0.383	+1.812	+0.729	+0.204	−0.225	+0.169	−0.729	−0.432	+0.634
11	−0.174	−0.154	+0.098	+0.393	−3.090	+1.762	+1.530	+0.028	+0.950	−0.935
12	+2.576	−0.684	−1.200	+0.002	+0.261	−0.415	+0.598	−0.769	−0.169	−1.498
13	−1.103	+1.398	−0.653	+1.739	+0.476	+0.510	+0.782	−0.634	+0.562	−0.053
14	+1.635	+0.448	−1.530	−0.043	+2.290	−0.063	−1.695	+0.199	+1.211	−1.360
15	−0.068	−0.860	−0.194	−1.616	+0.334	+0.189	+0.927	−1.454	+0.958	+0.404
16	−1.960	+1.076	−0.671	−0.103	+1.041	+2.226	+1.838	−0.510	−1.322	+2.366
17	+0.443	−0.912	+0.251	−0.574	+1.131	0.204	−0.324	−0.487	−1.287	+0.522
18	+1.360	+0.533	+1.094	+0.671	+0.582	−2.576	−0.539	−0.568	+0.225	−0.545

19	+0.810	+0.319	-1.514	+0.556	+1.112	-0.210	+0.292	+0.749	+0.882	+0.033
20	+0.616	+1.347	-1.866	-0.755	+0.329	+0.148	-0.058	-0.199	+0.048	+1.546
21	-0.598	-2.366	-0.831	+0.454	-0.118	-1.762	+0.493	+1.103	+0.361	+0.113
22	+0.426	+1.580	-1.112	+0.550	-1.254	-0.033	+0.143	-1.141	+0.366	-0.073
23	+0.831	-0.516	-1.717	-0.340	+1.655	+0.194	-0.388	-0.942	-1.243	-0.292
24	-0.640	-0.128	+1.276	-1.838	-0.410	+0.646	+2.075	-0.159	+1.695	+0.527
25	-0.927	+0.838	-1.546	+0.246	-0.742	-0.143	+2.457	+0.043	-1.058	-0.867
26	+1.232	+2.170	+0.088	-0.803	+0.574	+0.058	+0.282	+0.356	+0.350	-1.927
27	+0.935	+0.665	+2.034	-1.995	+0.703	-0.083	-1.468	+0.078	-0.966	-0.303
28	-1.739	-0.622	-1.563	+0.313	+0.220	-0.586	+0.272	+0.789	-1.335	+1.440
29	+0.990	-1.483	+0.154	-1.372	-1.896	+1.385	-1.041	+0.974	+0.482	-1.211
30	-0.189	-0.240	+0.133	-2.290	-0.616	-0.437	+0.459	-0.499	+0.845	+0.383
31	+1.866	-1.398	+0.068	+0.053	-2.034	+1.426	+1.254	+1.067	+0.592	+0.174
32	-0.018	+0.628	+0.230	+0.659	-0.298	+1.927	-0.282	+0.769	-0.690	+1.675
33	-0.646	-0.350	+0.324	-1.675	+1.190	-1.076	+1.287	-1.426	+0.345	-0.215
34	-1.150	-0.220	-0.533	+0.912	-0.710	-0.904	-0.817	-1.160	-0.919	-0.659
35	+0.103	+0.361	+1.024	-0.604	+0.966	-1.122	+0.604	-0.845	+0.736	-0.882
36	+1.243	+0.539	+0.684	-0.716	-0.482	-0.562	+0.277	-1.440	-0.366	-0.256
37	-0.093	-1.190	+0.580	-1.276	+0.653	-0.048	+0.742	-1.170	+1.960	+2.120
38	-0.261	-0.194	+0.303	+0.340	+1.498	-1.232	-0.078	-0.443	+1.141	+1.787
39	-0.230	-0.550	+0.266	-1.655	+0.999	-1.067	+1.058	+0.796	+0.415	+1.995
40	-0.148	+0.504	-0.028	+0.083	+0.824	-1.024	+1.412	-0.164	+1.150	-0.272
41	+1.122	+0.896	-0.789	+0.215	-0.426	-1.049	-0.974	+0.586	+1.311	-0.736
42	+0.499	-1.032	+0.159	+0.123	+2.748	-0.749	-0.665	-1.221	-1.180	+1.049
43	+0.678	-0.782	+0.470	+0.256	+0.298	-0.990	+0.287	+0.942	+0.128	+1.372
44	-1.347	+3.090	-0.896	+0.138	-0.838	+0.690	+1.007	+0.184	+0.164	+0.179
45	-1.094	-0.610	-0.287	+0.755	-0.459	-1.635	-0.108	-0.246	+1.032	-0.527
46	-0.088	-0.889	+0.803	-1.311	-0.703	+1.170	-0.113	+0.108	-0.874	+0.372
47	+0.093	-0.476	+1.265	-0.448	+1.015	-0.313	-0.958	+0.716	+1.483	+0.722
48	-0.950	-0.008	+0.012	+0.073	-0.762	-0.493	+1.896	+0.982	+1.616	+1.221
49	-0.329	-0.138	-0.504	-0.678	+1.335	-2.075	-1.385	-0.023	-0.356	-0.982

TABLE 7   Present values

Of £1 receivable at end of each period

Percentage

Year	1	2	3	4	5	6	7	8	9	10
1	0.990	0.980	0.971	0.962	0.952	0.943	0.935	0.926	0.917	0.909
2	0.980	9.961	0.943	0.925	0.907	0.890	0.873	0.857	0.842	0.826
3	0.971	0.942	0.915	0.889	0.864	0.840	0.816	0.794	0.772	0.751
4	0.961	0.924	0.888	0.855	0.823	0.792	0.763	0.735	0.708	0.683
5	0.951	0.906	0.863	0.822	0.784	0.747	0.713	0.681	0.650	0.621
6	0.942	0.888	0.837	0.790	0.746	0.705	0.666	0.630	0.596	0.564
7	0.933	0.871	0.813	0.760	0.711	0.665	0.623	0.583	0.547	0.513
8	0.923	0.853	0.789	0.731	0.677	0.627	0.582	0.540	0.502	0.467
9	0.914	0.837	0.766	0.703	0.645	0.592	0.544	0.500	0.460	0.424
10	0.905	0.820	0.744	0.676	0.614	0.558	0.508	0.463	0.422	0.386
11	0.896	0.804	0.722	0.650	0.585	0.527	0.475	0.429	0.388	0.350
12	0.887	0.788	0.701	0.625	0.557	0.497	0.444	0.397	0.356	0.319
13	0.879	0.773	0.681	0.601	0.530	0.469	0.415	0.368	0.326	0.290
14	0.870	0.758	0.661	0.577	0.505	0.442	0.388	0.340	0.299	0.263
15	0.861	0.743	0.642	0.555	0.481	0.417	0.362	0.315	0.275	0.239
16	0.853	0.728	0.623	0.534	0.458	0.394	0.339	0.292	0.252	0.218
17	0.844	0.714	0.605	0.513	0.436	0.371	0.371	0.270	0.231	0.198
18	0.836	0.700	0.587	0.494	0.416	0.350	0.296	0.250	0.212	0.180
19	0.828	0.686	0.570	0.475	0.396	0.331	0.277	0.232	0.194	0.164
20	0.820	0.673	0.554	0.456	0.377	0.312	0.258	0.215	0.178	0.149
21	0.811	0.660	0.538	0.439	0.359	0.294	0.242	0.199	0.164	0.135
22	0.803	0.647	0.522	0.422	0.342	0.278	0.226	0.184	0.150	0.123
23	0.795	0.634	0.507	0.406	0.326	0.262	0.211	0.170	0.138	0.112
24	0.788	0.622	0.492	0.390	0.310	0.247	0.197	0.158	0.126	0.102
25	0.780	0.610	0.478	0.375	0.295	0.233	0.184	0.146	0.116	0.092
30	0.742	0.552	0.412	0.308	0.231	0.174	0.131	0.099	0.075	0.057
35	0.706	0.500	0.355	0.253	0.181	0.130	0.094	0.068	0.049	0.036
40	0.672	0.453	0.307	0.208	0.142	0.097	0.067	0.046	0.032	0.022

TABLE 7 (contd)

Percentage

Year	11	12	13	14	15	16	17	18	19	20
1	0.901	0.893	0.885	0.877	0.870	0.862	0.855	0.847	0.840	0.833
2	0.812	0.797	0.783	0.769	0.756	0.743	0.731	0.718	0.706	0.694
3	0.731	0.712	0.693	0.675	0.658	0.641	0.624	0.609	0.593	0.579
4	0.659	0.636	0.613	0.592	0.572	0.552	0.534	0.516	0.499	0.482
5	0.593	0.567	0.543	0.519	0.497	0.476	0.456	0.437	0.419	0.402
6	0.535	0.507	0.480	0.456	0.432	0.410	0.390	0.370	0.352	0.335
7	0.482	0.452	0.425	0.400	0.376	0.354	0.333	0.314	0.296	0.279
8	0.434	0.404	0.376	0.351	0.327	0.305	0.285	0.266	0.249	0.233
9	0.391	0.361	0.333	0.308	0.284	0.263	0.243	0.225	0.209	0.194
10	0.352	0.322	0.295	0.270	0.247	0.227	0.208	0.191	0.176	0.162
11	0.317	0.287	0.261	0.237	0.215	0.195	0.178	0.162	0.148	0.135
12	0.286	0.257	0.231	0.208	0.187	0.168	0.152	0.137	0.124	0.112
13	0.258	0.229	0.204	0.182	0.163	0.145	0.130	0.116	0.104	0.093
14	0.232	0.205	0.181	0.160	0.141	0.125	0.111	0.099	0.088	0.078
15	0.209	0.183	0.160	0.140	0.123	0.108	0.095	0.084	0.074	0.065
16	0.188	0.163	0.141	0.123	0.107	0.093	0.081	0.071	0.062	0.054
17	0.170	0.146	0.125	0.108	0.093	0.080	0.069	0.060	0.052	—
18	0.153	0.130	0.111	0.095	0.081	0.069	0.059	0.051	—	—
19	0.138	0.116	0.098	0.083	0.070	0.060	0.051	—	—	—
20	0.124	0.104	0.087	0.073	0.061	0.051	—	—	—	—
21	0.112	0.093	0.077	0.064	0.053	—	—	—	—	—
22	0.101	0.083	0.068	0.056	—	—	—	—	—	—
23	0.091	0.074	0.060	—	—	—	—	—	—	—
24	0.082	0.066	0.053	—	—	—	—	—	—	—
25	0.074	0.059	—	—	—	—	—	—	—	—

TABLE 7 (contd)

Percentage

Year	21	22	23	24	25	26	27	28	29	30
1	0.826	0.820	0.813	0.806	0.800	0.794	0.787	0.781	0.775	0.769
2	0.683	0.672	0.661	0.650	0.640	0.630	0.620	0.610	0.601	0.592
3	0.564	0.551	0.537	0.524	0.512	0.500	0.488	0.477	0.466	0.455
4	0.467	0.451	0.437	0.423	0.410	0.397	0.384	0.373	0.361	0.350
5	0.386	0.370	0.355	0.341	0.328	0.315	0.303	0.291	0.280	0.269
6	0.319	0.303	0.289	0.275	0.262	0.250	0.238	0.227	0.217	0.207
7	0.263	0.249	0.235	0.222	0.210	0.198	0.188	0.178	0.168	0.159
8	0.218	0.204	0.191	0.179	0.168	0.157	0.148	0.139	0.130	0.123
9	0.180	0.167	0.155	0.144	0.134	0.125	0.116	0.108	0.101	0.094
10	0.149	0.137	0.126	0.116	0.107	0.099	0.092	0.085	0.078	0.073
11	0.123	0.112	0.103	0.094	0.086	0.079	0.072	0.066	0.061	0.056
12	0.102	0.092	0.083	0.076	0.069	0.062	0.057	0.052	—	—
13	0.084	0.075	0.068	0.061	0.055	—	—	—	—	—
14	0.069	0.062	0.055	—	—	—	—	—	—	—
15	0.057	0.051	—	—	—	—	—	—	—	—

Of £1 receivable annually at end of each year

Percentage

Year	1	2	3	4	5	6	7	8	9	10
1	0.990	0.980	0.971	0.962	0.952	0.943	0.935	0.926	0.917	0.909
2	1.970	1.942	1.913	1.886	1.859	1.833	1.808	1.783	1.759	1.736
3	2.941	2.884	2.829	2.775	2.723	2.673	2.624	2.577	2.531	2.487
4	3.902	3.803	3.717	3.630	3.546	3.465	3.387	3.312	3.240	3.170
5	4.853	4.713	4.580	4.452	4.329	4.212	4.100	3.993	3.890	3.791
6	5.795	5.601	5.417	5.242	5.076	4.917	4.767	4.623	4.486	4.355
7	6.728	6.472	6.230	6.002	5.786	5.582	5.389	5.206	5.033	4.868
8	7.652	7.325	7.020	6.733	6.463	6.210	5.971	5.747	5.535	5.335
9	8.566	8.162	7.786	7.435	7.108	6.802	6.515	6.247	5.995	5.759
10	9.471	8.983	8.530	8.111	7.722	7.360	7.024	6.710	6.418	6.145
11	10.368	9.787	9.253	8.760	8.306	7.887	7.499	7.139	6.805	6.495
12	11.255	10.575	9.954	9.385	8.863	8.384	7.943	7.536	7.161	6.814
13	12.134	11.348	10.635	9.986	9.394	8.853	8.358	7.904	7.487	7.103
14	13.004	12.106	11.296	10.563	9.899	9.295	8.745	8.244	7.786	7.367
15	13.865	12.849	11.938	11.118	10.380	9.712	9.108	8.559	8.061	7.606
16	14.718	13.578	12.561	11.652	10.838	10.106	9.447	8.851	8.313	7.824
17	15.562	14.292	13.166	12.166	11.274	10.477	9.763	9.122	8.544	8.022
18	16.398	14.992	13.754	12.659	11.690	10.828	10.059	9.372	8.756	8.201
19	17.226	15.678	14.324	13.134	12.085	11.158	10.336	9.604	8.950	8.365
20	18.046	16.351	14.877	13.590	12.462	11.470	10.594	9.818	9.129	8.514
21	18.857	17.011	15.415	14.029	12.821	11.764	10.836	10.017	9.292	8.649
22	19.660	17.658	15.937	14.451	13.163	12.042	11.061	10.201	9.442	8.772
23	20.456	18.292	16.444	14.857	13.489	12.303	11.272	10.371	9.580	8.883
24	21.243	18.914	16.936	15.247	13.799	12.550	11.469	10.529	9.707	8.985
25	22.023	19.523	17.413	15.622	14.094	12.783	11.654	10.675	9.823	9.077
30	25.808	22.396	19.600	17.292	15.372	13.765	12.409	11.258	10.274	9.427
35	29.409	24.999	21.487	18.665	16.374	14.498	12.948	11.655	10.567	9.644
40	32.835	27.355	23.115	19.793	17.159	15.046	13.332	11.925	10.757	9.779

Table 7 (contd)

Percentage

Year	11	12	13	14	15	16	17	18	19	20
1	0.901	0.893	0.885	0.877	0.870	0.862	0.855	0.847	0.840	0.833
2	1.713	1.690	1.668	1.647	1.626	1.605	1.585	1.566	1.546	1.528
3	2.444	2.402	2.361	2.322	2.283	2.246	2.210	2.174	2.140	2.106
4	3.102	3.037	2.974	2.914	2.855	2.798	2.743	2.690	2.639	2.589
5	3.696	3.605	3.517	3.433	3.352	3.274	3.199	3.127	3.058	2.991
6	4.231	4.111	3.998	3.889	3.784	3.685	3.589	3.498	3.410	3.326
7	4.712	4.564	4.423	4.288	4.160	4.039	3.922	3.812	3.706	3.605
8	5.146	4.968	4.799	4.639	4.487	4.344	4.207	4.078	3.954	3.837
9	5.537	5.328	5.132	4.946	4.772	4.607	4.451	4.303	4.163	4.031
10	5.898	5.560	5.426	5.216	5.019	4.833	4.659	4.494	4.339	4.192
11	6.207	5.939	5.687	5.453	5.234	5.029	4.836	4.656	4.486	4.327
12	6.492	6.194	5.918	5.660	5.421	5.197	4.988	4.793	4.610	4.439
13	6.650	6.424	6.122	5.842	5.583	5.342	5.118	4.910	4.715	4.533
14	6.982	6.628	6.302	6.002	5.724	5.468	5.229	5.008	4.802	4.611
15	7.191	6.811	6.462	6.142	5.847	5.575	5.324	5.092	4.876	4.675
16	7.379	6.974	6.604	6.265	5.954	5.669	5.405	5.162	4.938	4.730
17	7.549	7.120	6.729	6.373	6.047	5.749	5.475	5.222	4.990	4.775
18	7.702	7.250	6.840	6.467	6.128	5.818	5.534	5.273	5.033	4.812
19	7.839	7.366	6.938	6.550	6.198	5.877	5.584	5.316	5.070	4.844
20	7.963	7.469	7.025	6.623	6.259	5.929	5.628	5.353	5.101	4.870
21	8.075	7.562	7.102	6.687	6.312	5.973	5.665	5.384	5.127	4.891
22	8.176	7.645	7.170	6.743	6.359	6.011	5.696	5.410	5.149	4.909
23	8.266	7.718	7.230	6.792	6.399	6.044	5.723	5.432	5.167	4.925
24	8.348	7.784	7.283	6.835	6.434	6.073	5.746	5.451	5.182	4.937
25	8.422	7.843	7.330	6.873	6.464	6.097	5.766	5.467	5.195	4.948
30	8.694	8.055	7.496	7.003	6.566	6.177	5.829	5.517	5.235	4.979
35	8.855	8.175	7.586	7.070	6.617	6.215	5.858	5.539	5.251	4.992
40	8.951	8.244	7.634	7.105	6.642	6.234	5.871	5.548	5.258	4.997

Percentage

Year	21	22	23	24	25	26	27	28	29	30
1	0.826	0.820	0.813	0.806	0.800	0.794	0.787	0.781	0.775	0.769
2	1.509	1.492	1.474	1.457	1.440	1.424	1.407	1.392	1.376	1.361
3	2.074	2.042	2.011	1.981	1.952	1.923	1.896	1.868	1.842	1.816
4	2.540	2.494	2.448	2.404	2.362	2.320	2.280	2.241	2.203	2.166
5	2.926	2.864	2.803	2.745	2.689	2.635	2.583	2.532	2.483	2.436
6	3.245	3.167	3.092	3.020	2.951	2.885	2.821	2.759	2.700	2.643
7	3.508	3.416	3.327	3.242	3.161	3.083	3.009	2.937	2.868	2.802
8	3.726	3.619	3.518	3.421	3.329	3.241	3.156	3.076	2.999	2.925
9	3.905	3.786	3.673	3.566	3.463	3.366	3.273	3.184	3.100	3.019
10	4.054	3.923	3.799	3.682	3.571	3.465	3.364	3.269	3.178	3.092
11	4.177	4.035	3.902	3.776	3.656	3.544	3.437	3.335	3.239	3.147
12	4.278	4.127	3.985	3.851	3.725	3.606	3.493	3.387	3.286	3.190
13	4.362	4.203	4.053	3.912	3.780	3.656	3.538	3.427	3.322	3.223
14	4.432	4.265	4.108	3.962	3.824	3.695	3.573	3.459	3.351	3.249
15	4.489	4.315	4.153	4.001	3.859	3.726	3.601	3.483	3.373	3.268
16	4.536	4.357	4.189	4.033	3.887	3.751	3.623	3.503	3.390	3.283
17	4.576	4.391	4.219	4.059	3.910	3.771	3.640	3.518	3.403	3.295
18	4.608	4.419	4.243	4.080	3.928	3.786	3.654	3.529	3.413	3.304
19	4.635	4.442	4.263	4.097	3.942	3.799	3.664	3.539	3.421	3.311
20	4.657	4.460	4.279	4.110	3.954	3.808	3.673	3.546	3.427	3.316
21	4.675	4.476	4.292	4.121	3.963	3.816	3.679	3.551	3.432	3.320
22	4.690	4.488	4.302	4.130	3.970	3.822	3.684	3.556	3.436	3.323
23	4.703	4.499	4.311	4.137	3.976	3.827	3.689	3.559	3.438	3.325
24	4.713	4.507	4.318	4.143	3.981	3.831	3.692	3.562	3.441	3.327
25	4.721	4.514	4.323	4.147	3.985	3.834	3.694	3.564	3.442	3.329
30	4.746	4.534	4.339	4.160	3.995	3.842	3.701	3.569	3.447	3.332
35	4.756	4.541	4.345	4.164	3.998	3.845	3.703	3.571	3.448	3.333
40	4.760	4.544	4.347	4.166	3.999	3.846	3.703	3.571	3.448	3.333

TABLE 8   Areas in tail of normal distribution.

The function tabulated is $1 - \Phi(u)$, where $\Phi(u)$ is the cumulative distribution function of a standardised normal variable u. Thus $1 - \Phi(u) = 1/\sqrt{2\pi} \int_u^\infty e^{-x^2/2}\,dx$ is the probability that a standardised normal variable selected at random will be greater than a value of $u (= x - \mu/\sigma)$.

FIG. A.5

$\dfrac{(x-\mu)}{\sigma}$	0.00	0.01	0.02	0.03	0.04	0.05	0.06	0.07	0.08	0.09
0.0	0.5000	0.4960	0.4920	0.4880	0.4840	0.4801	0.4761	0.4721	0.4681	0.4641
0.1	0.4602	0.4562	0.4522	0.4483	0.4443	0.4404	0.4364	0.4325	0.4286	0.4247
0.2	0.4207	0.4168	0.4129	0.4090	0.4052	0.4013	0.3974	0.3936	0.3897	0.3859
0.3	0.3821	0.3783	0.3745	0.3707	0.3669	0.3632	0.3594	0.3557	0.3520	0.3483
0.4	0.3446	0.3409	0.3372	0.3336	0.3300	0.3264	0.3228	0.3192	0.3156	0.3121
0.5	0.3085	0.3050	0.3015	0.2981	0.2946	0.2912	0.2877	0.2843	0.2810	0.2776
0.6	0.2743	0.2709	0.2676	0.2643	0.2611	0.2578	0.2546	0.2514	0.2483	0.2451
0.7	0.2420	0.2389	0.2358	0.2327	0.2296	0.2266	0.2236	0.2206	0.2177	0.2148
0.8	0.2119	0.2090	0.2061	0.2033	0.2005	0.1977	0.1949	0.1922	0.1894	0.1867
0.9	0.1841	0.1814	0.1788	0.1762	0.1736	0.1711	0.1685	0.1660	0.1635	0.1611
1.0	0.1587	0.1562	0.1539	0.1515	0.1492	0.1469	0.1446	0.1423	0.1401	0.1379
1.1	0.1357	0.1335	0.1314	0.1292	0.1271	0.1251	0.1230	0.1210	0.1190	0.1170
1.2	0.1151	0.1131	0.1112	0.1093	0.1075	0.1056	0.1038	0.1020	0.1003	0.0985
1.2	0.1151	0.1131	0.1112	0.1093	0.1075	0.1056	0.1038	0.1020	0.1003	0.0985
1.3	0.0968	0.951	0.934	0.0918	0.0901	0.0885	0.0869	0.0853	0.0838	0.0823
1.4	0.0808	0.0793	0.0778	0.0764	0.749	0.0735	0.0721	0.0708	0.0694	0.0681

1.5	0.0668	0.0655	0.0643	0.0630	0.0618	0.0606	0.0594	0.0582	0.0571	0.0559
1.6	0.0548	0.0537	0.0526	0.0516	0.0505	0.0495	0.0485	0.0475	0.0465	0.0455
1.7	0.0446	0.436	0.0427	0.0418	0.0409	0.0401	0.0392	0.0384	0.0375	0.0367
1.8	0.0359	0.0351	0.0344	0.0336	0.0329	0.0322	0.0314	0.0307	0.0301	0.0294
1.9	0.0287	0.0281	0.0274	0.0268	0.0262	0.0256	0.0250	0.0244	0.0239	0.0233
2.0	0.02275	0.02222	0.02169	0.02118	0.02068	0.02018	0.01970	0.01923	0.01876	0.01831
2.1	0.01786	0.01743	0.01700	0.01659	0.01618	0.01578	0.01539	0.01500	0.01463	0.01426
2.2	0.01390	0.01355	0.01321	0.01287	0.01255	0.01222	0.01191	0.01160	0.01130	0.01101
2.3	0.01072	0.01044	0.01017	0.00990	0.00964	0.00939	0.00914	0.00889	0.00866	0.00842
2.4	0.00820	0.00798	0.00776	0.00755	0.00734	0.00714	0.00695	0.00676	0.00657	0.00639
2.5	0.00621	0.00604	0.00587	0.00570	0.00554	0.00539	0.00523	0.00508	0.00494	0.00480
2.6	0.00466	0.00453	0.00440	0.00427	0.00415	0.00402	0.00391	0.00379	0.00368	0.00357
2.7	0.00347	0.00336	0.00326	0.00317	0.00307	0.00298	0.00289	0.00280	0.00272	0.00264
2.8	0.00256	0.00248	0.00240	0.00233	0.00226	0.00219	0.00212	0.00205	0.00199	0.00193
2.9	0.00187	0.00181	0.00175	0.00169	0.00164	0.00159	0.00154	0.00149	0.00144	0.00139
3.0	0.00135									
3.1	0.00097									
3.2	0.00069									
3.3	0.00048									
3.4	0.00034									
3.5	0.00023									
3.6	0.00016									
3.7	0.00011									
3.8	0.00007									
3.9	0.00005									
4.0	0.00003									

Operational Research by Example

TABLE 9 Exponential functions

x	e^x	e^{-x}	x	e^x	e^{-x}	x	e^x	e^{-x}	x	e^x	e^{-x}
0·00	1·00000	1·00000	0·50	1·64872	0·60653	1·00	2·71828	0·36788	1·50	4·48169	0·22313
0·01	1·01005	0·99005	0·51	1·66529	0·60050	1·01	2·74560	0·36422	1·55	4·71147	0·21225
0·02	1·02020	0·98020	0·52	1·68203	0·59452	1·02	2·77319	0·36059	1·60	4·95303	0·20190
0·03	1·03045	0·97045	0·53	1·69893	0·58860	1·03	2·80107	0·35701	1·65	5·20698	0·19205
0·04	1·04081	0·96079	0·54	1·71601	0·58275	1·04	2·82922	0·35345	1·70	5·47395	0·18268
0·05	1·05127	0·95123	0·55	1·73325	0·57695	1·05	2·85765	0·34994	1·75	5·75460	0·17377
0·06	1·06184	0·94176	0·56	1·75067	0·57121	1·06	2·88637	0·34646	1·80	6·04965	0·16530
0·07	1·07251	0·93239	0·57	1·76827	0·56553	1·07	2·91538	0·34301	1·85	6·35982	0·15724
0·08	1·08329	0·92312	0·58	1·78604	0·55990	1·08	2·94468	0·33960	1·90	6·68589	0·14957
0·09	1·09417	0·91393	0·59	1·80399	0·55433	1·09	2·97427	0·33622	1·95	7·02869	0·14227
0·10	1·10517	0·90484	0·60	1·82212	0·54881	1·10	3·00417	0·33287	2·0	7·38906	0·13534
0·11	1·11628	0·89583	0·61	1·84043	0·54335	1·11	3·03436	0·32956	2·1	8·16617	0·12246
0·12	1·12750	0·88692	0·62	1·85893	0·53794	1·12	3·06485	0·32628	2·2	9·02501	0·11080
0·13	1·13883	0·87810	0·63	1·87761	0·53259	1·13	3·09566	0·32303	2·3	9·97418	0·10026
0·14	1·15027	0·86936	0·64	1·89648	0·52729	1·14	3·12677	0·31982	2·4	11·0232	0·09072
0·15	1·16183	0·86071	0·65	1·91554	0·52205	1·15	3·15819	0·31664	2·5	12·1825	0·08208
0·16	1·17351	0·85214	0·66	1·93479	0·51685	1·16	3·18993	0·31349	2·6	13·4637	0·07427
0·17	1·18530	0·84366	0·67	1·95424	0·51171	1·17	3·22199	0·31037	2·7	14·8797	0·06721
0·18	1·19722	0·83527	0·68	1·97388	0·50662	1·18	3·25437	0·30728	2·8	16·4446	0·06081
0·19	1·20925	0·82696	0·69	1·99372	0·50158	1·19	3·28708	0·30422	2·9	18·1741	0·05502
0·20	1·22140	0·81873	0·70	2·01375	0·49659	1·20	3·32012	0·30119	3·0	20·0855	0·04979
0·21	1·23368	0·81058	0·71	2·03399	0·49164	1·21	3·35348	0·29820	3·1	22·1980	0·04505
0·22	1·24608	0·80252	0·72	2·05443	0·48675	1·22	3·38719	0·29523	3·2	24·5325	0·04076
0·23	1·25860	0·79453	0·73	2·07508	0·48191	1·23	3·42123	0·29229	3·3	27·1126	0·03688
0·24	1·27125	0·78663	0·74	2·09594	0·47711	1·24	3·45561	0·28938	3·4	29·9641	0·03337
0·25	1·28403	0·77880	0·75	2·11700	0·47237	1·25	3·49034	0·28650	3·5	33·1155	0·03020
0·26	1·29693	0·77105	0·76	2·13828	0·46767	1·26	3·52542	0·28365	3·6	36·5982	0·02732
0·27	1·30996	0·76338	0·77	2·15977	0·46301	1·27	3·56085	0·28083	3·7	40·4473	0·02472
0·28	1·32313	0·75578	0·78	2·18147	0·45841	1·28	3·59664	0·27804	3·8	44·7012	0·02237
0·29	1·33643	0·74826	0·79	2·20340	0·45384	1·29	3·63279	0·27527	3·9	49·4024	0·02024
0·30	1·34986	0·74082	0·80	2·22554	0·44933	1·30	3·66930	0·27253	4·0	54·5982	0·01832
0·31	1·36343	0·73345	0·81	2·24791	0·44486	1·31	3·70617	0·26982	4·1	60·3403	0·01657
0·32	1·37713	0·72615	0·82	2·27050	0·44043	1·32	3·74342	0·26714	4·2	66·6863	0·01500
0·33	1·39097	0·71892	0·83	2·29332	0·43605	1·33	3·78104	0·26448	4·3	73·6998	0·01357
0·34	1·40495	0·71177	0·84	2·31637	0·43171	1·34	3·81904	0·26185	4·4	81·4509	0·01228
0·35	1·41907	0·70469	0·85	2·33965	0·42741	1·35	3·85743	0·25924	4·5	90·0171	0·01111
0·36	1·43333	0·69768	0·86	2·36316	0·42316	1·36	3·89619	0·25666	4·6	99·4843	0·01005
0·37	1·44773	0·69073	0·87	2·38691	0·41895	1·37	3·93535	0·25411	4·7	109·947	0·00910
0·38	1·46228	0·68386	0·88	2·41090	0·41478	1·38	3·97490	0·25158	4·8	121·510	0·00823
0·39	1·47698	0·67706	0·89	2·43513	0·41066	1·39	4·01485	0·24908	4·9	134·290	0·00745
0·40	1·49182	0·67032	0·90	2·45960	0·40657	1·40	4·05520	0·24660	5·0	148·413	0·00674
0·41	1·50682	0·66365	0·91	2·48432	0·40252	1·41	4·09596	0·24414	5·1	164·022	0·00610
0·42	1·52196	0·65705	0·92	2·50929	0·39852	1·42	4·13712	0·24171	5·2	181·272	0·00552
0·43	1·53726	0·65051	0·93	2·53451	0·39455	1·43	4·17870	0·23931	5·3	200·337	0·00499
0·44	1·55271	0·64404	0·94	2·55998	0·39063	1·44	4·22070	0·23693	5·4	221·406	0·00452
0·45	1·56831	0·63763	0·95	2·58571	0·38674	1·45	4·26311	0·23457	5·5	244·692	0·00409
0·46	1·58407	0·63128	0·96	2·61170	0·38289	1·46	4·30596	0·23224	5·6	270·426	0·00370
0·47	1·59999	0·62500	0·97	2·63794	0·37908	1·47	4·34924	0·22993	5·7	298·867	0·00335
0·48	1·61607	0·61878	0·98	2·66446	0·37531	1·48	4·39295	0·22764	5·8	330·300	0·00303
0·49	1·63232	0·61263	0·99	2·69123	0·37158	1·49	4·43710	0·22537	5·9	365·037	0·00274
									6·0	403·429	0·00248

Index